Computer Science, Technology and Applications

Mathematics Research Developments

nova
science publishers
New York

Computer Science, Technology and Applications

Additional books in this series can be found on Nova's website under the Series tab.

Additional e-books in this series can be found on Nova's website under the e-book tab.

Biswadip Basu Mallik, PhD
Sharmistha Ghosh, PhD
Binay Kumar Pandey
Digvijay Pandey
Vinay Kumar Nassa
Editors

Emerging Trends in Mathematical Sciences and Computing

nova
science publishers
New York

DOI: https://doi.org/10.52305/VTTP1252

NOTICE TO THE READER

Library of Congress Cataloging-in-Publication Data

ISBN: 979-8-89113-751-6 (hardcover)
ISBN: 979-8-89113-818-6 (e-book)

Published by Nova Science Publishers, Inc. † New York

Contents

Preface

Nearly every aspect of daily life involves mathematics, and the field has contributed to the development of useful modern technologies like internet searches, medical imaging, computer animation, numerical weather prediction, and all forms of digital communications. The foundation of computer science is also mathematics, which supports notions in computing and programming. Without it, understanding algorithms, data structures, differential equations, and other abstract concepts would be difficult which are all essential to understanding how computers operate. Mathematics is important to understand computer science as it teaches readers how to use abstract language, work with algorithms, analyze their own computational thinking, and accurately model real-world solutions, In computer programming, algebra is used to create mathematical software and algorithms. Additionally, it is involved in the design of numerical programs. Mathematical statistics uses quantified models, representations, and summaries to draw conclusions from data sets. A Handbook on Emerging Trends in Mathematical Sciences and Computing focuses on the amalgamation of Mathematics and Computer Science. With the help of case studies, it also illustrates how to apply mathematical models to numerous domains. The book contains the following chapters:

Chapter 1 is entitled "An Extension of Soft Set and its Application to Decision Making". In this chapter, the authors have introduced a generalized soft set as a dilatation of soft set where the domain of the function is extended to its power set. The utility of this generalized theory is shown through its application in decision making.

Chapter 2 entitled "Fermatean Fuzzy Aggregation Operator based Multi Criteria Group Decision Making for Green Supplier Selection" aims to introduce and integrate Fermatean fuzzy weighted power geometric operator (FFWPGO) based Stepwise weight assessment ratio analysis (SWARA) and multi-criteria group decision making (MCGDM) to solve the Green Supplier Selection Problem (GSSP).

Chapter 3 is entitled "An Integrated Multi-criteria Decision-making Approach for Material Selection by Waste Recycling". In this chapter, recycled agricultural and plastic wastes were used to produce floor tiles, a building material. Nine alternatives and five criteria have been chosen to model the issue. Stepwise Weight Assessment Ratio Analysis (SWARA) and Technique for Order Performance by Similarity to Ideal Solution (TOPSIS) have been blended to develop an integrated multi-criteria decision making (MCDM) technique that is used to find ideal composition for sustainable floor tiles by recycling waste plastic (WP) and agricultural waste (AW).

Chapter 4 is entitled "Potential of Optimal Coupling of Species Migration to Bring Synchrony in Seasonally Perturbed System". The authors investigated the impact of migration on the synchronization of two different habitats at different geographical locations. They demonstrate that unidirectional migration can lead to phase synchronization between the two patches that play a critical role in balancing the ecosystem in fluctuating environments. Through alteration of migration-associated coupling coefficient, the study identifies the best-suited coupling dimension for regulating fluctuating resources and establishing sustainable habitats.

Chapter 5 is entitled "Results on Best Proximity Point in b-Metric Space using Weak Contraction". The primary motto of this chapter is addressing a novel best proximity problem in b-metric structure associated with the idea of weak contraction. A result of the best proximity point has been shown following a suitable example.

Chapter 6 is entitled "Pre and Post Covid Scenario of Fuel Economy: A Survey through Statistical Analysis". This chapter gives an extensive Statistical Analysis to know about the swing in the price of fuels in pre-Covid stage and post-Covid stage and provides a proper interpretation about the real effect of Covid in fuel prices.

Chapter 7 is entitled "Modelling and Analysis of the Spread of Crime against Women in an Open Population". In this chapter, the authors propose a mathematical model and its analysis has been done for the study of spread of crime against women by considering open population. The modelling process involves the assumptions that women become victim after their interaction with criminals and criminals influenced non-susceptible to commit crime against women. Model possible equilibria is obtained and stability analysis has been discussed.

Chapter 8 is entitled "Boundedness Characterization of Pseudo-Differential Operators on W_M (R^n)". In this chapter, boundedness characteristics of infinite order pseudo-differential operators using fractional Fourier transform on W_M (R^n) space have been studied.

Chapter 9 is entitled "Study of a G1/M/1/N Queue including Negative Consumers, Disasters and Working Vacations". This chapter unifies a large number of killing tactics for the classic single-server queue, wherein arrivals occur as a general process with exponential service time distribution. As early as the service facility realizes that the system is dormant, he will go on a working vacation and the service will be delivered at a reduced rate. The model is analyzed at steady state with the help of supplementary variable and iterative techniques.

Chapter 10 is entitled "Provable Secure Proxy Signature scheme over Elliptic Curves using Chaotic Map". The authors have proposed a new digital proxy signature scheme (PSS) using Chaotic maps (CMs) over elliptic curves. Security of their PSS relies on "elliptic curve discrete logarithm (ECDL) and integer factorization (FAC) problems". Implementation of it requires only low-complexity computation, which increases efficiency. It can be highly used digitally in Pandemic durations like COVID-19.

Chapter 11 is entitled "Numerical Modelling of Dispersion of Suspended Particles in a Turbulent Open Channel Flow: A Fitted Operator Approach". In this chapter, a mathematical model based on convection-diffusion equation with the Dirichlet boundary conditions has been simulated to study the process of longitudinal spreading of the particles with suspension and settling velocity into turbulent shear flows over an uneven bottom surface. The computed solution exhibits adumbration of settling of particles as the equi-concentration contour plots.

Chapter 12 is entitled "Propagation of SH-wave in Anisotropic Porous Layer Lying over Viscoelastic Sandy Half-space". This chapter discusses the SH-wave propagating in a pre-stressed anisotropic porous layer overlying viscoelastic sandy half-space. Variable separation method is applied to derive the expressions for displacement for the half-space and layer. The findings of the current study could be useful in earthquake engineering, geophysics, and seismology.

Chapter 13 is entitled "A Pythagorean Fuzzy Distance Measure with Hesitancy Degree and Application in Decision Making". In this chapter the authors proposed a new metric incorporating a hesitancy degree for Pythagorean fuzzy sets. This novel measure is compared to the prevailing distance metrics to demonstrate its improved efficacy. Numerical examples have been provided here that have successfully assessed the efficiency and feasibility of the introduced measure in the problem of decision-making.

Chapter 14 is entitled "Stability of General Radical Quadratic Functional Equation in Modular Spaces". The goal of this chapter is to study the Generalized Hyers - Ulam – Rassias (H.U.R.) stability of general radical quadratic functional equation (RQFE) in Modular spaces using fixed point (FP) and direct method.

Chapter 15 entitled "Health Care Waste Recycling Technology Selection using Fermatean Fuzzy Multi-Criteria Group Decision Making". The aim of this chapter is to identify best health care waste recycling technique (HCWRT) for sustainable environmental development using Fermatean Fuzzy Aggregation Operator (FFAO) based multi criteria group decision making (MCGDM). To carry out this research, FF weighted power average operator (FFWPAO) based Stepwise Weight Assessment Ratio Analysis (SWARA) and Weighted Aggregated Sum Product Assessment (WASPAS) method have been developed.

The editors thank Almighty God for granting them the opportunity to finish this book. We appreciate Nova Science Publishers for believing in us and providing us the chance to edit this book. We want to thank all the writers who contributed significantly to this book project; due to scale and quality, we were unable to accept many excellent chapters, but we are convinced that the work in this book will be helpful to emerging scholars and members of the industry.

Although the chapters and writers' work have been carefully chosen and have undergone rigorous peer review and monitoring, the authors' or readers' evaluations and feedback would be extremely helpful for us in ensuring that one's issues are addressed in our upcoming volumes.

Chapter 1

An Extension of Soft Set and Its Application to Decision Making

Avijit Nemu[1], MSc
Sharmistha Ghosh[2,*], PhD
[1]Department of Basic Science and Humanities,
University of Engineering and Management, Kolkata, India
[2]Department of Basic Science and Humanities, Institute of Engineering and Management, Kolkata, India

Abstract

In this work, the authors have introduced a generalized soft set as a dilatation of soft set where the domain of the function is extended to its power set. The utility of this generalized theory is shown through its application in decision making. It is used to calculate merit list for the admission of students in various courses in an institute according to the importance of the subjects for different courses. It is shown that the merit list (full list/up-to desired list) may vary for admission from one course to another course and thus can contribute to right judgment and consequently proper selection of candidates.

Keywords: fuzzy set, soft set, generalized soft set, choice value, decision making

---

* Corresponding Author's Email: sharmisthag2023@gmail.com.

In: Emerging Trends in Mathematical Sciences and Computing
Editors: B. Basu Mallik, S. Ghosh, B. Kumar Pandey et al.
ISBN: 979-8-89113-751-6

Introduction

Data sets are readily available in a wide range of fields in the modern world. Most of the data sets contain information that is usually vague or inaccurate and is not always clear to the human mind. Varied situations contain different forms of uncertainty, and we cannot always apply the standard approaches to analyze them. The predominant existing theories, namely, the theory of probability, fuzzy set theory, (Zadeh, 1965), vague set theory (Gau et al., 1993 and Mishra et al., 2014), rough set theory (Pawlak, 1982), intuitionistic fuzzy set (Deli et al., 2015) have been designed as mathematical methods to deal with various kinds of uncertainties. However, different theories have their own constraints and there are situations where we cannot always analyze the data set properly. Such adversities might arise due to some inherent deficiency of the theoretical parameterization tools. Consequently, Molodtsov (1999) initiated the theory of soft sets as a novel method for treating hesitancy that is devoid of the above limitations. Soft sets have strong potential for application in varied directions, as pointed out by Molodtsov himself in his great effort in 1999. Soft sets and their applications in decision making have also been investigated extensively by Maji et al. (2002, 2003) and Yang (2008). Several authors have contributed in extension of soft sets (Nasef et al., 2017) that leads to different hybrid models as fuzzy soft set (Liu et al., 2017), intuitionistic fuzzy soft set (Deli et al., 2015), vague soft set (Alhazaymeh et al., 2012), soft rough set (Liu et al., 2017), neutrosophic soft set (Maji, 2013) and many more (Xia et al., 2021; Dalkilic, 2021 and Ali et al., 2022). Such models play important roles in different decision support systems as demonstrated by many authors in recent years.

In the present work, the authors have put forth another extension of soft sets where the domain of the function has been extended to its power set and is called a *generalized soft set.* The applicability of the new definition has been demonstrated through its application in real life problems and different case studies.

Preliminaries

Basic Definitions

Soft Set: Let U be the universal set and G be a set of parameters. The pair (F, G) is said to be a soft set over the initial universe U if and only if F maps from G into the power set of U, i.e., $F: G \rightarrow P(U)$ (Molodtsov, 1999).

Example: Let us consider the example given by Maji et al. in 2003. Mr. X is willing to buy an attractive house. Let the soft set (F, G) characterize the attractiveness of houses, where $U = \{u_1, u_2, u_3, u_4, u_5, u_6\}$, is the set of houses considered for the study. Also, let us take the parameter set G given by

$G = \{p_1, p_2, p_3, p_4, p_5, p_6, p_7, p_8\}$
= {beautiful; expensive; modern; in the green surroundings; in good repair; in bad repair;
cheap; wooden}.

Now the soft set (F, G) describes the attractiveness of houses like, *beautiful* houses, *expensive* houses, *modern* houses ... and so on; i.e.:

$F(p_1) = \{u_3, u_4, u_6\}$
$F(p_2) = \{u_1, u_6\}$
$F(p_3) = \{u_1, u_4\}$ and so on.

Generalized Soft Set: We have considered $P(G)$, power set of the set of parameters, as the domain of the function in a soft set and thus, we have defined the extended soft set which is termed as *generalized soft set.*

Definition: Let the initial universe be considered as U and the parameter set be G. A pair $(F, P(G))$ is called a *generalized soft set* over the initial universe U if and only if F maps from $P(G)$ into the power set of U, i.e., $F: P(G) \rightarrow P(U)$.

Example: Let $U = \{s_1, s_2, s_3, s_4, s_5, s_6\}$, be a set of six students and

$G = \{p_1 = \text{1st Language}, p_2 = \text{English}, p_3 = \text{Mathematics}, p_4 = \text{Physics}, p_5 = \text{Chemistry}, p_6 = \text{Programming}\}$ be a set of parameters (subjects).

Here, the generalized soft set would determine the 1st, 2nd and 3rd rankers and so on, i.e.:

$$F(\{p_3\}) = \{s_5, s_4, s_1, s_3, s_6, s_2\}$$
$$F(\{p_1, p_2\}) = \{s_3, s_4, s_1\}$$
$$F(\{p_2, p_3, p_4, p_6\}) = \{s_4, (s_1, s_5)\} \text{ and so on.}$$

Application of Generalized Soft Set Theory

Problem Statement: Prepare merit list (full/up-to certain limit) of students for the admission in the following courses: (I) General Bachelor Degree course (like, Science, Arts, Commerce etc.), (II) B.Tech. in Computer Science, (III) Mathematics Honours and (IV) B.Sc. in Computer Science. The marks obtained by the students in different subjects are shown in Table 1.

Table 1. Marks obtained by the students under consideration

U \ G	p_1	p_2	p_3	p_4	p_5	p_6
s_1	75	98	97	88	78	91
s_2	79	93	82	97	84	94
s_3	87	91	91	80	88	93
s_4	83	99	99	79	84	95
s_5	70	78	100	90	82	97
s_6	77	96	84	99	80	92

Here, $U = \{s_1, s_2, s_3, s_4, s_5, s_6\}$ is a set of six students, $G = \{p_1 =$ 1st Language, $p_2 =$ English, $p_3 =$ Mathematics, $p_4 =$ Physics, $p_5 =$ Chemistry, $p_6 =$ Programming$\}$ is the set of parameters i.e the subjects.

In order to determine the desired rank for the purpose of admission to different courses, the choice value for each student is calculated using the following formulae:

Formula for un-weighted data set:

$$c_i = \left(\sum_j \frac{h_{ij}}{100}\right) / (\text{No. of parameters}) \quad (1)$$

where, $c_i =$ Choice value and $h_{ij} =$ Marks obtained out of 100.

Formula for weighted data set :

$$c_i = \left(\sum_j \frac{h_{ij} \times w_j}{100}\right) / \left(\sum w_j\right) \tag{2}$$

where, c_i = Choice value and w_j = Weights of subjects.

Algorithm for finding choice value for un-weighted data set:

The following algorithm is used to find the choice value for each student as element of initial universe with respect to all/some parameters with equal weight one (i.e., no weight) to calculate the rank for admission purpose.

Algorithm - 1: Choice value evaluation process for un-weighted data set:

Input: Marks h_{ij} (i.e., assigned value of parameters) obtained in the corresponding subject p_j for each student s_i.

Output: A choice value between zero and one.

Method:

Step - 1: Row sum of all h_{ij} for each s_i i.e., $\sum_j h_{ij}$.

Step - 2: Divide Step - 1 value by number of parameters i.e., $\left(\frac{\sum_j h_{ij}}{\text{No.of parameters}}\right)$ for each i.

Step - 3: Divide Step - 2 values by 100 to convert the choice value in $[0, 1]$ for each i.

Step - 4: Arranging the choice values in descending order to make the merit list.

Algorithm for finding choice value for weighted data set:

The following algorithm determines the choice value of each student with respect to all/some parameters with their assigned weights to calculate the rank of the student. The weights designate the relevance or importance of the corresponding subject for admission to a particular discipline.

Algorithm - 2: Choice value evaluation process for weighted data set:

Input: Marks h_{ij} (i.e., assigned value of parameters) obtained in the corresponding subject p_j for each student s_i and the weights w_j for a parameter p_j.

Output: A choice value between zero and one.

Method:

Step - 1: Weighted row sum of all h_{ij} for each s_i i.e., $\sum_j h_{ij} \times w_j$.

Step - 2: Divide Step – 1 value by the total weight of parameters i.e., $\left(\frac{\sum_j h_{ij} \times w_j}{\sum w_j}\right)$ for each i.

Step - 3: Divide Step – 2 values by 100 to convert the choice value in $[0, 1]$ for each i.

Step - 4: Arranging the choice values in descending order to prepare the merit list.

Different Case Studies

In this section, we shall calculate choice values to prepare merit list for the admission of students in the four courses: (I) General Bachelor Degree course (like, Science, Arts, Commerce etc.), (II) B.Tech. in Computer Science (CS), (III) Mathematics Honours and (IV) B.Sc. in Computer Science.

Case 1: Un-weighted Table (with all parameters)

Table 2. Choice values for all un-weighted parameters

U \ G	p_1	p_2	p_3	p_4	p_5	p_6	Choice Value (c_i)
s_1	75	98	97	88	78	91	$c_1 = 0.878$ (5)
s_2	79	93	82	97	84	94	$c_2 = 0.882$ (3)
s_3	87	91	91	80	88	93	$c_3 = 0.883$ (2)
s_4	83	99	99	79	84	95	$c_4 = 0.898$ (1)
s_5	70	78	100	90	82	97	$c_5 = 0.862$ (6)
s_6	77	96	84	99	80	92	$c_6 = 0.880$ (4)

Arranging these choice values in descending order, we get the following:
Observation: $s_4 > s_3 > s_2 > s_6 > s_1 > s_5$.

This first case is considered to produce a merit list for General Bachelor Degree course. Here we consider all the subjects as parameters with equal weight one (i.e., un-weighted) and calculate choice values by the formula (**1**) for each student of the initial universe U which are indicated in the last column of Table 2.

Case 2: Weighted Table (with all parameters)

This second case is considered to make a merit list for B.Tech. in Computer Science course. Here we consider all the subjects as parameters with different weights which are supposed to be decided by the institute (in our calculation we have considered one sample). We then calculate the choice values by the formula (**2**) for each student element of the universe U which are indicated in the last column of Table 3:

Table 3. Choice values for all weighted parameters

G / U	p_1, $w_1 = 1$	p_2, $w_2 = 1$	p_3, $w_3 = 4$	p_4, $w_4 = 3$	p_5, $w_5 = 3$	p_6, $w_6 = 3$	Choice Value (c_i)
s_1	75	98	97	88	78	91	$c_1 = 0.888$ (3)
s_2	79	93	82	97	84	94	$c_2 = 0.883$ (4)
s_3	87	91	91	80	88	93	$c_3 = 0.883$ (4)
s_4	83	99	99	79	84	95	$c_4 = 0.901$ (2)
s_5	70	78	100	90	82	97	$c_5 = 0.903$ (1)
s_6	77	96	84	99	80	92	$c_6 = 0.881$ (5)

Arranging these choice values in descending order, we get the following:
Observation: $\boldsymbol{s_5 > s_4 > s_1 > s_3 = s_2 > s_6}$.

Case 3: Un-weighted Table (with some parameters)

This third case is considered for the preparation of merit list for Mathematics Honours course. Here we consider some parameters ($p_2 =$ English, $p_3 =$ Mathematics, $p_4 =$ Physics, $p_6 =$ Programming) with equal weight one (i.e., un-weighted) as set by the institute. We then calculate the choice values by the formula (**1**) for each student of the given universe U and are indicated in last column of the Table 4.

Table 4. Choice value for some un-weighted parameters

U \ G	p_2	p_3	p_4	p_6	Choice Value (c_i)
s_1	98	97	88	91	$c_1 = 0.935$ (1)
s_2	93	82	97	94	$c_2 = 0.915$ (4)
s_3	91	91	80	93	$c_3 = 0.888$ (6)
s_4	99	99	79	95	$c_4 = 0.930$ (2)
s_5	78	100	90	97	$c_5 = 0.912$ (5)
s_6	96	84	99	92	$c_6 = 0.928$ (3)

Arranging these choice values in descending order, we get the following:
Observation: $s_1 > s_4 > s_6 > s_2 > s_5 > s_3$.

Case 4: Weighted Table (with some parameters)

This fourth case is considered to make merit list for B.Sc. in Computer Science course. Here we consider some parameters ($p_2 =$ English, $p_3 =$ Maths, $p_4 =$ Physics, $p_6 =$ Programming) with different weights which are decided by the institute (one such sample is considered). The choice values are now calculated for each student using the formula (**2**) and are indicated at the last column of the Table 5:

Table 5. Choice value for some weighted parameters

U \ G	p_2, $w_2 = 2$	p_3, $w_3 = 4$	p_4, $w_4 = 2$	p_6, $w_6 = 4$	Choice Value (c_i)
s_1	98	97	88	91	$c_1 = 0.937$ (2)
s_2	93	82	97	94	$c_2 = 0.903$ (4)
s_3	91	91	80	93	$c_3 = 0.898$ (5)
s_4	99	99	79	95	$c_4 = 0.943$ (1)
s_5	78	100	90	97	$c_5 = 0.937$ (2)
s_6	96	84	99	92	$c_6 = 0.917$ (3)

Arranging these choice values in descending order, we get the following:
Observation: $s_4 > s_1 = s_5 > s_6 > s_2 > s_3$.

Analysis of the Different Cases of Study

We have obtained the following four observations in the four different cases:

Case 1: Observation: $s_4 > s_3 > s_2 > s_6 > s_1 > s_5$
Case 2: Observation: $s_5 > s_4 > s_1 > s_3 = s_2 > s_6$
Case 3: Observation: $s_1 > s_4 > s_6 > s_2 > s_5 > s_3$
Case 4: Observation: $s_4 > s_1 = s_5 > s_6 > s_2 > s_3$

It is clear from these observations that the merit list varies from one course to another. In certain cases, there exists a tie at particular ranks, which may be eradicated by using some other condition (like, a candidate whose marks of one particular subject is greater than that of the other, may be considered as first and so on). In Table 6, we have shown the merit list up to the desired rank (here, top three students out of six students) for each of the four case studies considered in this work. Very often, for admission purpose, an institute may not publish the full merit list. Instead, the institute may display the merit list only up to a certain rank for which institute can admit students according to sanctioned number of seats in a particular course.

Table 6. Merit list of top three students

Course	Merit list
General course (all p_i with $w_i = 1$)	$\{s_4, s_3, s_2\}$
B.Tech. in Computer Science (all p_i with different w_i)	$\{s_5, s_4, s_1\}$
Mathematics Honours (some p_i with $w_i = 1$)	$\{s_1, s_4, s_6\}$
B.Sc. in Computer Science (some p_i with different w_i)	$\{s_4, (s_1, s_5)\}$

Conclusion

In the present study, we have extended the definition of soft set by considering the domain of the function as power set of the parameter set G (i.e., $P(G)$) instead of simply, G. The limitation of binary values of the parameters is removed which can now take any real value as considered in this work for marks obtained by a student in any subject. We have considered choice value formulae for both un-weighted and weighted data as a function such that outcome or result of the function is considered as merit list to retain the similar concept of a function in analytical mathematics. As demonstrated by many authors in literature, this study reconfirms that the soft set theory can be considered as a powerful mathematical tool that has the ability to give right decision for various real life problems. Here, we have presented an application of extended soft set theory (we call it as generalized soft set) for preparation of merit list based on the marks obtained by students and norms of the institution (assigned different weights to different subjects for varied courses). This work will help an institute to prepare merit list (full/up to desired rank) with large data set for different courses. The students may as well get the right direction for future study in a suitable course. Thus, this kind of analysis can be an added advantage for counselling purposes.

References

Alhazaymeh, K. A., and Hassan, N. (2012). Generalized Vague Soft Set and its Application. *International Journal of Pure and Applied Mathematics,* 77(3), 391-401.

Ali, B., Saleem, N., Sundus, N., Khaleeq, S., Saeed, M., and George, R. (2022). A Contribution to the Theory of Soft Sets via Generalized Relaxed Operations. *Mathematics, 10*(15), 2636.

Dalkilic, O. (2021). A Novel Approach to Soft Set Theory in Decision-Making under Uncertainty. *International Journal of Computer Mathematics, 98*(10), 1935-1945.

Deli, I. and Cagman, N. (2015). Intuitionistic Fuzzy Parameterized Soft Set Theory and its Decision Making, *Applied Soft Computing, 28*, 109-113.

Gau W. L., Buehrer. D. J. (1993). Vague Sets. *IEEE Transactions on Systems, Man, and Cybernetics, 23*(2), 610-614.

Liu, Y., Luis, M. and Qin, K. (2017). A Comparative Study of Some Soft Rough Sets. *Symmetry, 9*(11), 252.

Liu, Z., Qin, K. and Pei, Z. (2017). A Method for Fuzzy Soft Sets in Decision-Making Based on an Ideal Solution. *Symmetry, 9*(10), 246.

Maji, P. K. (2013). Neutrosophic Soft Set. *Annals of Fuzzy Mathematics and Informatics, 5*(1), 157-168.

Maji, P. K., Biswas, R. and Roy, A. R. (2003). Soft Set Theory. *Computers and Mathematics with Applications, 45*(4-5), 555-562.

Maji, P. K., Roy, A. R. and Biswas, R. (2002). An Application of Soft Set in a Decision Making Problem. *Computers and Mathematics with Applications, 44*(8-9), 1077-1083.

Mishra, J. and Ghosh, S. (2014). Uncertain Query Processing Using Vague Set or Fuzzy Set: Which One is Better? *International Journal of Computers, Communications and Control, 9*(6), 730-740.

Molodtsov, D. (1999). Soft Set Theory-First Results. *Computers and Mathematics with Applications, 37*(4-5), 19-31.

Nasef, A. A. and Sayed-EL, M. K. (2017). Molodtsov's Soft Set Theory and its Applications in Decision Making. *International Journal of Engineering Science Invention, 6*(2), 86-90.

Pawlak, Z. (1982). Rough Sets. *International Journal of Computer and Information Sciences, 11*, 341-356.

Xia, S., Yang, H. and Chen, L. (2021). An Incomplete Soft Set and its Application in MCDM Problems with Redundant and Incomplete Information. *International Journal of Applied Mathematics and Computer Science, 31*(3), 417-430.

Yang. C. F. (2008). A note on "Soft Set Theory" [Comput. Math. Appl. 45 (4-5) (2003) 555-562]. *Computers and Mathematics with Applications, 56*(7), 1899-1900.

Zadeh, L. A. (1965). Fuzzy Sets. *Information and Control, 8*(3), 338-353.

Chapter 2

Fermatean Fuzzy Aggregation Operator-Based Multi Criteria Group Decision Making for Green Supplier Selection

Mampi Debnath*
Sayanta Chakraborty
Debasish Bhattacharya
Department of Mathematics, NIT Agartala, India

Abstract

The aim of this study is to introduce two Fermatean fuzzy weighted power geometric (FFWPG) aggregation operator (AO) based multi criteria group decision making (MCGDM) techniques, namely FFWPGAO based Stepwise weight assessment ratio analysis (SWARA) and FFWPGAO based MCGDM. They are integrated to solve the Green Supplier Selection (GSS) problem for an automobile company. The consistency and robustness of this technique have been examined through comparative analysis (CA) and sensitivity analysis (SA).

Keywords: green supplier selection, FFWPGAO, MCGDM, SWARA

* Corresponding Author's Email: tejaswitadebnath@gmail.com.

In: Emerging Trends in Mathematical Sciences and Computing
Editors: B. Basu Mallik, S. Ghosh, B. Kumar Pandey et al.
ISBN: 979-8-89113-751-6

Introduction

Choosing between two or more choices is the first step in making a decision. Yet, it is crucial to remember that considerations may not always result in the best decision. In a multi-criteria decision-making (MCDM) conundrum, possibilities are implicitly understood. A rapid solution can be made by solving a mathematical problem. In real MCDM (Chakraborty and Saha, 2022(b); Soni et al., 2022) problems, numerous qualities will be related to one another.

In real-world scenarios, uncertainty is common due to the existence of multiple constraints and unpredictability of a situation. Numerous real-world decision-making challenges have been successfully addressed using fuzzy sets (FSs) (Zadeh, 1965). Even while FS theory is great at handling ambiguity and partial truth, it is limited in its ability to account for all ambiguity in handling imprecise data and inherent inference of human thinking. Later, intuitionistic fuzzy set (IFS) was proposed by Atanassov (1986), which associates each element with both membership degrees (MDs) and non-membership degrees (NMDs) rather than just a single MD, with the sum of two grades between 0 and 1. But in some complex situations, the sum of MD and NMD exceeds one. To deal with these situations, Yager (2014) introduced Pythagorean fuzzy set (PFS), where the sum of the squares of MD and NMD lies between 0 and 1. Senapati and Yager (2019(a); 2019(b)) suggested the concept of Fermatean Fuzzy Sets (FFSs) to overcome limitations of PFS. FFSs are characterized by the sum of cubes of MD and NMD lies between 0 and 1. Due to the capability of handling data present in the larger domain, FFSs are more influential and effective in solving uncertain MCDM problems in comparison with IFSs and PFSs.

When dealing with MCDM issues, it may be necessary to solicit feedback from a variety of decision makers (DMs) in order to choose the best option out of numerous competing options. AOs are crucial in combining evaluations of different DMs. There are numerous AOs available, including weighted average (WA) operator (Chakraborty and Saha, 2023), the weighted geometric operator (WG) operator(Chakraborty and Saha, 2023), weighted Bonferroni mean operator (BMO)(Chakraborty and Saha, 2023)and weighted geometric BMO (Chakraborty and Saha, 2023), FFBMO and FFWBMO (Chakraborty and Saha, 2023), FF Hamy Mean operator (FFHMO) and FFWHMO (Chakraborty and Saha, 2022(a)), power geometric operator (PGO) and weighted PGO (Senapati and Yager, 2019(c)) etc. Aggregation of DM's judgment in real-world MCGDM situations is a very difficult process when

DM's preferences can change. A desirable AO should be general and flexible enough to adapt to such variation. Also, there are generally interrelationships among the criteria considered in a problem. Information aggregation is a process that fuses images data from various resources by using a proper aggregation operator. The investigation on information of aggregation has received extensive attention from researchers and practitioners over the past few decades. However, most of the existing AOs do not take into account information about the inter-relationship between values being fused. Then Yager (2019(c)) introduced FFWGOs namely Fermatean Fuzzy Power Geometric (FFPG) and FFWPGO which help us to aggregate assessments in MCGDM problems.

Selection of a potential supplier has been acknowledged as one of the critical issues that an organization faces while maintaining a strategically competitive position. Supplier selection (SS) has a direct effect on probability and cash flow. But now due to increasing awareness of environmental issues and environmental regulatory mandates, both private and public sectors are facing tremendous stress and pressure to consider environmental aspects in their supply chain practices. The combination of environmental concerns with supply chain management practices is termed as "green supply chain management (GSCM)". GSCM comprises of different stages from raw material purchase to the end user product delivery. These stages require proper selection of a supplier among many by considering the need and expectations of the organization. Therefore, organizations need to go beyond their boundaries to look at the performance of their suppliers in order to meet high quality and environmental standards. Hence, it can be believed that the selection of a potential supplier is a complex decision-making procedure with the goal of reducing the preliminary set of suppliers to the final choices. A high degree of uncertainty is associated with these decision-making processes. Therefore, the problem of GSS could be viewed as MCGDM problem under FF environment (FFE).

Motivation of the Research

From the literature, it is evident that FFS acts as an important tool to accomplish decision making in a complex and vague setting and successfully overcome shortcomings of IFS and PFS theories. On the other hand, appropriate GSS is also a very important task for both the public and the environment. So amalgamation of these two facts seems to be inevitable. This issue motivated us for the present study.

Novelty

Novelty of this work is twofold:

- For the first time, the problem of GSS has been modeled in the form of MCGDM under FFE.
- As far as our knowledge is concerned, again for the first time FFWPGAO based SWARA and FFWPGAO based MCGDM have been introduced and integrated to solve GSS problem.

Contributions of the Study

Followings are main contributions of this study:

- We have presented FFWPGAO based SWARA approach for aggregating preference values and establishing weights of GSS criterion.
- Rank of alternatives has been determined by proposed FFWPGAO based MCGDM.
- The proposed FFWPGAO-based integrated MCGDM technique has been used to simulate and solve GSS problems.
- CA and SA have been used to examine the proposed integrated model's (Pandey, B. K. et al., 2024) consistency and robustness.

The organization of the rest of the paper is as follows: in "Related work" section, we have discussed about the related literature on GSS. In section "Basic concepts of FSS", basic definitions, operational laws and examples FFPGO and FFWPGO are discussed. In section "Proposed FFWPGAO based MCGDMs", FFAO based SWARA and FFAO based MCGDM have been introduced. Section "Application of proposed integrated MCGDM in GSS" contains solution of GSS problem using proposed integrated MCGDM technique. In "Results and discussion" section, the comparative and sensitivity analyses have been carried out. The last section includes a conclusion and the future scope of research.

Related Work

In this section, the current literature related to GSS using MCDM technique has been discussed as follows:

In order to solve GSS problem, Wu et al. (2019) presented an integrated methodology based on the BWM and VIKOR technique in an interval type-2 fuzzy environment. In a low-carbon paper industry, Govindan et al. (2016) presented a two-phase hybrid strategy employing fuzzy TOPSIS and MOLPP for GSS and order allocation. To evaluate a supplier's sustainability performance using a triple bottom line approach, Govindan et al. (2013) suggested a fuzzy MCDM approach. To address problems with decision-making like GSS, Baki (2013) suggested an approach based on fuzzy logic in which criterion weights were established using SEM. A fuzzy multi-criteria approach was presented by Shen et al. (2013) for assessing GS's performance in GSC with linguistic preferences. The GSS problem was resolved by Freeman and Chen (2015) utilizing AHP-Entropy-TOPSIS framework. Sarkis (2018) used combined rough sets and fuzzy TOPSIS methodology to offer GSC practices evaluation to the mining industry. A fuzzy MCDM strategy for GSS incorporating economic and environmental factors was proposed by Chen et al. (2016). Fuzzy AHP is used in the suggested approach to identify the crucial weights of criteria in a hazy environment. Using MCDM in a fuzzy context, Gupta et al. (2019) solved GSS problem using a case study from automotive industry. The various performance metrics and sub-indicators accountable for GSCM implementation through AHP were investigated by Sharma et al. (2017). Using fuzzy AHP and TOPSIS, Jain et al. (2018) solved GSS problem using a case study from the Indian automotive sector. Using entropy-TOPSIS-F, Santosh et al. (2019) presented performance evaluation of GSs. Mavi et al. (2016) conducted supply chain risk management SS using fuzzy TOPSIS and Shannon entropy. The mining industry's GSC practices were assessed by Kusi-Sarpong et al. (2016) using combined rough sets and fuzzy TOPSIS technique. Using an FFWBMO-based MCGDM, Chakraborty and Saha (2023) addressed and solved the GSS problem.

Basic Concepts of FFS

Here basics of FFSs, their operational laws, FFPGO and FFWPGO and examples are discussed.

Definition (FSS)

Senapati and Yager (2019(a); 2019(b)) defined mathematical form of FFS given as –

$$\hat{F}=\{<z_i, t_{\hat{F}}(z_i), f_{\hat{F}}(z_i) | z_i € \Omega\}$$

Here Ω denotes universe of discourse, $t_{\hat{F}} € \Omega\,[0,\ 1]$ and $f_{\hat{F}} € \Omega\,[0,\ 1]$ symbolize MD and NMD respectively for an element of Ω satisfying

$$0 \leq t_{\hat{F}}^{3}(z_i)+f_{\hat{F}}^{3}(z_i) \leq 1 \qquad (1)$$

Score and Accuracy Function

For a FFN $O = (t_o, f_o)$, Senapati and Yager (2019(a)) defined score and accuracy function respectively as follows:

$$\S(o)=(t_o)^3-(f_o)^3; \S(o)€[-1,1] \qquad (2)$$

$$\hat{h}(o)=(t_o)^3+(f_o)^3; \hat{h}(o)€[0,1] \qquad (3)$$

Operational Laws

For three FFNs, $O = (t_o, f_o)$, $O_1= (t_{o_1}, f_{o_1})$, $O_2= (t_{o_2}, f_{o_2})$, basic set operational laws defined by Senapati and Yager (2019(a), 2019(b)) are

$$O^c=(f_o, t_o)$$
$$O_1 \cap O_2= (\min\{t_{o_1}, t_{o_2}\},\max\{f_{o_1}, f_{o_2}\})$$
$$O_1 \cup O_2=(\max\{t_{o_1}, t_{o_2}\},\min\{f_{o_1}, f_{o_2}\})$$
$$O_1 \oplus O_2=((t_{o_1}{}^3 + t_{o_2}{}^3 - t_{o_1}{}^3 t_{o_2}{}^3)^{\frac{1}{3}}, f_{o_1} f_{o_2})$$
$$O_1 \otimes O_2= (t_{o_1} t_{o_2}, (f_{o_1}{}^3 + f_{o_2}{}^3 - f_{o_1}{}^3 f_{o_2}{}^3)^{\frac{1}{3}})$$
$$\lambda O =(\left(1-(1-t_o{}^3)^{\lambda}\right)^{\frac{1}{3}}, f_o{}^{\lambda}) , \lambda > 0$$
$$O^{\lambda} = (t_o{}^{\lambda}, \left(1-\left(1-f_o{}^3\right)^{\lambda}\right)^{\frac{1}{3}}) , \lambda > 0$$

FFPGO

Let $F_i = (\alpha_i, \beta_i)$ (i= 1, 2, 3… n) be a number of FFNs and $w = (w_1, w_2, \ldots, w_n)^T$ be weight vector of F_i with $\sum_{i=1}^{n} w_i = 1$, then FFPGO is a function, where $FFPGO(F_1, F_2, \ldots, F_n) = \left(\prod_{i=1}^{n} \alpha_i^{w_i}, \prod_{i=1}^{n} \beta_i^{w_i}\right)$.

FFWPGO

Let $F_i = (\alpha_i, \beta_i)$ (i = 1, 2, 3… n) be a number of FFNs and $w = (w_1, w_2, \ldots, w_n)^T$ be weight vector of F_i with $\sum_{i=1}^{n} w_i = 1$, then FFWPGO is a function, where

$$FFWPGO(F_1, F_2, \ldots, F_n) = \left(\left(1 - \prod_{i=1}^{n} (1 - \alpha_i^3)^{w_i}\right)^{\frac{1}{3}}, \left(1 - \prod_{i=1}^{n} (1 - \beta_i^3)^{w_i}\right)^{\frac{1}{3}} \right)$$

Example 1:

Let $F_1 = (0.8, 0.6), F_2 = (0.9, 0.3), F_3 = (0.7, 0.5), F_4 = (0.5, 0.8)$ and $F_5 = (0.6, 0.4)$ be FFNs and $w = (0.15, 0.35, 0.25, 0.15.0.10)^T$ be weight vector.

$$FFWPGO(F_1, F_2, \ldots, F_5) = \Big((1 - ((1 - 0.8^3)^{0.15}) \times ((1 - 0.9^3)^{0.35} \times ((1 - 0.7^3)^{0.25} \times ((1 - 0.5^3)^{0.15} \times ((1 - 0.6^3)^{0.10})^{\frac{1}{3}}, (1 - ((1 - 0.6^3)^{0.15}) \times ((1 - 0.3^3)^{0.35} \times ((1 - 0.5)^{0.25} \times ((1 - 0.8^3)^{0.15} \times ((1 - 0.4^3)^{0.10})^{\frac{1}{3}} \Big) = (0.554326, 0.223890),$$ which is also a FFN.

Proposed FFWPGAO Based MCGDMs

In this section, two FFAO based MCGDM techniques, namely FFWPGAO based SWARA and FFWPGAO based MCGDM have been introduced.

FFWPGAO – Based SWARA

SWARA method was first introduced by Kersuilene et al. (2011). This method helps DMs to express their decisions freely as they are not based on fixed measures. By considering the decision of experts, this method resolves the computational complexity of the decision-making problem and gives a near optimal solution. This method can be used in real-life decision-making problems under complex situations.

This algorithm has been modified by integrating assessments of DMs by using FFWPGO and is discussed below:

Step 1. Formulate the FF aggregated decision matrix (ADM) using FFWPGO for the criteria and defuzzify those using (2).

Step 2. Rank the preference values of criteria in descending order according to their relative importance and calculate s_j using

$$s_j=\bar{p}_{j-1}-\bar{p}_j \quad (4)$$

Step 3. Calculate $c_j = \left.\begin{matrix} 1\,, j=1 \\ s_j+1\,, j=2,3,\ldots,n \end{matrix}\right\}$ (5)

Step 4. Calculate corrected CWs (CWs) using

$$\acute{s}_j=\begin{cases} 1, j=1 \\ \frac{\acute{s}_{j-1}}{c_j}\,, j=,3\ldots,n \end{cases} \quad (6)$$

Step 5. Calculate final CWs using

$$w_j=\frac{\acute{s}_j}{\sum_{j=1}^{n}\acute{s}_j}, j=2,3\ldots,n. \quad (7)$$

FFWPGAO Based MCGDM

This method comprises of following steps:

Step 1. Normalize decision matrices corresponding to each DM using

$$f_{ij}^k=(h_{ij}^k, g_{ij}^k)=\begin{cases} (x_{ij}^k, y_{ij}^k), \text{for beneficiary criteria (BC)} \\ (y_{ij}^k, x_{ij}^k), \text{for cost criteria (CC)} \end{cases} \quad (8)$$

where i= (1,2,...,m) and k= (1,2,...,l) are no of alternatives and DMs respectively.

Step 2. Utilize FFWPGO as $f_i^k=(h_i^k, g_i^k)=FFWPG^{s,t}(f_{i1}^k, f_{i2}^k, \ldots\ldots, f_{in}^k)$ (9)

to aggregate DM's assessments to find overall preference f_i^k with respect to each alternative corresponding to each DM.

Step 3. To derive overall preference value of f_i, utilize FFWPGO as

$f_i=(h_i, g_i)=(f_i^1, f_i^2, \ldots\ldots, f_i^l)$ (10)

Step 4. Calculate $S(f_i)$ and $H(f_i)$ (if required) of f_i.

Step 5. Rank alternative as per $S(f_i)$.

Application of Proposed Integrated MCGDM in GSS

Over the past few decades, it has been widely observed that environmental awareness is continuously increasing among people and governments. However, various kinds of environmental rules and regulations pushed organizations to accept affirmative changes like GSCM. Choosing proper GS is a challenging task in real-world situations. Four (04) GS alternatives under nine (09) criteria have been chosen here to implement proposed MCGDM. Criteria are described in Table 1. Here, linguistic evaluations (LEs) are gathered from three (03) DMs and are described in terms of FFNs through a FF scale (Table 2). Here DMs are assigned weights as (0.33, 0.34 and 0.33). Algorithm of proposed method is as follows:

Algorithm

Step 1. LEs of DMs are converted to FFNs using Table 2 and placed in Table 3.

Step 2. Using proposed FFWPGO based SWARA, CWs are calculated (Table 4).

Step 3: Decision matrices are normalized using Eqn. (8). Using FFWPGO, corresponding to each alternative and each DM, performance of all criteria are aggregated (Table 5).

Step 4: Using FFWPGO, corresponding to each alternative, overall performance of alternatives corresponding to all DMs have been aggregated.

Step 5: Using Eqn. (2), score of each alternative is calculated and furnished in Table 6. Alternatives are ranked and shown in Figure 1.

Table 1. Description of criterias

Criteria	Name	Type
C1	Resource consumption	CC
C2	Staff Training	BC
C3	Service	BC
C4	Eco design	BC
C5	Green Image	BC
C6	Environmental management System	BC
C7	Cost	CC
C8	Pollution control	BC
C9	Quality	BC

Table 2. Description of linguistic evaluations

Linguistic Terms	Absolutely Low	Reasonably Low	Low	Fair	Medium	High	Reasonably High	Absolutely High
LE	AL	RL	L	F	M	H	RH	EH
FFNs	(.1,.9)	(.2,.8)	(.4,.6)	(.6,4)	(.75,.25)	(.8,.2)	(.85,.25)	(.9,.1)

Table 3. DMs assessments for criteria

	DM1	DM2	DM3
C1	(0.554,0.233)	(0.443,0.568)	(0.776,0.326)
C2	(0.446,0.267)	(0.773,0.422)	(0.557,0.328)
C3	(0.669,0.224)	(0.884,0.334)	(0.553,0.114)
C4	(0.668,0.256)	(0.669,0.334)	(0.663,0.221)
C5	(0.543,0.331)	(0.886,0.441)	(0.774,0.334)
C6	(0.442,0.289)	(0.773,0.331)	(0.674,0.331)
C7	(0.556,0.256)	(0.853,0.356)	(0.554,0.145)
C8	(0.578,0.221)	(0.665,0.387)	(0.732,0.556)
C9	(0.489,0.209)	(0.557,0.267)	(0.889,0.441)

Table 4. CWs

Criteria	C1	C2	C3	C4	C5	C6	C7	C8	C9
FFN	(0.508, 0.551)	(0.680, 0.421)	(0.611, 0.485)	(0.649, 0.486)	(0.866, 0.152)	(0.926, 0.123)	(0.858, 0.196)	(0.914, 0.130)	(0.868, 0.174)
Score	0.27184	0.43624	0.35987	0.39679	0.75628	0.83597	0.70420	0.8116	0.7226
Rank	9	6	8	7	3	1	5	2	4

Table 5. DM's assessments

	A1	A2	A3	A4
DM1	(0.831,0.260)	(0.841,0.242)	(0.787,0.288)	(0.816,0.298)
DM2	(0.875,0.157)	(0.774,0.319)	(0.756.0.370)	(0.748,0.389)
DM3	(0.845,0.266)	(0.668,0.113)	(0.667,0.229)	(0.823,0.371)

Table 6. Ranking

Alternatives	Overall performance	Score	Rank
A1	(0.22766,0.68721)	-0.31274	3
A2	(0.99432,0.22567)	0.971564	1
A3	(0.29953,0.89971)	-0.70142	4
A4	(0.77643,0.33876)	0.42919	2

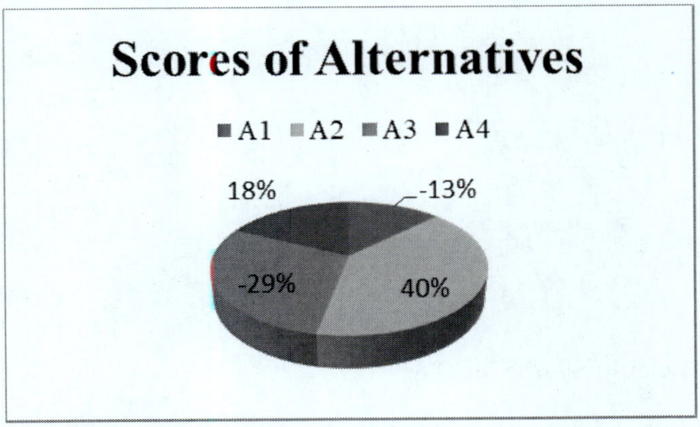

Figure 1. Ranking of alternatives.

Results and Discussions

It could be observed that A2 is ranked as the best GS. To check reliability and consistency of proposed method, CA and SA are executed as follows:

Comparison with Existing MCDMs

Proposed FFWPGAO-based MCGDM has been compared with FF-WASPAS, FF-TOPSIS, FF-WSM, FF-WPM, FF-MOORA. A2 has been identified as the best alternative for all methods and ranks of alternatives remain same. So ranking results derived from proposed MCGDM (Table 7 and Figure 2) is consistent.

Table7. Comparative analysis

Methods	Ranking
Proposed method	$A_2 > A_4 > A_1 > A_3$
FF-WASPAS	$A_2 > A_4 > A_1 > A_3$
FF-TOPSIS	$A_2 > A_4 > A_1 > A_3$
FF-WSM	$A_2 > A_4 > A_1 > A_3$
FF-WPM	$A_2 > A_4 > A_1 > A_3$
FF-MOORA	$A_2 > A_4 > A_1 > A_3$

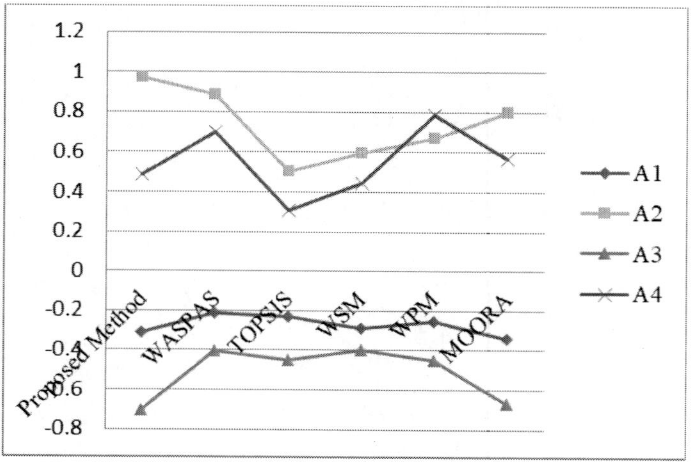

Figure 2. Comparison with MCDMs.

For further validation of results, a SA on variation of CWs is performed below:

Sensitivity Analysis

Table 8. SA by varying CWs

Sl. No	Weigh ratio (BC-CC)	Ranking of alternatives
Case 1	Proposed Method	$A_2 > A_3 > A_1 > A_4$
Case 2	80-20	$A_2 > A_1 > A_4 > A_3$
Case 3	60-40	$A_1 > A_4 > A_2 > A_3$
Case 4	50-50	$A_2 > A_3 > A_4 > A_1$
Case 5	90-10	$A_3 > A_4 > A_1 > A_2$
Case 6	35-65	$A_1 > A_4 > A_2 > A_3$
Case 7	25-75	$A_1 > A_4 > A_2 > A_3$

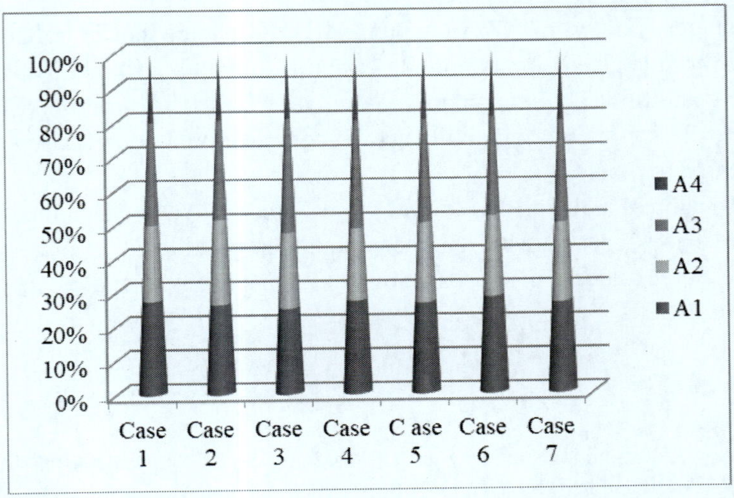

Figure 3. Variation of CWs.

SA has been done for examining consistency and robustness of ranking results. In order to validate the model, ranking results checked by varying CWs (Table 8 and Figure 3) and observed that the proposed technique is sensitive enough as there are variations in ranking of alternatives in respect of criteria.

Perspectives

Proper supplier selection is a major objective for all industries for developing a smooth supply chain management scheme. Day by day with the advent of industrialization, green supplier selection can be regarded as a strategy by which supply chain members get more value. Nowadays competititve markets/companies have been focused on environmental issues with other critical factors to meet the production demand. Therefore green supplier selection is a complex decision making process and to identify the best supplier, the present study has modelled this problem as a MCGDM problem.

Conclusion

In this study, an integrated MCGDM strategy has been proposed based on FFWPGAO to address GSS issue. A variety of comparisons and SA have been performed to assess consistency and robustness. The proposed method has two advantages. Firstly, in SWARA method DM's choice can be reflected and secondly, it is also computationally easier as only two arithmetic operations, namely addition and division are required. Moreover, the proposed MCGDM requires less computation and hence its computational complexity is low as compared to others.

To address real world MCGDM issues, other FFAOs can be introduced in future. The suggested MCGDM technique can be utilized to address issues like resource allocation, site selection, waste management and recycling etc.

References

Atanassov K. T. Intuitionistic fuzzy sets (1986). *Fuzzy Sets & Systems* 20(1): 87–96.

Baki R. An Integrated Multi-criteria Structural Equation Model for Green Supplier Selection (2022). *Int. J. of Precis Eng. and Manuf.-Green Tech.* vol. 9, pp. 1063–1076.

Chakraborty S. and Saha A. K. Selection of optimal lithium ion battery recycling process: A multi- criteria group decision making approach (2022a). *Journal of Energy Storage*, Vol 55, Part B, https://doi.org/10.1016/j.est.2022.105557. Elsevier, 2022(a).

Chakraborty S. and Saha A. K. Selection of Forklift Unit for Transport Handling using Integrated MCDM under Neutrosophic Environment 2022(b). Facta Universitatis, Series. *Mechanical Engineering*: 1087-1098.

Chakraborty S. and Saha A. K. A framework of LR fuzzy AHP and fuzzy WASPAS for health care waste recycling technology (2022c). *Appl. Soft Comput.* 127 (109388).

Chakraborty S. and Saha A. K. Novel Fermatean Fuzzy Bonferroni Mean aggregation operators for selecting optimal health care waste treatment technology (2023). *Engineering Applications of Artificial Intelligence,* Volume119 105752, https://doi.org/10.1016/j.engappai.2022.105752, Elsevier.

Chen H. M. W., Chou S. Y., Luu Q. D. and Yu T. H. K. A fuzzy MCDM approach for green supplier selection from the economic and environmental aspects (2016). *Mathematical Problems in Engineering*. 127(109876).

Dos Santos B. M., Godoy L. P. and Lucila Campos M. P. Performance evaluation of green suppliers Using entropy-TOPSIS-F (2019). *Journal of Cleaner Production*. 207, 498-509.

Freeman J. and Chen T. Green supplier selection using an AHP-Entropy-TOPSIS framework: Supply Chain Management (2015). *An International Journal*, 20(3): 327-340.

Gupta S., Soni U. and Kumar G. Green supplier selection using multi-criterion decision making under fuzzy environment: A case study in automotive industry (2019). *Computers & Industrial Engineering*. Vol. 136, pp. 663-680.

Govindan K. and Sivakumar R. Green supplier selection and order allocation in a low-carbon paper industry: integrated multi-criteria heterogeneous decision-making and multi-objective linear programming approaches (2016). *Annals of Operations Research*. vol. 238(1), pp. 243-276.

Govindan K., Khodaverdi R. and Jafarian A. A fuzzy multi criteria approach for measuring sustainability performance of a supplier based on triple bottom line approach (2013). *IntellSyst.* 114(3), pp. 505–518.

Jain V., Sangaiah A. K., Sakhuja S., Thoduka N. and Aggarwal R. Supplier selection using fuzzy AHP and TOPSIS: a case study in the Indian automotive industry (2018). *Neural Computing and Applications*, 29(7), 555-564.

Kusi Sarpong S., Bai C., Sarkis J. and Wang X. Green supply chain practices evaluation in the mining industry using a joint rough sets and fuzzy TOPSIS methodology (2015). *Resources Policy*, vol. 46, pp. 86-100.

Kersulien V., Zavadskas E. K. and Turskis Z. Selection of rational dispute resolution method by applying new step-wise weight assessment ratio analysis (SWARA) (2011). *Journal of Business Economics and Management*, vol. 11(2), pp. 243-258.

Shen L., Olfat L., Khanna G., Khodaverdi R. and Diabat A. A fuzzy multi criteria approach for evaluating green supplier's performance in green supply chain with linguistic preferences (2013). *Resources, Conservation and Recycling,* 74, 170-179.

Sarkis J. A boundaries and flows perspective of green supply chain management (2012). *Journal of environmental management*;28(5):1079–1093,2012.

Shen L., Olfat L., Govindan K., Khodaverdi R. and Diabat A. A fuzzy multi criteria approach for evaluating green supplier's performance in green supply chain with linguistic preferences (2013). *Resources, Conservation and Recycling*, 74, 170-179, 2013.

Senapati T. and Yager R. R. Fermatean fuzzy sets (2019a). *J Ambient Intell Hum Computing*. https://doi.org/10.1007/s12652-019-01377-0.

Senapati T. and Yager R R. Some new operations over Fermatean fuzzy numbers and application of Fermatean fuzzy WPM in multiple criteria decision making (2019b). *Informatica* 30(2):391–412.

Senapati T. and Yager R. R. Fermatean fuzzy weighted averaging/geometric operators and its application in multi-criteria (2019c). *Eng Appl Artif Intell.* 85:112–121.

Soni A., Chakraborty S., Das P. K. and Saha A. K. Materials selection of reinforced sustainable composites by recycling waste plastics and agro-waste: an integrated multi-criteria decision making approach (2022c). *Constr. Build. Mater* 348(2022):128- 608, https://doi.org/10.1016/j.conbuildmat.2022.128608. Elsevier.

Wu Q., Zhou L., Chen Y. and Chen H. An integrated approach to green supplier selection based on the interval type-2 fuzzy best-worst and extended VIKOR methods (2019). *Information Sciences*. vol. 502, pp: 394-417.

Yager R. R. Pythagorean membership grades in multicriteria decision making (2014). *IEEE Trans Fuzzy Syst* 22(4):958–965.

Yager R. R. and Atanaasov A M. Pythagorean membership grades, complex numbers, and decision making (2013). *Int J of Intelligent Systems* 28(5):436–452.

Zadeh L. A. Fuzzy sets (1965): *Information & Control* 8(3):338–353.

Chapter 3

An Integrated Multi-Criteria Decision-Making Approach for Material Selection by Waste Recycling

Ankita Pareek*
Sayanta Chakraborty
Apu Kumar Saha
Department of Mathematics, NIT Agartala, India

Abstract

Recycling waste involves gathering and processing waste materials to create fresh, useful products that protect the environment and public health. In the current study, recycled agricultural and plastic wastes were used to produce floor tiles, a building material. Nine alternatives and five criteria have been chosen to model the issue. Stepwise Weight Assessment Ratio Analysis (SWARA) and Technique for Order Performance by Similarity to Ideal Solution (TOPSIS) have been blended to develop an integrated multi-criteria decision making (MCDM) technique that is used to find ideal composition for sustainable floor tiles by recycling waste plastic (WP) and agricultural waste (AW). To test the integrity, dependability and reliability of the suggested integrated method, comparative analysis (CA) and sensitivity analysis (SA) have been conducted.

Keywords: waste recycling, MCDM, SWARA, TOPSIS

---

* Corresponding Author's Email: ankitapareek97689@gmail.com.

In: Emerging Trends in Mathematical Sciences and Computing
Editors: B. Basu Mallik, S. Ghosh, B. Kumar Pandey et al.
ISBN: 979-8-89113-751-6

Introduction

MCDM is a process for publicly assessing a wide range of conflicting considerations while making decisions in real-world scenarios including business, government, healthcare (Chakraborty and Saha, 2022) etc. When making daily judgments, people typically make implicit considerations of a variety of aspects and if their decisions are completely based on intuition, they may be happy with the outcomes. On the other hand, when the stakes are high, it is critical to clearly define the problem and assess a variety of factors. Making good decisions demands framing complex problems carefully and considering a variety of criteria. Basically, two important tasks are performed in MCDM (Choudhury et al. 2021; Saha et al. 2017): one is finding the weights (Pandey, B. K. et al., 2023) of criteria based on which decision will be made; the second is ranking the alternatives based on selection criteria. There are several MCDM techniques (Chakraborty and Saha, 2022; Soni et al. 2022) present in literature among which SWARA (Kersuliene et al. 2010) and TOPSIS (Yoon and Hwang, 1995) are considered in this paper for calculating criteria weights and ranking of alternatives respectively. The SWARA method basically contains two mathematical operations addition and division. In this method, based on the decision maker's (DM's) preference, criteria weights are calculated. On the other hand, TOPSIS always leads to the result which is nearer to the positive ideal solution (PIS) and farther from negative IS (NIS).

Effects of the rise in volume and variety of municipal solid waste include exponential growth in population, industrialization, and urbanization, as well as a rise in consumption levels and an increase in living standards (Yang et al. 2018; Senyigit and Demirel, 2018). The nation's strained waste disposal infrastructure is having a negative impact on both the environment and public health (Dev et al. 2020). Recycling of waste (Chakraborty and Saha, 2022) has now become a crying need for the safety of public health and sustainable environmental development. Recycling of waste is a part of waste management.

On the other hand, one of the fundamental requirements of humankind is shelter. There is a high demand for construction materials in order to accommodate the rising population's need for housing. Because of remarkable qualities of polymers, plastics and their composites have an extensive range of engineering applications, so the industrial sector has a bright future with development of green composites using recycled waste polymers and reinforcement from renewable fillers. The use of natural fillers and AW has produced many successful outcomes that have improved the workability of polymeric composites. Utilizing recycled plastics, rice husk ash, and silica sand, polymeric composites can be created as floor tiles, focusing on sustainability in housing.

As a result, it is possible to view the problem of choosing suitable material for a desirable combination of attributes as an MCDM problem (Choudhury et al. 2020). Here nine (09) compositions of waste materials have been considered as alternatives out of five selection criteria, namely compressive strength (C1), flexural strength (C2), density (C3), abrasive wear (C4), and water absorption (C5). A brief literature on MS through MCDM has been discussed below:

Literature Review

In this subsection, a few recent literatures where MSs have been performed through MCDM techniques are furnished.

In (Emovon and Oghenenyerovwho, 2020), a methodical review of application of MCDM method in material selection (MS) has been presented. Haq et al. (2022) integrated MEREC and MARCOS under the SVNSs environment for MS of a lightweight aircraft wing spar. Moradian et al. (2019) developed Entropy-AHP model to find criteria weights and used MOORA, TOPSIS, VIKOR for selecting braking booster valve body material. Yang et al. (2018) proposed an AHP-TOPSIS based model for phase change MS. Yadav et al. (2019) proposed a hybrid TOPSIS-PSI approach for MS in marine applications. Malanoand Magdaluyo (2018) used DLM-COPRAS method in MS of Laminated Glass Interlayer for a Fuel-Efficient Concept Vehicle. Dev et al. (2020) developed Entropy-VIKOR model for materials selection for automotive piston component. Soni et al. (2022) introduced integrated AHP-WASPAS model for selecting building material by recycling WP and AW. Aires et al. (2022) used TOPSIS for sustainable MS. Aghazadeh et al. (2022) developed Delphi-SWARA-ARAS model to choose optimal structural system in accordance with sustainable materials in mass-housing projects.

Contribution

Contributions of this paper are:

- Two popular MCDM techniques, namely SWARA and TOPSIS have been integrated.
- The problem of MS is modeled as MCDM problem and solved by the proposed integrated technique.
- The proposed method has been compared with existing MCDM techniques to check reliability and integrity of results.
- SA has been carried out to check robustness.

Remaining paper has been organized as:

Section "Proposed integrated SWARA-TOPSIS" contains proposed integrated SWARA-TOPSIS method. In section "Application of proposed integrated SWARA-TOPSIS in materials selection", application of proposed method in MS has been discussed. Section 4 contains the discussion on the obtained results. In section 5, the concluding remarks and future research direction have been discussed.

Proposed integrated SWARA-TOPSIS

In this section, the proposed integrated SWARA-TOPSIS method has been discussed. In SWARA, introduced by Kersuliene et al. (2010), the criteria that should be used in evaluating alternatives are prioritized from the most significant weight to the least significant one. Then DMs choose each criterion, discarding less critical ones. On the other hand, TOPSIS, introduced by Yoon and Hwang (1995) is basically based on finding the shortest distance from PIS and farthest from NIS. The algorithm of the proposed integrated method is as follows:

Step 1: Arrange n criteria $C_j (j = 1,2, \dots, n)$according to their importance. Here experts perform ranking of defined criteria according to their preference, denoted as p_j.

Step 2: Determine scientific criteria (s_j) to evaluate comparative significance of average value using $s_j = p_{j-1} - p_j$ (1)

Step 3: Calculate c_j as follows: $c_j = \begin{cases} 1, j = 1 \\ s_j + 1, j > 1 \end{cases}$ (2)

Step 4: Determine recalculated weight, $s'_j = \begin{cases} 1, j = 1 \\ \frac{s'_{j-1}}{c_j}, j = 2, \ldots, n \end{cases}$ (3)

Step 5: Calculate weights of criteria using

$$w_j = \frac{s'_j}{\sum_{j=1}^{n} s'_j} \tag{4}$$

where w_j represents relative weight.

Step 6: Consider the decision matrix $= [a_{ij}]_{m \times n}$, where a_{ij} represents the performance value of ith alternative $A_i (i = 1,2, \ldots, m)$ with respect to j^{th} criterion C_j.

Step 7: Calculate normalized and weighted normalized matrices.

Step 8: Calculate ideal best (v_j^+) and ideal worst (v_j^-) and Euclidean distance (S_i^+ and S_i^-) for each row from ideal worst and ideal best.

$$S_i^+ = \sqrt{\sum_{j=1}^{n} (v_{ij} - v_j^+)^2} \text{ and } S_i^- = \sqrt{\sum_{j=1}^{n} (v_{ij} - v_j^-)^2}$$

Step 9: Calculate closeness coefficient $CC_i = \frac{S_i^-}{S_i^- + S_i^+}$ and hence rank alternatives.

Application of Proposed Integrated SWARA-TOPSIS in Materials Selection

In this section, the problem formulation and solution using proposed integrated technique have been discussed. Table 1 describes the suggested alternatives of different compositions of polythene, rice husk and sand.

The relation between criteria is assigned by the decision maker as C1>C2>C3>C4>C5. Using SWARA, the criteria weights are calculated as (0.252, 0.215, 0.192, 0.173, 0.166). Finally, TOPSIS has identified A9 as the the best alternative, which is composed of 90% PP, 5% RHA and 5% sand. The result is presented in Table 2 and shown in Figure 1. Thus, the proposed integrated approach has successfully identified the best material for building construction by recycling WP and AW.

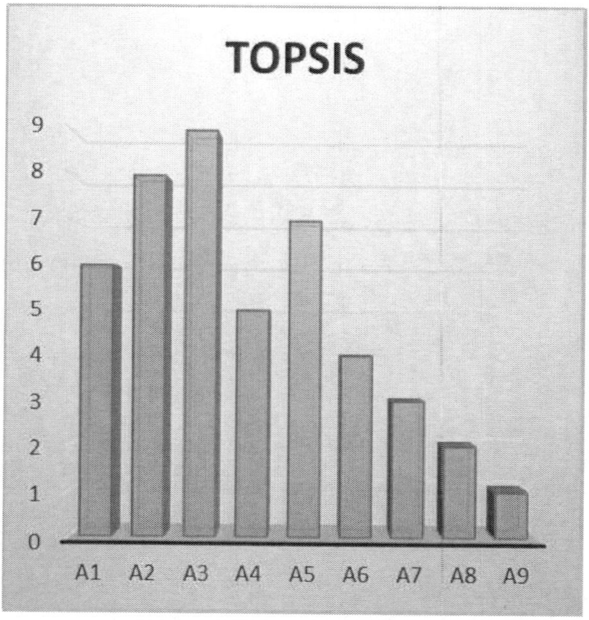

Figure 1. Ranking of alternatives.

Table 1. Description of Alternatives

Alternatives	Sample	Composition				
		LDPE (Wt. %)	HDPE (Wt. %)	PP (Wt. %)	RHA (Wt. %)	Sand (Wt. %)
A1	LD70R15S15	70			15	15
A2	LD80R10S10	80			10	10
A3	LD90R5S5	90			5	5
A4	HD70R15S15		70		15	15
A5	HD80R10S10		80		10	10
A6	HD90R5S5		90		5	5
A7	PP70R15S15			70	15	15
A8	PP80R10S10			80	10	10
A9	PP90R5S5			90	5	5

Table 2. Ranking of alternatives

	S_i^+	S_i^-	CC_i	RANK
A1	.148	.089	.374	6
A2	.174	.074	.297	8
A3	.173	.047	.215	9
A4	.136	.110	.446	5
A5	.154	.071	.316	7
A6	.114	.097	.460	4
A7	.105	.164	.611	3
A8	.057	.146	.719	2
A9	.025	.185	.882	1

Results and Discussions

To check reliability and robustness of proposed technique, CA and SA are performed and discussed below.

Comparative Analysis

Proposed techniques compared with various popular MCDM techniques. Ranking results are furnished in Table 3 and shown in Figure 2.

Table 3. Comparative Analysis

Methods	Ranking of Alternatives								
	A1	A2	A3	A4	A5	A6	A7	A8	A9
TOPSIS	6	8	9	5	7	4	3	2	1
MOORA	7	8	9	5	6	4	3	2	1
CoCoSo	8	7	6	9	5	3	4	2	1
ARAS	8	9	6	4	7	5	2	3	1
WSM	7	9	6	5	8	4	1	3	2
WPM	5	9	8	6	7	4	1	3	2
WASPAS	7	9	6	5	8	4	1	3	2

It could be observed that MOORA, CoCoSo, ARAS have identified A9 as the best alternative, whereas A7 has been selected as the best option by WSM, WPM and WASPAS. The variation in the ranking order occurred because different MCDM techniques use different methodologies to rank the alternatives. To check consistency of various ranking results obtained by

MCDM techniques, the Spearman's rank correlation coefficients (SRCCs) (Chakraborty and Saha, 2022(a); 2023; 2022(b)) have been calculated. It could be observed that the SRCCs between TOPSIS and other MCDMs are (0.98, 0.7, 0.85, 0.85, 0.917, 0.85), which indicates the strong correlation between the ranking orders of the results obtained by the various MCDM techniques.

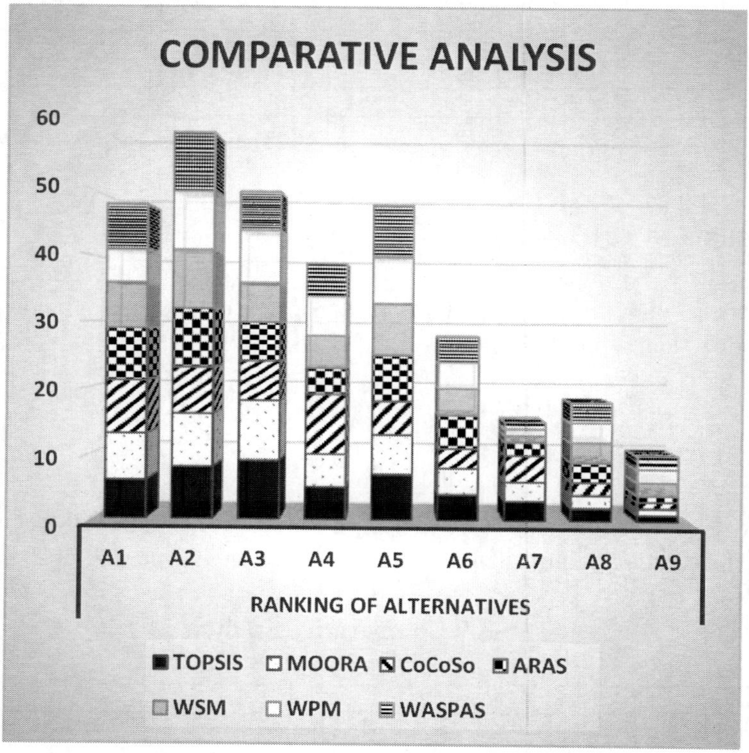

Figure 2. Comparative analysis.

Sensitivity Analysis

For further validation of results obtained by proposed technique, SA has been performed by varying criteria weights (Pandey, B. K. et al., 2021). Various cases have been investigated and results are furnished in Table 4 and shown in Figure 3. From Table 4, it is clear that ranking of alternatives changes according to variation of criteria weights, which indicates that ranking results are sensitive with respect to change in criteria weights.

Table 4. Variation in criteria weights

Cases	Criteria Weights		Ranking of alternatives								
			A1	A2	A3	A4	A5	A6	A7	A8	A9
Case 1	Weights obtained from SWARA		6	8	9	5	7	4	3	2	1
Case 2	Equal Weights		6	7	9	5	8	4	3	2	1
Case 3	50% weights for beneficiary criteria (BC)	50% weights for cost criteria (CC)	6	8	9	5	7	4	3	2	1
Case 4	60% weights forBC	40% weights forCC	6	8	9	5	7	4	3	1	2
Case 5	70% weights forBC	30% weights forCC	6	9	8	5	7	4	3	1	2
Case 6	80% weights forBC	20% weights forCC	6	9	8	5	7	2	4	1	3

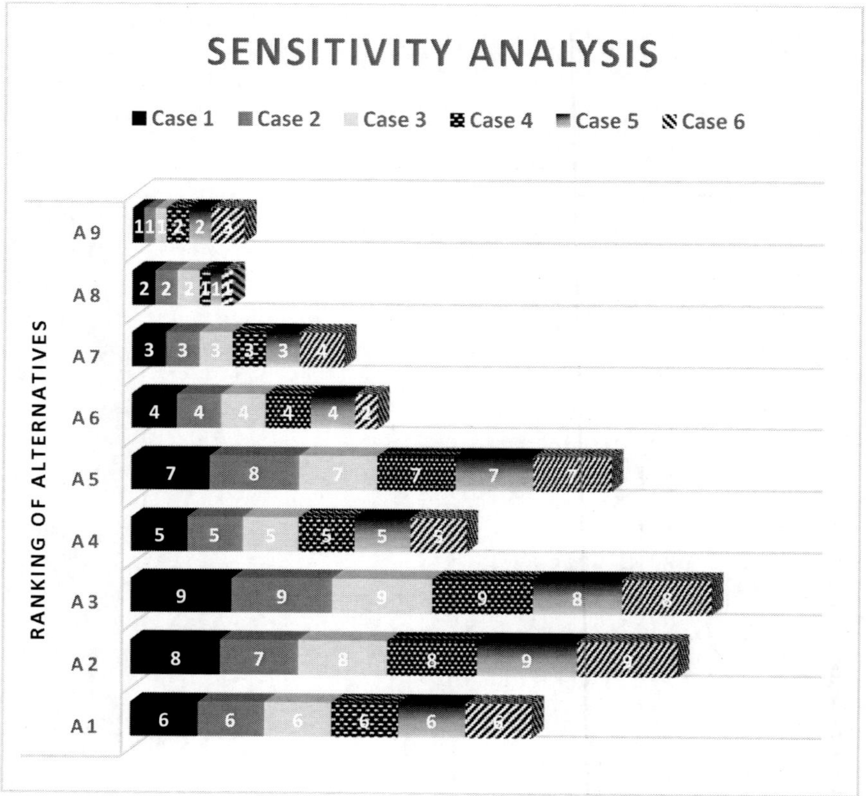

Figure 3. Variation in criteria weights.

Perspectives

When choosing recyclable materials, one can analyze their environmental impact and priorities of those with the smallest carbon footprint. This aligns with sustainability goals and contributes to lowering the total environmental impact of recycling procedures. The development of any sustainable material involves material selection, as it increases the life of any product while conserving important resources. Composites are developed in the current work by recycling several types of WP with RHA and sand reinforcement. MCDM is a continuous process, not a one-time decision. It is critical to assess and update material selection factors and decisions regularly in response to changing situations, technology, and market conditions in order to optimize waste recycling processes.

Conclusion

One of the most effective ways of waste management is recycling of waste, which reduces waste volume and helps to have pollution free safe environment. In the present treatise and AW are recycled for developing polymeric composites such as floor tiles, which offers sustainable, low-cost and alternative building construction material. Here the problem of MS has been modeled and solved using proposed SWARA-TOPSIS technique and has identified "A9" as the best composition for floor tiles. Furthermore, the proposed technique has been compared with various MCDM techniques and the results are consistent and reliable. SA is performed to check robustness of proposed method. The proposed approach will be helpful for industrialists and engineers for selecting building material through recycling of solid waste. So, the proposed method is advantageous both in environmental and economical aspect.

In future, the problem of materials selection could be modeled under various fuzzy environments and also can be solved by integrating other MCDM techniques. In this regard, several decision makers can be involved and aggregation operators can be developed for aggregating decision maker's assessments.

References

Aghazadeh E., Yildirim H., Kuruoglu M. A Hybrid Fuzzy MCDM Methodology for Optimal Structural System Selection Compatible with Sustainable Materials in Mass-Housing Projects. *Sustainability* (2022) vol. 14(20), 13559, https://doi.org/10.3390/su142013559.

Aires R. F. d. F., FerreiraL. A. New Multi-Criteria Approach for Sustainable MS Problem. *Sustainability* (2022) vol. 14, 11191, https://doi.org/10.3390/su141811191.

Chakraborty S., Saha A. K. A framework of LR fuzzy AHP and fuzzy WASPAS for health care waste recycling technology. *Applied Soft Computing* (2022) 127. 109388, https://doi.org/10.1016/j.asoc.2022.109388.

Chakraborty S., Saha A. K. Selection of Forklift Unit for Transport Handling using Integrated MCDM under Neutrosophic Environment. *Facta Universitatis, Series: Mechanical Engineering* (2022) (a).

Chakraborty S., Saha A. K. Novel Fermatean Fuzzy Bonferroni Mean aggregation operators for selecting optimal health care waste treatment technology. *Engineering Applications of Artificial Intelligence* (2023) vol. 119 105752, https://doi.org/10.1016/j.engappai.2022.105752.

Chakraborty S., Saha A. K. Selection of optimal lithium-ion battery recycling process: A multi-criteria group decision making approach. *Journal of Energy Storage* (2022) (b) Volume 55, Part B, https://doi.org/10.1016/j.est.2022.105557.

Choudhury S., Majumdar A., Saha A. K., Majumdar P., Evaluating the preparedness of Indian States against COVID-19 pandemic risk: a fuzzy multi-criteria decision-making approach, *Risk Anal*(2022) 42 (1) 85–96 2021 Aug 23, https://doi.org/10.1111/risa.13808.

Choudhury S., Saha A. K., Majumder M., Optimal location selection for installation of surface water treatment plant by gini coefficient-based analytical hierarchy process, *Environ. Dev. Sustain* (2020) 22 (5), 4073–4099, https://doi.org/10.1007/s10668-019-00373-w.

Dev S., Aherwar A., Patnaik A., MS for automotive piston component using entropy-VIKOR method, *Silicon* (2020) vol. 12 (1), pp. 155-169, https://link.springer.com/article/10.1007/s12633-019-00110-y.

Emovon I., Oghenenyerovwho O. S. Application of MCDM method in MS for optimal design: A review. *Results in Materials* (2020) vol. 7, 100115, https://doi.org/10.1016/j.rinma.2020.100115.

Haq R. S. U., Saeed M., Mateen N., Siddiqui F., Naqvi M., Yi J. B., Ahmed S. Sustainable MS with crisp and ambiguous data using single-valued neutrosophic-MEREC-MARCOS framework. *Applied Soft Computing* (2022) vol 128, 109546, https://doi.org/10.1016/j.engappai.2023.106177.

Kersuliene V., Zavadskas E. K. and Turskis Z. Selection of rational dispute resolution method by applying new step-wise weight assessment ratio analysis (SWARA). *Journal of Business Economics and Management* (2010) vol. 11(2). pp. 243-258, https://doi.org/10.3846/jbem.2010.12.

Moradian M., Modanloo V., Aghaie S. Comparative analysis of multi criteria decision making techniques for MS of brake booster valve body. *Journal of Traffic and Transportation Engineering* (2019) vol 6 (5), pp. 526-534, https://doi.org/10.1016/j.jtte.2018.02.001.

Manalo M. V. G., Magdaluyo Jr. E. R. Integrated DLM-COPRAS method in materials selection of laminated glass interlayer for a fuel-efficient concept vehicle. *Proceedings of the World Congress on Engineering* (2018) vol. 2, International Association of Engineers London, https://doi.org/10.1016/j.eswa.2022.118268.

Soni A., Chakraborty S., Das P. K., Saha A. K. MS of reinforced sustainable composites by recycling waste plastic and agro-waste: An integrated multi-criteria decision-making approach. *Construction and Building Materials* (2022) vol. 348. 128608, 2022, https://doi.org/10.1016/j.conbuildmat.2022.128608.

Saha A. K., Choudhury S., Majumder M. Performance efficiency analysis of water treatment plants by using MCDM and neural network model,*MATTER: international, J. Sci. Technol* (2017) 3 (1), 27–35, https://doi.org/10.20319/MIJST.2017.31.2735.

Senyigit E., Demirel B. The selection of material in dental implant with entropy based simple additive weighting and analytic hierarchy process methods. *Sigma Journal of Engineering and Natural Sciences*. (2018) vol. 36 (3), pp. 731-740.

Yang K., Zhu N., Chang C., Wang D., Yang S., Ma S. A methodological concept for phase change MS based on multi-criteria decision making (MCDM): A case study. *Energy* (2018) vol. 165, Part B, pp. 1085-1096, https://doi.org/10.1016/j.energy.2018.10.022.

Yoon K. P., Hwang C. L. Multiple attribute decision making: an introduction. *Sage publications* (1995).

Yadav S., Pathak V. K., Gangwar S. A novel hybrid TOPSIS-PSI approach for MS in marine applications. *Sādhanā* (2019) vol. 44(3), http://dx.doi.org/10.1007/s12046-018-1020-x.

Chapter 4

Potential of Optimal Coupling of Species Migration to Bring Synchrony in Seasonally Perturbed System

Shubhangi Dwivedi*
Nitu Kumari
School of Mathematical and Statistical Sciences
Indian Institute of Technology Mandi, Himachal Pradesh, India

Abstract

The study investigates phase synchronization within a two-habitat system, specifically focusing on the unidirectional migration of species induced by seasonal perturbations. Each habitat has the base dynamics of the classical Hastings-Powell model, where species flow in a simple in-line motif from prey to top predator via intermediate predators. In the system, the first habitat experiences seasonal fluctuations, whereas the growth function of prey in the second is subject to refugia and the Allee effect. The study begins by analyzing the properties of the seasonally perturbed model and then the role of migration in balancing the dynamics of the two-habitat system is assessed. Through adjustment in the coupling coefficient, the study identifies the best-suited coupling dimension for establishing sustainable habitats. Numerical computations suggest that migration of single species from a habitat under seasonal effects to a relatively more suitable habitat can promote synchrony within a two-habitat system. A key finding of the study is that migration is a mechanism that can induce synchronization within an eco-network, which paves the way for further investigation.

Keywords: seasonality, two-habitat system, synchronization

---

* Corresponding Author's Email: shubhangi.dwivedi176@gmail.com.

In: Emerging Trends in Mathematical Sciences and Computing
Editors: B. Basu Mallik, S. Ghosh, B. Kumar Pandey et al.
ISBN: 979-8-89113-751-6

Introduction

With no denial, migration plays a crucial role in shaping the dynamics of ecosystems, particularly in areas where resources are scarce or subject to extreme or unpredictable conditions. This survival strategy of species has the strength to induce synchrony or balance within coupled habitats. However, if not carefully managed, disruption can also take place. Due to the limited resources available in the host habitat, disruption caused by migration can have detrimental effects on both individual species and entire ecosystems of coupled habitats Therefore, it is important to understand the factors that can induce balanced synchrony, and subsequently a delicate balance of an ecosystem can be maintained.

To understand this, we use Hastings-Powell model as a starting point for the investigation and further extend it to include seasonal effects (Hastings, 1988). The model flows linearly from prey species to top-predator via intermediate predator. Additionally, the growth of the prey population in the system is considered under the refugia and the Allee effect (Nath, Kumari, Kumar, & Das, 2019).

Our study extends the Hastings-Powell model to two coupled habitats and investigates synchrony under species migration. In the two-habitat configuration, the first patch represents an adverse habitat with seasonal disturbances whereas the second patch refers to a favourable habitat with Allee and refugia effects. These two habitats are coupled through a uni-directional migration scheme, where species migrate from the habitat under seasonal effects to the favourable one. Unidirectional migration means that the species only moves in one direction, rather than moving back and forth or in multiple directions.

We examine each possible coupling coefficient associated with migration. The phase-space projection method has been used to identify the best-suited coupling scheme for synchrony with two-habitat system (Pikovsky, Rosenblum, Osipov, & Kurths, 1997; Pikovsky, Rosenblum, & Kurths, 2000). The results of the study are validated through numerical simulation. The inferences from this study can have important implications for the management of natural resources, particularly in areas where resources are scarce or subject to extreme or unpredictable perturbations.

Model

The mathematical equations of HP model (Hastings, 1988), where prey (X_1) conventionally points to top predator X_3 via intermediate predator X_2, are given as

$$\begin{aligned}
\dot{X}_1(t) &= R_0 X_1(1-\tfrac{X_1}{k_0}) - \tfrac{C_1 A_1 X_1 X_2}{1+B_1 X_1}, \\
\dot{X}_2(t) &= \tfrac{A_1 X_1 x_2}{1+B_1 X_1} - \tfrac{A_2 X_2 X_3}{1+B_2 X_2} - \Gamma_1 x_2, \\
\dot{X}_3(t) &= \tfrac{C_2 A_2 X_2 X_3}{1+B_2 X_2} - \Gamma_2 X_3.
\end{aligned} \tag{1}$$

where R_0 is the natural growth rate, k_0 is the carrying capacity of the prey population, which means that the prey population cannot grow indefinitely. The interaction between intermediate predator and top predator is incorporated by a Holling type II functional response (Dawes & Souza, 2013). The functional response of the predators is of Holling type II, which means that the rate of prey consumption by the predators increases as the prey density increases but at a decreasing rate. C_1^{-1} and C_2 are the conversion rates of prey to predator, Γ_i (for $i \in \{1, 2\}$) are the constant death rate. A_i and B_i (for $i \in \{1, 2\}$) are the maximal predation rate and a half-saturation constant for the middle and the top predator.
Nath and coauthors (Nath et al., 2019) further extended the Hastings-Powell model with two bio-controlling parameters refugia and Allee effects (we call it as eHPM). In the model, refugia refers to that fraction of prey who hide themselves and avoid being consumed by intermediate predators. It is assumed that a portion m of the prey always escapes from the intermediate predator and the remaining $(1-m)$ portion takes part in the interaction with intermediate predators. Whereas, the Allee effect refers to the phenomenon where a population's growth rate decreases as population density decreases. $\Theta > 0$ denotes the Allee effect imposed on the prey population. This can occur when the cost of finding a mate or other resources exceeds the benefits of increased population size. The mathematical equations of eHPM are given as (see details in (Nath et al., 2019)).

$$\begin{aligned} \dot{X}_1(T) &= R_0 X_1 (1 - \tfrac{X_1}{k_0})(\tfrac{X_1}{X_1+\Theta}) - \tfrac{C_1 A_1 (1-m) X_1 X_2}{1+B_1(1-m)X_1}, \\ \dot{X}_2(T) &= \tfrac{A_1(1-m)X_1 X_2}{1+B_1(1-m)X_1} - \tfrac{A_2 X_2 X_3}{1+B_2 X_2} - \Gamma_1 X_2, \\ \dot{X}_3(T) &= \tfrac{C_2 A_2 X_2 X_3}{1+B_2 X_2} - \Gamma_2 X_3. \end{aligned} \tag{2}$$

Next, we consider a model introduced in the article (Dwivedi & Kumari, 2023). In previous work, researchers (Gakkhar & Naji, 2003), (Sauve, Taylor, & Barraquand, 2020) integrated seasonal effects using sinusoidal functions because of the periodic nature of seasonal forces. The study (Dwivedi & Kumari, 2023) followed a similar approach and assumed that seasonal effects primarily affect the prey and subsequently cascade to affect the mortality rates of predators dependent on its prey. Specifically, the natural growth rate of prey, denoted by X_1, the death rates of intermediate predators, denoted by Γ_1, and the death rates of top predators, denoted by Γ_2, are modeled as functions of time, denoted by T. It allows the Hastings-Powell to capture the dynamic effects of seasonal variation on the food chain. Now, we consider the model () that has time varying growth rate of prey $R_0(T)$, and mortality rates of $\Gamma_{1,2}(T)$. Expressions of seasonally perturbed parameters are as follows:

$$\begin{aligned} R_0(T) &= R_0(1 + \epsilon_1 \sin(\Psi T)), \\ \Gamma_1(T) &= (1 + \epsilon_2 \sin(\Psi T + h))\Gamma_1, \\ \Gamma_2(T) &= (1 + \epsilon_3 \sin(\Psi T + h))\Gamma_2. \end{aligned} \tag{3}$$

Here, $R_0(T)$ represents the natural growth rate of the prey, which is affected by seasonal fluctuations. The parameter ϵ_i represents the magnitude of the perturbations in $R_0(T)$ and $\Gamma_{1,2}(T)$ due to seasonality respectively, with $0 < \epsilon_i < 1$. The term Ψ is the angular frequency of seasonal fluctuations. The death rate of intermediate predators, $\Gamma_1(T)$, is also affected by seasonality. The term h is the phase angle between the seasonality of $R_0(T)$ and $\Gamma_1(T)$. The death rate of top predators, $\Gamma_2(T)$, are similarly affected by seasonality. The term h is again the phase angle between the seasonality of $R_0(T)$ and $\Gamma_2(T)$. In these equations, the average values of $\Gamma_1(T)$ and $\Gamma_2(T)$ are denoted by Γ_1 and Γ_2, respectively.
The non-dimensionalized version of the model can be obtained by choosing the relation given below (for more detail, see the discussion in (Nath et al., 2019))-

$$x_1 = \frac{X_1}{K_0}, \quad x_2 = \frac{C_1 X_2}{K_0}, \quad x_3 = \frac{C_1 X_3}{C_2 K_0}, \quad t = R_0 T.$$

Making these substitutions and simplifying yields the following system of equations,

$$\begin{aligned} \dot{x}_1(t) &= R_0(t)x_1(1-x_1)\tfrac{x_1}{x_1+\theta} - \tfrac{\alpha_1(1-m)x_1x_2}{1+\beta_1(1-m)x_1}. \\ \dot{x}_2(t) &= \tfrac{\alpha_1(1-m)x_1x_2}{1+\beta_1(1-m)x_1} - \tfrac{\alpha_2x_2x_3}{1+\beta_2x_2} - \gamma_1(t)x_2, \\ \dot{x}_3(t) &= \tfrac{\alpha_2x_2x_3}{1+\beta_2x_2} - \gamma_2(t)x_3. \end{aligned} \tag{4}$$

where

$$\begin{aligned} R_0(t) &= (1+\epsilon_1 \sin(\nu t)), \\ \gamma_1(T) &= (1+\epsilon_2 \sin(\nu t + p))\gamma_1, \\ \gamma_2(T) &= (1+\epsilon_3 \sin(\nu t + p))\gamma_2. \end{aligned} \tag{5}$$

The substitution of equation (5) into the model (4) forms the eHPM to a seasonally perturbed eHPM where dimensionless parameters are taken as

$$\epsilon_i = \mu_i, \forall i \in \{1,2,3\}, p = h, \nu = \frac{\Psi}{R_0}.$$

The remaining dimensionless parameters are provided in the table 1 along with their ecologically feasible numerical values:

Two-habitat Configuration

The configuration considers the seasonally perturbed eHPM, introduced in the recent article (Dwivedi & Kumari, 2023). The study (Dwivedi & Kumari, 2023) has referred the synchrony as an adaptability mechanism exhibited by species in response to fluctuating seasonal influences within an isolated habitat. The model is now followed by inducing the migration of species to a favourable habitat which is represented by the eHPM model with refugia and Allee effects. The migration

Table 1. Parameter values used in the simulations.

Non-dimensional Parameters	Dimensional Parameters	Values of parameters used in the simulations
θ	$\frac{\Theta}{K_0}$	0.01
m	m	0.04
α_1	$\frac{A_1K_0}{B_1R_0}$	5
α_2	$\frac{A_2C_2K_0}{B_2C_1R_0}$	0.1
β_1	$\frac{K_0}{B_1}$	3
β_2	$\frac{K_0}{B_2C_1}$	2
γ_1	$\frac{\Gamma_1}{R_0}$	0.4
γ_2	$\frac{\Gamma_2}{R_0}$	0.01

strength of the prey, intermediate predator, and top predator are represented by ψ_{x_1}, ψ_{x_2}, and ψ_{x_3}, respectively. These strengths indicate the individual's likelihood to leave the habitat under seasonal effects for a relatively favorable one. The mathematical equations of the two-habitat system are given as:

Habitat: 1

$$\begin{aligned} \dot{x}_1(t) &= (1+\mu_1 \sin(\nu t))(1-x_1)\tfrac{x_1^2}{x_1+\theta} - \tfrac{\alpha_1(1-m)x_1x_2}{1+\beta_1(1-m)x_1} - \psi_{x_1}\, d_1x_1, \\ \dot{x}_2(t) &= \tfrac{\alpha_1(1-m)x_1x_2}{1+\beta_1(1-m)x_1} - \tfrac{\alpha_2x_2x_3}{1+\beta_2x_2} - (1+\mu_2\sin(\nu t+p))\gamma_1x_2 - \psi_{x_2}\, d_1x_2, \\ \dot{x}_3(t) &= \tfrac{\alpha_2x_2x_3}{1+\beta_2x_2} - (1+\mu_3\sin(\nu t+p)\gamma_2x_3 - \psi_{x_3}\, d_1x_3. \end{aligned} \tag{6}$$

Habitat: 2

$$\begin{aligned} \dot{y}_1(t) &= y_1(1-y_1)\tfrac{y_1}{y_1+\theta} - \tfrac{\alpha_1(1-m)y_1y_2}{1+\beta_1(1-m)y_1} + \psi_{x_1}\, d_1x_1, \\ \dot{y}_2(t) &= \chi_2\, \tfrac{\alpha_1(1-m)y_1y_2}{1+\beta_1(1-m)y_1} - \tfrac{\alpha_2y_2y_3}{1+\beta_2} - \gamma_1y_2 + \psi_{x_2}\, d_1x_2, \\ \dot{y}_3(t) &= \tfrac{\alpha_2y_2y_3}{1+\beta_2y_2} - \gamma_2y_3 + \psi_{x_3}\, d_1x_3. \end{aligned} \tag{7}$$

In order to gain insight into the broader collective dynamics of the network, we consider the identical migration strength of species from both communities, denoted by

$$\psi_{x_1} = \psi_{x_2} = \psi_{x_3} = \psi.$$

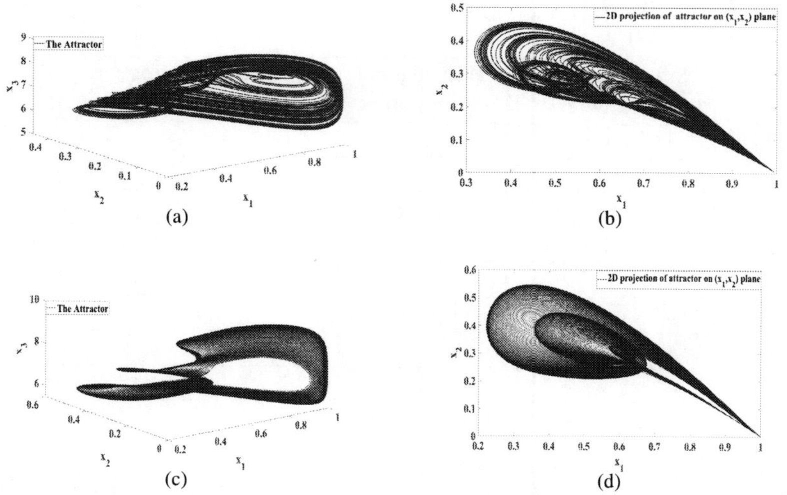

Figure 1. (a), (b): $\nu = 0.13, p = \frac{\pi}{12}$; (c), (d): $\nu = 2 \times 10^{-4}, p = \frac{3\pi}{4}$.

The coupling dimension coefficient for each i is denoted by d_i, where $i \in \{1, 2, 3\}$, and ψ represents the strength of coupling. Two different natural frequencies for the communities are described as $\chi_1 = \chi_0 + \Delta\chi$ and $\chi_2 = \chi_0 - \Delta\chi$, where $\Delta\chi$ is the natural frequency mismatch and χ_0 is the normalized natural frequency of the communities.

We first study the dynamics of isolated habitat under seasonal effects (6) in the absence of coupling ($d_i = 0$ for all $i \in \{1, 2, 3\}$). We consider five sets of parameter values, where the parameters associated with seasonal fluctuation vary for each set and the other parameters are the same as in Table 1. A regime shift in the system from chaos to a periodic cycle just by a minor change in the frequency ν of seasonal forces is an important ecological phenomenon. Using ν and p as control parameters, we plot the three-dimensional attractor and its projection on the (x_1, x_2)-plane for different parameter sets but with the same initial condition. The numerical value of magnitude of seasonal perturbation $\{\mu_1, \mu_2, \mu_3\}$, are kept fixed at $\{0.109, 0.169, 0.109\}$. The system is numerically simulate with the initial condition $(x_1(0), x_2(0), x_3(0)) = (0.63564, 0.24691, 6.6392)$ for all the three figures 1, 2, 3. The results show vastly different dynamics for each set, as evidenced in these figures, which reveal a transition from a strange attractor to a stable limit cycle. This highlights the significant impact of seasonality on the dynamics of an isolated habitat. Next, to understand the role of initial conditions on the seasonally perturbed system, we plot the time trajectories of species with two sets of initial

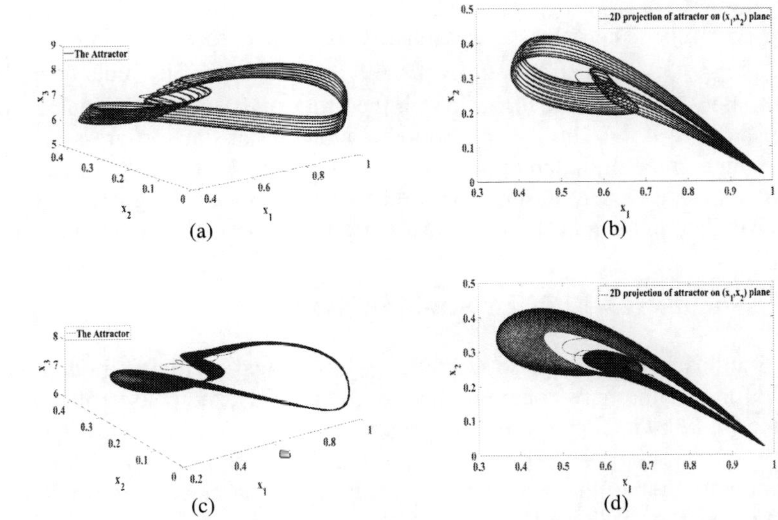

Figure 2. (a), (b): $\nu = 3 \times 10^{-3}, p = 0$; (c) (d): $\nu = \frac{\pi}{3}, p = \frac{2\pi}{3}$.

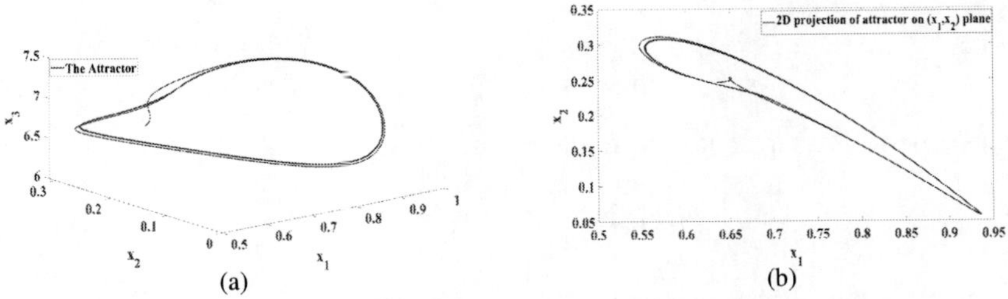

Figure 3. (a), (b): $\nu = 10^{-7}, p = \frac{\pi}{2}$.

values as $(x_1(0), x_2(0), x_3(0))$ and$(x_1(0) + 0.001, x_2(0) + 0.001, x_3(0) + 0 : 001)$ respectively. The values of seasonality associated parameters are chosen as $\nu = \frac{pi}{3}, p = \frac{2\pi}{3}, \mu_1 = 0.399, \mu_2 = 0.169, \mu_3 = 0.309$. The plots depicted in Figure 4 show that a minute alteration on the order of 10^{-3} in the initial densities of species can lead to a significant change in dynamics as time progresses. Thus, a minor change in the initial condition of each state variable of the system can make the system evolve closely to quasi-periodically. Ecologically, it gives a sense that species oscillate in abundance with quasi-periodic (closely) peaks and phases.

Phase Synchrony within Two-habitat System

Figure 3 indicates that the phase extraction of ecological oscillators in *habitat:1* is possible for certain phase-coherent attractors. Similarly, the phases of ecological oscillators in *habitat: 2* can also be extracted. As the projection of the attractor in the x_1, x_2 plane resembles a limit cycle (along the direction where neither expansion nor contraction of the phase volume occurs), and the trajectories rotate around the origin (see Fig. 5). The limit cycle is obtained by taking the specific values for the parameters of habitat-2

$$\alpha_1 = 4.996, \alpha_2 = 0.691, \beta_1 = 3, \beta_2 = 1.99, \gamma_1 = 0.5,$$

$$\gamma_2 = 0.02, \theta = 0.91, m = 0.01.$$

Now, we investigate the phase synchrony in two habitats using the phase-space projection method. Note that the smeared limit cycles presented in figures 3 and 5 for *habitat: 2* and *habitat:1* can be approximated by circle with center $(h_{1,2}, k_{1,2})$ (located in positive quadrant) and radius as $A_{1,2}$ respectively. Here, we introduce the phase as the angle between the projection of the phase point on the plane and a given direction on the plane. For *habitat:1* and *habitat:2*, the polar coordinates of the limit cycle approximated to a circle are taken as:

$$\begin{aligned} x_1 &= h_1 + A_1 \cos\phi_1, \quad x_2 = k_1 + A_1 \sin\phi_1, \\ y_1 &= h_2 + A_2 \cos\phi_2, \quad y_2 = k_2 + A_2 \sin\phi_1. \end{aligned} \tag{8}$$

We use the following equations to define the phases:

$$\phi_1 = \arctan\left(\frac{x_2}{x_1}\right), \quad \phi_2 = \arctan\left(\frac{y_2}{y_1}\right).$$

To calculate the observed frequency based on the phase angle ϕ_i for $i \in \{1, 2\}$ during observation time T, we define the mean frequency as the average of $\frac{d\phi_i}{dt}$ during observation time T. The observed frequency can be defined as follows:

$$\Omega_i = \lim_{T\to\infty} \frac{\phi_i(T) - \phi_i(0)}{T}, \quad for \quad i \in \{1, 2\} \tag{9}$$

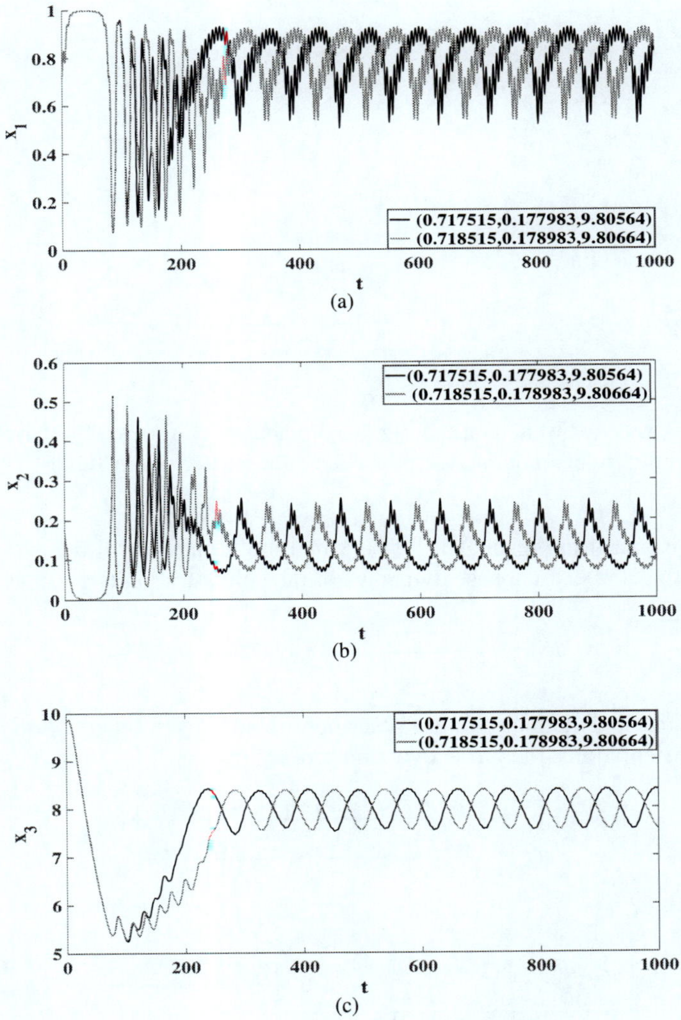

Figure 4. Divergence of trajectories when seasonally perturbed system exhibits quasi-periodic dynamics. Trajectories of species x_1, x_2 and x_3 are plotted for two different initial conditions $(0.717515, 0.177983, 9.80564)$ and $(0.718515, 0.178983, 9.80664)$ (in red and black colour respectively), in figures (a), (b), and (c) respectively.

For a system of two-coupled patches, we simply calculate the difference of two mean observed frequencies. The observed frequency mismatch is defined as

$$\Omega = |\Omega_2 - \Omega_1| \tag{10}$$

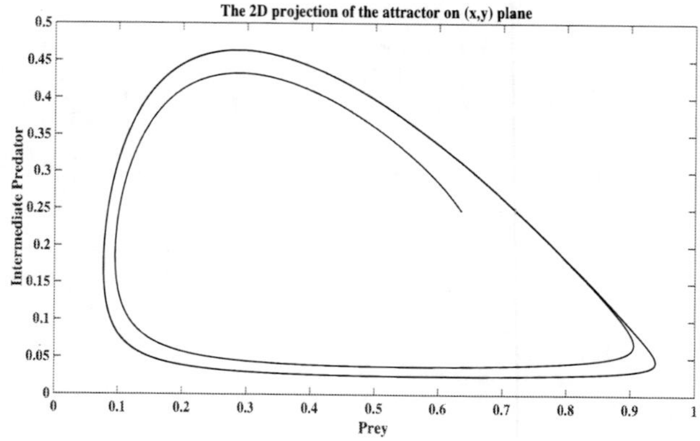

Figure 5. Projection of habitat-2 on (x_1, x_2) plane which forms a limit cycle attractor and performs periodic motion. The parameter values are given in Table 1.

The idea is that if the mismatch $\Delta\Omega$ is small, both phases will behave almost the same. To check this, the phase dynamics of the configuration is given as

$$\dot{\phi}_1 = \frac{x_1\dot{x}_2 - x_2\dot{x}_1}{(A_1)^2}, \quad \dot{\phi}_2 = \frac{y_1\dot{y}_2 - y_2\dot{y}_1}{(A_2)^2}.$$

For these phase dynamics, we use polar coordinates given by equation (8). Using these representations, the phase dynamics are follows as:

$$\begin{aligned} \dot{\phi}_1 &= \frac{(h_1+A_1\cos(\phi_1))\dot{x}_2-(k_1+A_1\sin(\phi_1))\dot{x}_1}{{A_1}^2}, \\ \dot{\phi}_2 &= \frac{(h_2+A_2\cos(\phi_2))\dot{y}_2-(k_2+A_2\sin(\phi_2))\dot{y}_1}{{A_2}^2}. \end{aligned} \tag{11}$$

where

$$\begin{aligned} \dot{x}_1(t) &= (1+\mu_1\sin(\nu t))(1-(h_1+A_1\cos(\phi_1)))\frac{(h_1+A_1\cos(\phi_1))^2}{h_1+A_1\cos(\phi_1)+\theta} \\ &\quad -\frac{(2h_1k_1+2A_1(k_1\cos(\phi_1)+h_1\sin(\phi_1))+{A_1}^2\alpha_1(1-m)\sin(2\phi_1))}{2(1+\beta_1(1-m)(h_1+A_1\cos(\phi_1)))} - \psi\, d_1\,(h_1+A_1\cos(\phi_1)), \\ \dot{x}_2(t) &= \chi_1\,\frac{(2h_1k_1+2A_1(k_1\cos(\phi_1)+h_1\sin(\phi_1))+{A_1}^2\alpha_1(1-m)\sin(2\phi_1))}{2(1+\beta_1(1-m)(h_1+A_1\cos(\phi_1)))} \\ &\quad -\frac{\alpha_2(k_1+A_1\sin(\phi_1))x_3}{1+\beta_2(k_1+A_1\sin(\phi_1))} - ((1+\mu_2\sin(\nu t+p))\,\gamma_1 - \psi d_2(k_1+A_1\sin(\phi_1)), \\ \dot{y}_1(t) &= (1-(h_2+A_2\cos(\phi_2)))\frac{(h_2+A_2\cos(\phi_2))^2}{h_2+A_2\cos(\phi_2)+\theta} \\ &\quad -\frac{(2h_2k_2+2A_2(k_2\cos(\phi_2)+h_2\sin(\phi_2))+{A_2}^2\alpha_2(1-m)\sin(2\phi_1))}{2(1+\beta_2(1-m)(h_2+A_2\cos(\phi_2)))} + \psi\, d_1\,(h_1+A_1\cos(\phi_1)), \\ \dot{y}_2(t) &= \chi_2\,\frac{(2h_2k_2+2A_2(k_2\cos(\phi_2)+h_2\sin(\phi_2))+{A_2}^2\alpha_1(1-m)\sin(2\phi_2))}{2(1+\beta_1(1-m)(h_2+A_2\cos(\phi_2)))} - \frac{\alpha_2(k_2+A_2\sin(\phi_2))y_3}{1+\beta_2(k_2+A_2\sin(\phi_2))}, \\ &\quad -\gamma_1(k_2+A_2\sin(\phi_2)) + \psi\, d_2\,(k_1+A_1\sin(\phi_1)). \end{aligned} \tag{12}$$

Numerical Simulation: Best-suited Coupling

We initialize the two-habitat configuration with the initial condition $(0.80556, 0.178, 6.8646)$, $(0.91389, 0.177983, 9.80564)$, The parameters associated to seasonality are considered as $\mu_1 = 0.34599, \mu_2 = 0.189, \mu_3 = 0.0978, \nu = 1.057, p = \frac{\pi}{2}$. The natural frequency mismatch between the two communities is set as $\Delta\chi = 0.015$. We pick all eight possible choices of CDC $(d_1, d_2, d_3) \in \{(0,0,0), (1,0,0), (0,1,0), (0,0,1), (1,0,0), (1,1,0), (0,1,1), (1,0,1), (1,1,1)\}$ with fixed coupling strength $\psi = 0.102$. The results, as shown in Fig. 6, indicate that CDC $(0, 1, 0)$ is the most suitable for achieving synchronous states in coupled habitats. For easy comparison, the maximum values of the numerically calculated phase difference for all coupling dimensions considered are listed in Table 2. We here emphasize the importance of the dimension of coupling in inducing synchrony within coupled communities in a patchy ecosystem network.

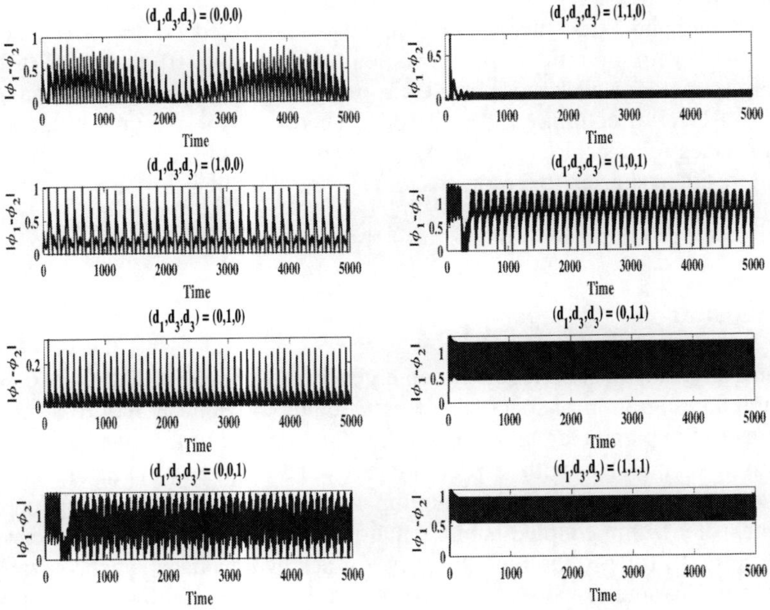

Figure 6. Relative phase difference $\Delta\Omega$ of two communities coupled with eight different scenarios of coupling dimension while the considered natural frequency mismatch $\Delta\chi$ and migration strength ψ is fixed for all eight cases.

After careful assessment of Table 2, we claim that if only the intermediate predator

Table 2. Maximum difference of two mean observed frequencies $\Delta\Omega$ of two coupled habitats with eight different scenarios of coupling dimension while the considered natural frequency mismatch $\Delta\chi$ and migration strength ψ is fixed.

S.N.	1	2	3	4	5	6	7	8
(d_1, d_2, d_3)	$(0,0,0)$	$(1,0,0)$	$(0,1,0)$	$(0,0,1)$	$(1,1,0)$	$(0,1,1)$	$(1,0,1)$	$(1,1,1)$
$\Delta\Omega_{Max}$	0.85802	1.0355	0.26243	1.4815	0.59149	1.3205	1.4078	1.0919

of the habitat under seasonal effects migrates with migration strength $\psi = 0.102$, then phase-synchronized oscillators within the two-habitat system can be obtained as phase difference is relatively smaller.
To verify this statement, we numerically solve the coupled equations of the configuration using the Runge-Kutta method and extract the instantaneous phase of the oscillators. With reference to time, we plot the relative phase for two choices of coupling dimensions $(d_1, d_2, d_3) = (0,0,0), (0,1,0)$. Fig. 7 shows weakly synchronous and non-synchronous states for uncoupled ($\psi = 0$) and coupled ($\psi = 0.108$) communities. For uncoupled habitats ($\psi = 0$), the phase difference performs a random-walk motion whereas regimes of phase-locking are initiated for the small level of coupling ($\psi = 0.108$). Therefore, the minimal number of migrant species in an ecological setting offers advantages by decreasing competition among resident species for resources, thus promoting their thriving.

Conclusion

We investigated a scenario of the emergence of synchrony within two habitats through the migration of species. We first studied the delicate nature of model (6) with respect to parameter values and initial conditions. For this, we have shown the sensitivity of model (6) with respect to severity and frequency of season. Thereafter, we have studied the role of the coupling dimension coefficient on the emergence of synchrony within coupled habitats. Our results have indicated that the coupling dimension $(0,1,0)$ is the most effective in achieving phase synchronization under certain parameter values. In particular, this coupling allows some species to remain in habitat under seasonal effects, reducing the strain on resource availability for the other habitat. Phase synchronization within the coupled patches under seasonal perturbation can help in thriving the species living in both habitats. Our findings demonstrate that species can coexist with balanced population density in each community, leading to a stable state that can recover after a transient time under a perturbation, if the coupling dimension coefficient is chosen carefully.

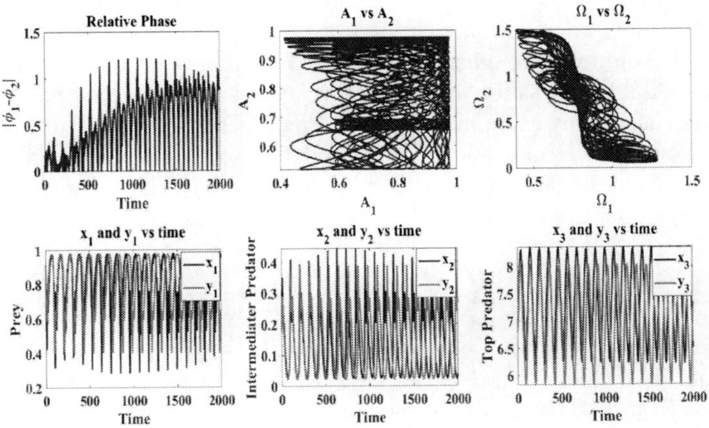

(a)

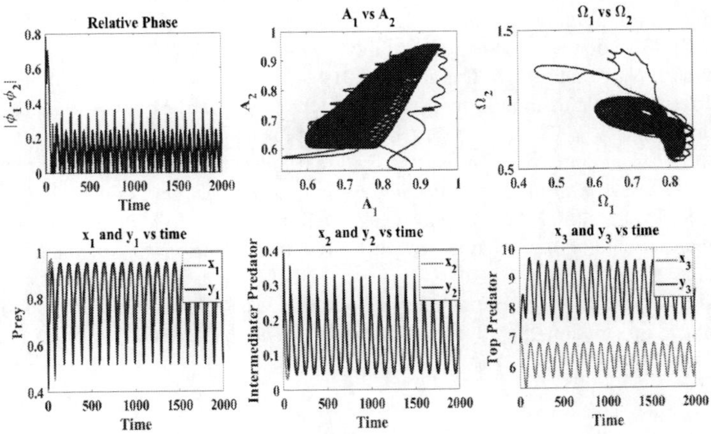

(b)

Figure 7. $|\phi_1 - \phi_2|$ versus time, amplitude A_1 vs A_2, ϕ_1 vs ϕ_2 and time series of each species are shown for two scenarios: (a) uncoupled patches ($\psi = 0$), (b) $(d_1, d_2, d_3) = (0, 1, 0)$ and $\psi = 0.108$. $\Delta\chi$ of the communities is taken as 0.015. Seasonality associated parameters are taken as: $\mu_1 = 0.34599, \mu_2 = 0.189, \mu_3 = 0.0978, \nu = 1.057, p = \frac{\pi}{2}, \psi = 0.108$.

Notably, the two-habitat configuration can be applied to a wide range of scenarios. These scenarios include climate change caused by human activities such as deforestation, mining, and pollution, which destroy or make natural habitats uninhabitable, forcing species to migrate. Moreover, some species migrate to areas where food is more abundant like caribou or wildebeest moving to new grazing grounds. Also, some species migrate to specific breeding or nesting sites to reproduce. It is crucial to assess the impact of species migration on their survival and the ecosystem at large by examining these different scenarios. The results from the study, based on minor modifications in the model presented here, can offer a valuable contribution to the field of experimental ecology. These insights can aid in the development of effective ecosystem conservation strategies.

References

Dawes, J., & Souza, M. (2013). A derivation of holling's type i, ii and iii functional responses in predator–prey systems. *Journal of theoretical biology*, *327*, 11–22.

Dwivedi, S., & Kumari, N. (2023). Effectiveness of phase synchronization in chaotic food chain model with refugia and allee effects during seasonal fluctuations. *Chaos: An Interdisciplinary Journal of Nonlinear Science*, *33*(6).

Gakkhar, S., & Naji, R. K. (2003). Chaos in seasonally perturbed ratio-dependent prey–predator system. *Chaos, Solitons & Fractals*, *15*(1), 107–118.

Hastings, A. (1988). Food web theory and stability. *Ecology*, *69*(6), 1665–1668.

Nath, B., Kumari, N., Kumar, V., & Das, K. P. (2019). Refugia and allee effect in prey species stabilize chaos in a tri-trophic food chain model. *Differential Equations and Dynamical Systems*, 1–27.

Pikovsky, A. S., Rosenblum, M. G., & Kurths, J. (2000). Phase synchronization in regular and chaotic systems. *International Journal of Bifurcation and Chaos*, *10*(10), 2291-2305.

Pikovsky, A. S., Rosenblum, M. G., Osipov, G. V., & Kurths, J. (1997). Phase synchronization of chaotic oscillators by external driving. *Physica D: Nonlinear Phenomena*, *104*(3-4), 219–238.

Sauve, A. M., Taylor, R. A., & Barraquand, F. (2020). The effect of seasonal strength and abruptness on predator–prey dynamics. *Journal of Theoretical Biology*, 110175.

Chapter 5

Results on Best Proximity Point in b-Metric Space Using Weak Contraction

Deb Sarkar[1]**, MSc**
Ramakant Bhardwaj[2]**, PhD**
P.R.S. Choudhary[3]**, PhD**
Pulak Konar[4,*]**, PhD**
[1,2]Department of Mathematics, Amity University, Kolkata, WB, India
[3]Department of Mathematics and Computer Science, Govt. Science College, Jabalpur, M.P., India
[4]Department of Mathematics, VIT University, Chennai, Vandalur, Kelsmbakkam Road, Tamil Nadu, India

Abstract

This chapter introduces a novel best proximity point problem in b-metric structure associated with the idea of weak contraction. Here, a result of the best proximity point has been shown following a suitable example. Also, some consequences have been presented here.

Keywords: fixed point, b-Metric space, weak contraction, best proximity point

[*] Corresponding Author's Email: pulakkonar@gmail.com

In: Emerging Trends in Mathematical Sciences and Computing
Editors: B. Basu Mallik, S. Ghosh, B. Kumar Pandey et al.
ISBN: 979-8-89113-751-6

Introduction

The notion of fixed point plays a crucial role not only in non-linear studies but also in practical life. Besides mathematics, the usage of this theory is in diverse fields like physics, engineering, economics, computing, etc. In 1922, Stefan Banach (1922) brought a revolution in mathematics by introducing the famous Banach contraction principle, and by using this principle he found a fixed point result. After that Kannan (1968, 1969) and Chatterjea (1972) worked on this field and discovered their respective contractions and invariant point results. In 1989, a mathematician I. A. Bhatkin (1989) introduced b-MS and presented some fixed point results which have been modified by S. Czerwik (1993). Later, Czerwik (1998) found some invariant point results in b-MS using set-valued mappings. In 2004, the idea of weak contraction has been revealed by Berinde (2004). Several mathematicians (V. Berinde, 2008; Choudhury et. al., 2011 & Raghuwanshi et. al., 2021) worked on this field at different times.

In 2006, the idea of best proximity point came into mathematics by A. A. Eldred and P. Veeramani (2006). Later, Abkar, Gabeleh (2013) worked on this. In 2022, Rossafi et. al. (2022) worked on proximal type contractive non-self mapping to present their results. In 2015, George et. al. (2015) showed some works in b-metric space.

Motivated by the works (Jleli. et. al., 2013; Raj, 2011; Gabaleh, 2015 & Sarkar et. al., 2022), in this article, a β-$\wp$ mapping has been taken to show the result supported by a suitable example.

Prelimineries

Assume that there subsists a metric space $(\mathbb{W}, \bar{\mathfrak{d}})$ and $\widetilde{\mathfrak{D}}, \widehat{\mathfrak{E}} \subseteq \mathbb{W}$. We can write:

$$\bar{\mathfrak{d}}(\widetilde{\mathfrak{D}}, \widehat{\mathfrak{E}}) = \{inf\, \bar{\mathfrak{d}}(\mathfrak{i}, \mathfrak{p}) : \mathfrak{i} \in \widetilde{\mathfrak{D}}, \mathfrak{p} \in \widehat{\mathfrak{E}}\}$$
$$\widetilde{\mathfrak{D}}_0 = \{\mathfrak{i} \in \widetilde{\mathfrak{D}} : \bar{\mathfrak{d}}(\mathfrak{i}, \mathfrak{p}) = \bar{\mathfrak{d}}(\widetilde{\mathfrak{D}}, \widehat{\mathfrak{E}}) \text{ for some } \mathfrak{p} \in \widehat{\mathfrak{E}}\}$$
$$\widehat{\mathfrak{E}}_0 = \{\mathfrak{p} \in \widehat{\mathfrak{E}} : \bar{\mathfrak{d}}(\mathfrak{i}, \mathfrak{p}) = \bar{\mathfrak{d}}(\widetilde{\mathfrak{D}}, \widehat{\mathfrak{E}}) \text{ for some } \mathfrak{i} \in \widetilde{\mathfrak{D}}\}$$

We define the following:

Definition-1 (Best Proximity Point): Assume that there subsists a metric space $(\mathbb{W}, \bar{\mathfrak{d}})$ and $\widetilde{\mathfrak{D}}, \widehat{\mathfrak{E}} \subseteq \mathbb{W}$ such that $\widetilde{\mathfrak{D}}, \widehat{\mathfrak{E}} \neq \phi$. An element $\mathfrak{v}_* \in \widetilde{\mathfrak{D}}$ is known as a BPP of $\mathfrak{Q} : \widetilde{\mathfrak{D}} \longrightarrow \widehat{\mathfrak{E}}$ when $\bar{\mathfrak{d}}(\mathfrak{v}_*, \mathfrak{Q}(\mathfrak{v}_*)) = \bar{\mathfrak{d}}(\widetilde{\mathfrak{D}}, \widehat{\mathfrak{E}})$.

Definition-2 (P-property): Presuming two non-void sets $\widetilde{\mathfrak{D}}, \widehat{\mathfrak{E}} \subseteq (\mathbb{W}, \bar{\mathfrak{d}})$ such that $\widetilde{\mathfrak{D}}_0 \neq \phi$. So, $(\widetilde{\mathfrak{D}}, \widehat{\mathfrak{E}})$ satisfies $\mathbb{P}$-property iff $\bar{\mathfrak{d}}(\mathfrak{s}, \mathbf{f}) = \bar{\mathfrak{d}}(\mathbf{j}, \mathfrak{r}) = \bar{\mathfrak{d}}(\widetilde{\mathfrak{D}}, \widehat{\mathfrak{E}})$

connotates that $\bar{\mathfrak{d}}(\mathfrak{s},\mathbf{j}) = \bar{\mathfrak{d}}(\mathbf{f},\mathfrak{r})$ in which $\mathfrak{s},\mathbf{j} \in \widetilde{\mathfrak{D}}$ and $\mathbf{f},\mathfrak{r} \in \widehat{\mathfrak{E}}$

Definition-3 (b-Metric Space): Assuming $\mathbb{W} \neq \phi$ be a set and $\bar{\mathfrak{d}} : \mathbb{W} \times \mathbb{W} \to [0,\infty)$ such that $\forall\, \mathbf{o}, \mathbf{l}, \mathbf{s} \in \mathbb{W}$,
i) $\bar{\mathfrak{d}}(\mathbf{o},\mathbf{l}) \geq 0$
ii) $\bar{\mathfrak{d}}(\mathbf{o},\mathbf{l}) = 0$ iff $\mathbf{o} = \mathbf{l}$.
iii) $\bar{\mathfrak{d}}(\mathbf{o},\mathbf{l}) = \bar{\mathfrak{d}}(\mathbf{l},\mathbf{o})$.
iv) There subsists $\mathfrak{b} \in [1,\infty)$ in which $\bar{\mathfrak{d}}(\mathbf{o},\mathbf{s}) \leq \mathfrak{b}[\bar{\mathfrak{d}}(\mathbf{o},\mathbf{l}) + \bar{\mathfrak{d}}(\mathbf{l},\mathbf{s})]$.
Then, $(\mathbb{W},\bar{\mathfrak{d}})$ can be known as a b-metric space.
Throughout this chapter, we write fixed point as FP, best proximity point as BPP and b-metric space as b-MS.

The Result

Definition-4: Π, Λ be the collections of all $\beta, \wp : [0,\infty) \to [0,\infty)$ in which
i) $\beta, \wp$ are increasing.
ii) Both must attain continuity.
iii) $\beta(0) = 0, \quad \beta(\mathfrak{h}) < \mathfrak{h}$ for each $\mathfrak{h} \in [0,\infty)$.

Theorem-1: Assuming $\widetilde{\mathfrak{D}}, \widehat{\mathfrak{E}} \neq \phi$ be two closed subsets of a b-MS $(\mathbb{W},\bar{\mathfrak{d}})$ that is complete with $\mathfrak{b} \geq 1$ in which $\widetilde{\mathfrak{D}}_0 \neq \phi$. Let, $\beta \in \Pi, \wp \in \Lambda$ and consider a mapping $\mathfrak{Q} : \widetilde{\mathfrak{D}} \to \widehat{\mathfrak{E}}$ defined as

$$\bar{\mathfrak{d}}(\mathfrak{Q}(\mathfrak{q}),\mathfrak{Q}(\mathfrak{w})) \leq \frac{\mathfrak{h}}{\mathfrak{h}+1}\,\beta(\bar{\mathfrak{d}}(\mathfrak{q},\mathfrak{w})) - \wp\left(\frac{\bar{\mathfrak{d}}(\mathfrak{q},\mathfrak{w})}{\aleph}\right)$$

for all $\mathfrak{q},\mathfrak{w} \in \widetilde{\mathfrak{D}}$, $\aleph \geq 1$ such that $\mathfrak{b}\mathfrak{h} < 1$ for some $\mathfrak{h} \in (0,1)$ satisfying the following:
i) $\mathfrak{Q}(\widetilde{\mathfrak{D}}_0) \subseteq \widehat{\mathfrak{E}}_0$ and $(\widetilde{\mathfrak{D}},\widehat{\mathfrak{E}})$ accomplishes $\mathbb{P}$-property.
ii) There subsist $\mathfrak{i}_0, \mathfrak{i}_1 \in \widetilde{\mathfrak{D}}_0$ such that

$$\bar{\mathfrak{d}}(\mathfrak{i}_1,\mathfrak{Q}(\mathfrak{i}_0)) = dist(\widetilde{\mathfrak{D}},\widehat{\mathfrak{E}})$$

iii) $\mathfrak{Q}$ attains continuity.
Then, $\mathfrak{Q}$ has a sole BPP in $\widetilde{\mathfrak{D}}$.

Proof 1 *Considering the condition (ii), there subsist* $\mathfrak{i}_0, \mathfrak{i}_1 \in \widetilde{\mathfrak{D}}_0$ *such that*

$$\bar{\mathfrak{d}}(\mathfrak{i}_1,\mathfrak{Q}(\mathfrak{i}_0)) = dist(\widetilde{\mathfrak{D}},\widehat{\mathfrak{E}})$$

Since, $\mathfrak{Q}(\widetilde{\mathfrak{D}}_0) \subseteq \widehat{\mathfrak{E}}_0$*, there subsists* $\mathfrak{i}_2 \in \widetilde{\mathfrak{D}}_0$ *such that*

$$\bar{\mathfrak{d}}(\mathfrak{i}_2, \mathfrak{Q}(\mathfrak{i}_1)) = dist(\widetilde{\mathfrak{D}}, \widehat{\mathfrak{E}})$$

Thus, by mathematical induction, we obtain $\{\mathfrak{i}_\mathfrak{n}\} \in \widetilde{\mathfrak{D}}_0$ *such that*

$$\bar{\mathfrak{d}}(\mathfrak{i}_{\mathfrak{n}+1}, \mathfrak{Q}(\mathfrak{i}_\mathfrak{n})) = dist(\widetilde{\mathfrak{D}}, \widehat{\mathfrak{E}}) \quad \textit{for every } \mathfrak{n} \in \mathbf{N}$$

Since, $(\widetilde{\mathfrak{D}}, \widehat{\mathfrak{E}})$ *accomplishes* $\mathbb{P}$*-property,*

$$\bar{\mathfrak{d}}(\mathfrak{i}_\mathfrak{n}, \mathfrak{i}_{\mathfrak{n}+1}) = \bar{\mathfrak{d}}(\mathfrak{Q}(\mathfrak{i}_{\mathfrak{n}-1}), \mathfrak{Q}(\mathfrak{i}_\mathfrak{n}))$$

Now, we want to show,

$$\lim_{\mathfrak{n}\to\infty} \bar{\mathfrak{d}}(\mathfrak{i}_\mathfrak{n}, \mathfrak{i}_{\mathfrak{n}+1}) = 0$$

Here,

$$\begin{aligned}
\bar{\mathfrak{d}}(\mathfrak{i}_\mathfrak{n}, \mathfrak{i}_{\mathfrak{n}+1}) &= \bar{\mathfrak{d}}(\mathfrak{Q}(\mathfrak{i}_{\mathfrak{n}-1}), \mathfrak{Q}(\mathfrak{i}_\mathfrak{n})) \\
&\leq \frac{\mathfrak{h}}{\mathfrak{h}+1}\,\beta(\bar{\mathfrak{d}}(\mathfrak{i}_{\mathfrak{n}-1}, \mathfrak{i}_\mathfrak{n})) - \wp\left(\frac{\bar{\mathfrak{d}}(\mathfrak{i}_{\mathfrak{n}-1}, \mathfrak{i}_\mathfrak{n})}{\aleph}\right) \\
&\leq \frac{\mathfrak{h}}{\mathfrak{h}+1}\,\beta(\bar{\mathfrak{d}}(\mathfrak{i}_{\mathfrak{n}-1}, \mathfrak{i}_\mathfrak{n})) \\
&< \frac{\mathfrak{h}}{\mathfrak{h}+1}\,\bar{\mathfrak{d}}(\mathfrak{i}_{\mathfrak{n}-1}, \mathfrak{i}_\mathfrak{n}) \\
&\;\;\vdots \\
&< \left(\frac{\mathfrak{h}}{\mathfrak{h}+1}\right)^{\mathfrak{n}} \bar{\mathfrak{d}}(\mathfrak{i}_0, \mathfrak{i}_1)
\end{aligned}$$

Since, $\mathfrak{h} \in (0, 1)$, $\left(\frac{\mathfrak{h}}{\mathfrak{h}+1}\right)^{\mathfrak{n}} \to 0$ *as* $\mathfrak{n} \to \infty$
$\therefore \lim_{\mathfrak{n}\to\infty} \bar{\mathfrak{d}}(\mathfrak{i}_\mathfrak{n}, \mathfrak{i}_{\mathfrak{n}+1}) = 0$
Now, we have to establish that $\{\mathfrak{i}_\mathfrak{n}\}$ *is Cauchy.*

For $\mathfrak{m} > \mathfrak{n}$,

$$\begin{aligned}\bar{\mathfrak{d}}(\mathfrak{i}_n, \mathfrak{i}_m) &\leq \mathfrak{b}(\bar{\mathfrak{d}}(\mathfrak{i}_\mathfrak{n}, \mathfrak{i}_{\mathfrak{n}+1}) + \bar{\mathfrak{d}}(\mathfrak{i}_{\mathfrak{n}+1}, \mathfrak{i}_\mathfrak{m}))\\ &\leq \mathfrak{b}\,\bar{\mathfrak{d}}(\mathfrak{i}_\mathfrak{n}, \mathfrak{i}_{\mathfrak{n}+1}) + \mathfrak{b}^2(\bar{\mathfrak{d}}(\mathfrak{i}_{\mathfrak{n}+1}, \mathfrak{i}_{\mathfrak{n}+2}) + \bar{\mathfrak{d}}(\mathfrak{i}_{\mathfrak{n}+2}, \mathfrak{i}_\mathfrak{m}))\\ &\leq \mathfrak{b}\,\bar{\mathfrak{d}}(\mathfrak{i}_\mathfrak{n}, \mathfrak{i}_{\mathfrak{n}+1}) + \mathfrak{b}^2\,\bar{\mathfrak{d}}(\mathfrak{i}_{\mathfrak{n}+1}, \mathfrak{i}_{\mathfrak{n}+2}) + \mathfrak{b}^3\,\bar{\mathfrak{d}}(\mathfrak{i}_{\mathfrak{n}+2}, \mathfrak{i}_{\mathfrak{n}+3})\\ &+ \cdots + \mathfrak{b}^{\mathfrak{m}-\mathfrak{n}-1}\,\bar{\mathfrak{d}}(\mathfrak{i}_{\mathfrak{m}-2}, \mathfrak{i}_{\mathfrak{m}-1}) + \mathfrak{b}^{\mathfrak{m}-\mathfrak{n}-1}\,\bar{\mathfrak{d}}(\mathfrak{i}_{\mathfrak{m}-1}, \mathfrak{i}_\mathfrak{m})\\ &< \mathfrak{b}\left(\frac{\mathfrak{h}}{\mathfrak{h}+1}\right)^{\mathfrak{n}}\bar{\mathfrak{d}}(\mathfrak{i}_0, \mathfrak{i}_1) + \mathfrak{b}^2\left(\frac{\mathfrak{h}}{\mathfrak{h}+1}\right)^{\mathfrak{n}+1}\bar{\mathfrak{d}}(\mathfrak{i}_0, \mathfrak{i}_1) + \mathfrak{b}^3\left(\frac{\mathfrak{h}}{\mathfrak{h}+1}\right)^{\mathfrak{n}+2}\bar{\mathfrak{d}}(\mathfrak{i}_0, \mathfrak{i}_1)\\ &+ \cdots + \mathfrak{b}^{\mathfrak{m}-\mathfrak{n}-1}\left(\frac{\mathfrak{h}}{\mathfrak{h}+1}\right)^{\mathfrak{m}-2}\bar{\mathfrak{d}}(\mathfrak{i}_0, \mathfrak{i}_1) + \mathfrak{b}^{\mathfrak{m}-\mathfrak{n}-1}\left(\frac{\mathfrak{h}}{\mathfrak{h}+1}\right)^{\mathfrak{m}-1}\bar{\mathfrak{d}}(\mathfrak{i}_0, \mathfrak{i}_1)\\ &= \Bigg[\left(\frac{\mathfrak{b}\mathfrak{h}}{\mathfrak{h}+1}\right)^{\mathfrak{n}}\frac{1}{\mathfrak{b}^{\mathfrak{n}-1}} + \left(\frac{\mathfrak{b}\mathfrak{h}}{\mathfrak{h}+1}\right)^{\mathfrak{n}+1}\frac{1}{\mathfrak{b}^{\mathfrak{n}-1}} + \left(\frac{\mathfrak{b}\mathfrak{h}}{\mathfrak{h}+1}\right)^{\mathfrak{n}+2}\frac{1}{\mathfrak{b}^{\mathfrak{n}-1}}\\ &+ \cdots + \left(\frac{\mathfrak{b}\mathfrak{h}}{\mathfrak{h}+1}\right)^{\mathfrak{m}-2}\frac{1}{\mathfrak{b}^{\mathfrak{n}-1}} + \left(\frac{\mathfrak{b}\mathfrak{h}}{\mathfrak{h}+1}\right)^{\mathfrak{m}-1}\frac{1}{\mathfrak{b}^{\mathfrak{n}}}\Bigg]\bar{\mathfrak{d}}(\mathfrak{i}_0, \mathfrak{i}_1)\end{aligned}$$

Since, $\mathfrak{b} \geq 1$ *such that* $\mathfrak{b}\mathfrak{h} < 1$ *for some* $\mathfrak{h} \in (0, 1)$,
Letting $\mathfrak{m}, \mathfrak{n} \to \infty$,

$$\lim_{\mathfrak{m},\mathfrak{n}\to\infty} \bar{\mathfrak{d}}(\mathfrak{i}_\mathfrak{n}, \mathfrak{i}_\mathfrak{m}) = 0$$

$\therefore \{\mathfrak{i}_\mathfrak{n}\}$ *is Cauchy.*
By completeness of $\mathbb{W}$ *and closedness of* $\widetilde{\mathfrak{D}}$ *in* $\mathbb{W}$, $\{\mathfrak{i}_\mathfrak{n}\}$ *is convergent to some* $\mathfrak{i}_* \in \widetilde{\mathfrak{D}}$.
As $\mathfrak{Q}$ *attains continuity,*

$$\mathfrak{Q}(\mathfrak{i}_\mathfrak{n}) \to \mathfrak{Q}(\mathfrak{i}_*) \quad as \quad \mathfrak{n} \to \infty$$

Hence, we have,

$$dist(\widetilde{\mathfrak{D}}, \widehat{\mathfrak{E}}) = \bar{\mathfrak{d}}(\mathfrak{i}_{\mathfrak{n}+1}, \mathfrak{Q}(\mathfrak{i}_\mathfrak{n})) \to \bar{\mathfrak{d}}(\mathfrak{i}_*, \mathfrak{Q}(\mathfrak{i}_*)) \quad as \quad \mathfrak{n} \to \infty$$

$$\therefore \bar{\mathfrak{d}}(\mathfrak{i}_*, \mathfrak{Q}(\mathfrak{i}_*)) = dist(\widetilde{\mathfrak{D}}, \widehat{\mathfrak{E}})$$

Thus, $\mathfrak{Q}$ *has a best proximity point* $\mathfrak{i}_* \in \widetilde{\mathfrak{D}}$.
If possible, suppose $\mathfrak{i}' \in \widetilde{\mathfrak{D}}$ *be another BPP of* $\mathfrak{Q}$.
Now,

$$\bar{\mathfrak{d}}(\mathfrak{i}_*, \mathfrak{Q}(\mathfrak{i}_*)) = \bar{\mathfrak{d}}(\mathfrak{i}', \mathfrak{Q}(\mathfrak{i}')) = dist(\widetilde{\mathfrak{D}}, \widehat{\mathfrak{E}})$$

Using $\mathbb{P}$-property,

$$\begin{aligned}\bar{\mathfrak{d}}(\mathfrak{i}_*, \mathfrak{i}') &= \bar{\mathfrak{d}}(\mathfrak{Q}(\mathfrak{i}_*), \mathfrak{Q}(\mathfrak{i}'))\\ &\leq \frac{\mathfrak{h}}{\mathfrak{h}+1}\,\beta(\bar{\mathfrak{d}}(\mathfrak{i}_*, \mathfrak{i}')) - \wp\left(\frac{\bar{\mathfrak{d}}(\mathfrak{i}_*, \mathfrak{i}')}{\aleph}\right)\\ &\leq \frac{\mathfrak{h}}{\mathfrak{h}+1}\,\beta(\bar{\mathfrak{d}}(\mathfrak{i}_*, \mathfrak{i}'))\\ &< \beta(\bar{\mathfrak{d}}(\mathfrak{i}_*, \mathfrak{i}'))\\ &< \bar{\mathfrak{d}}(\mathfrak{i}_*, \mathfrak{i}')\end{aligned}$$

attaining a contradiction.
$\therefore$ *The uniqueness of BPP for $\mathfrak{Q}$ has been established.*

Illustration

Example-1: Let, $\mathbb{W} = \mathbb{R}$ endowing the metric defined by

$$\bar{\mathfrak{d}}(\mathfrak{w}, \mathfrak{g}) = \frac{(\mathfrak{w} - \mathfrak{g})^2}{4}$$

$\forall\, \mathfrak{w}, \mathfrak{g} \in \mathbb{W}$.
Now, for each $\mathfrak{w}, \mathfrak{g}, \mathfrak{j} \in \mathbb{W}$,

$$\bar{\mathfrak{d}}(\mathfrak{w}, \mathfrak{j}) \leq \mathfrak{b}\,(\bar{\mathfrak{d}}(\mathfrak{w}, \mathfrak{g}) + \bar{\mathfrak{d}}(\mathfrak{g}, \mathfrak{j}))$$

Here, $\mathfrak{b} = 2$, so $(\mathbb{W}, \bar{\mathfrak{d}})$ is a b-metric.
Let, $\widetilde{\mathfrak{D}} = [0, \frac{3}{4}]$, $\widehat{\mathfrak{E}} = [1, \frac{19}{16}]$.
Consider, $\mathfrak{Q} : \widetilde{\mathfrak{D}} \to \widehat{\mathfrak{E}}$ defined by

$$\mathfrak{Q}(\mathbf{c}) = 1 + \frac{\mathbf{c}}{4} \quad \forall\, \mathbf{c} \in \widetilde{\mathfrak{D}}$$

We have,

$$\bar{\mathfrak{d}}(0, \mathfrak{Q}(0)) = \frac{1}{4} = dist(\widetilde{\mathfrak{D}}, \widehat{\mathfrak{E}})$$

Let, $\beta, \wp : [0, \infty) \to [0, \infty)$ be the functions defined by

$$\beta(\mathfrak{o}) = \frac{99\mathfrak{o}}{100}$$
$$\wp(\mathfrak{o}) = \frac{\mathfrak{o}}{16}$$

So, $\beta \in \Pi$ and $\wp \in \Lambda$
Now, we prove the inequality.
We have,

$$\mathfrak{d}(\mathfrak{Q}(\mathfrak{w}), \mathfrak{Q}(\mathfrak{g})) = \mathfrak{d}\left(1 + \frac{\mathfrak{w}}{4}, 1 + \frac{\mathfrak{g}}{4}\right) = \frac{1}{4}\left(\frac{\mathfrak{w}}{4} - \frac{\mathfrak{g}}{4}\right)^2 = \frac{1}{64}(\mathfrak{w} - \mathfrak{g})^2$$

Taking $\mathfrak{h} = \frac{29}{60}$, $\aleph = 4$,

$$\frac{\mathfrak{h}}{\mathfrak{h}+1}\beta(\mathfrak{d}(\mathfrak{w}, \mathfrak{g})) - \wp\left(\frac{\mathfrak{d}(\mathfrak{w}, \mathfrak{g})}{\aleph}\right) = \frac{29}{89}\beta\left(\frac{1}{4}(\mathfrak{w} - \mathfrak{g})^2\right) - \wp\left(\frac{1}{4} \times \frac{(\mathfrak{w} - \mathfrak{g})^2}{4}\right) = \frac{2871(\mathfrak{w} - \mathfrak{g})^2}{35600} - \frac{(\mathfrak{w} - \mathfrak{g})^2}{256} = \frac{43711}{569600}(\mathfrak{w} - \mathfrak{g})^2$$

Clearly,

$$\frac{1}{64}(\mathfrak{w} - \mathfrak{g})^2 \leq \frac{43711}{569600}(\mathfrak{w} - \mathfrak{g})^2 \quad \forall\, \mathfrak{w}, \mathfrak{g} \in \widetilde{\mathfrak{D}}$$

i.e.

$$\mathfrak{d}(\mathfrak{Q}(\mathfrak{w}), \mathfrak{Q}(\mathfrak{g})) \leq \frac{\mathfrak{h}}{\mathfrak{h}+1}\beta(\mathfrak{d}(\mathfrak{w}, \mathfrak{g})) - \wp\left(\frac{\mathfrak{d}(\mathfrak{w}, \mathfrak{g})}{\aleph}\right) \quad \forall\, \mathfrak{w}, \mathfrak{g} \in \widetilde{\mathfrak{D}}$$

Thus, each assertion of theorem(1) is established.
$\therefore$ 0 is the sole BPP of $\mathfrak{Q}$.

Consequences

Corollary-1: Presuming $\widetilde{\mathfrak{D}}$, $\widehat{\mathfrak{E}}$ be two non-null closed subsets of a b-MS $(\mathbb{W}, \mathfrak{d})$ that is complete with $\mathfrak{b} \geq 1$ such that $\widetilde{\mathfrak{D}}_0$ is non-empty. Consider a mapping $\mathfrak{Q} : \widetilde{\mathfrak{D}} \to \widehat{\mathfrak{E}}$ defined as

$$\mathfrak{d}(\mathfrak{Q}(\mathfrak{q}), \mathfrak{Q}(\mathfrak{w})) \leq \frac{\mathfrak{h}}{\mathfrak{h}+1}\mathfrak{d}(\mathfrak{q}, \mathfrak{w})^{\mathfrak{r}} - \wp\left(\frac{\mathfrak{d}(\mathfrak{q}, \mathfrak{w})}{\aleph}\right)$$

for all $\mathfrak{q}, \mathfrak{w} \in \widetilde{\mathfrak{D}}$, $\aleph \geq 1$ such that $\mathfrak{b}\mathfrak{h} < 1$ for some $\mathfrak{h}, \mathfrak{r} \in (0, 1)$
satisfying the following:

i) $\mathfrak{Q}(\widetilde{\mathfrak{D}}_0) \subseteq \widehat{\mathfrak{E}}_0$ and $(\widetilde{\mathfrak{D}}, \widehat{\mathfrak{E}})$ accomplishes $\mathbb{P}$-property.
ii) There subsist $\mathfrak{v}_0, \mathfrak{v}_1 \in \widetilde{\mathfrak{D}}_0$ such that

$$\bar{\mathfrak{d}}(\mathfrak{v}_1, \mathfrak{Q}(\mathfrak{v}_0)) = dist(\widetilde{\mathfrak{D}}, \widehat{\mathfrak{E}})$$

iii) $\mathfrak{Q}$ must attain continuity.
Then, the uniqueness of BPP for $\mathfrak{Q}$ attains in $\widetilde{\mathfrak{D}}$.

Proof: Let, $\beta(\mathbf{t}) = \mathbf{t}^{\mathbf{r}}$. Obviously, $\beta \in \Pi$. So, it accomplishes all the hypotheses of theorem(1).
Thus, the uniqueness of BPP has been established. □

Corollary-2: Assuming $(\mathbb{W}, \bar{\mathfrak{d}})$ be a b-MS that is complete with $\mathfrak{b} \geq 1$. Consider a continuous operator $\mathfrak{Q} : \mathbb{W} \to \mathbb{W}$ defined as

$$\bar{\mathfrak{d}}(\mathfrak{Q}(\mathfrak{q}), \mathfrak{Q}(\mathfrak{w})) \leq \frac{\mathfrak{h}}{\mathfrak{h}+1}\,\beta(\bar{\mathfrak{d}}(\mathfrak{q}, \mathfrak{w})) - \wp\left(\frac{\bar{\mathfrak{d}}(\mathfrak{q}, \mathfrak{w})}{\aleph}\right)$$

for all $\mathfrak{q}, \mathfrak{w} \in \mathbb{W}$, $\aleph \geq 1$ such that $\mathfrak{b}\mathfrak{h} < 1$ for some $\mathfrak{h} \in (0, 1)$.
Then, $\mathfrak{Q}$ has a sole invariant point in $\mathbb{W}$.

Proof: Considering $\widetilde{\mathfrak{D}} = \widehat{\mathfrak{E}} = \mathbb{W}$ in theorem(1), the uniqueness of fixed point in $\mathbb{W}$ can be obtained. □

Conclusion

In this article, a result on the best proximity point in b-metric space has been presented by using a weak inequality with the help of control functions. This article will be worthy for those researchers who want to work further on this space and there can be an open problem for them to further investigate the real life applications of b-metric space. Overall, this research underscores the importance of b-metric space in modifying the optimal results, paving the way for further exploration and application in mathematical analysis and related fields.

References

Abkar, A., & Gabeleh, M. (2013). Best proximity points of non-self mappings. *Top*, 21, 287-295.
Bakhtin, I. A. (1989). The contraction principle in quasi metric spaces, *Funct. Anal. Unianowsk Gos. Ped. Inst*, 30, 26-37.
Banach, S. (1922). Sur les opÃľrations dans les ensembles abstraits et leur application aux Ãľquations intÃľgrales. *Fundamenta mathematicae*, 3(1), 133-181.

Berinde, V. (2004). Approximating fixed points of weak contractions using the Picard iteration. In *Nonlinear Analysis Forum* (Vol. 9, pp. 43-54).

Berinde, V. (2008). General constructive fixed point theorems for ÄĘiriÄĞ-type almost contractions in metric spaces. *Carpathian Journal of Mathematics*, 10-19.

Chatterjea, S., K. (1972), Fixed-point theorems, *C. R. Acad. Bulgare Sci.* 25, 727-730.

Choudhury, B. S., Konar, P., Rhoades, B. E., & Metiya, N. (2011). Fixed point theorems for generalized weakly contractive mappings. *Nonlinear Analysis: Theory, Methods & Applications*, 74(6), 2116-2126.

Czerwik, S. (1993). Contraction mappings in *b*-metric spaces. *Acta mathematica et informatica universitatis ostraviensis*, 1(1), 5-11.

Czerwik, S. (1998). Nonlinear set-valued contraction mappings in b-metric spaces. *Atti Sem. Mat. Fis. Univ. Modena*, 46, 263-276.

Eldred, A. A., & Veeramani, P. (2006). Existence and convergence of best proximity points. *Journal of Mathematical Analysis and Applications*, 323(2), 1001-1006.

Gabeleh, M. (2015). Best proximity point theorems via proximal non-self mappings. *Journal of Optimization Theory and Applications*, 164(2), 565-576.

George, R., Alaca, C., & Reshma, K. P. (2015). On best proximity points in b-metric space. *Nonlinear Anal. Appl*, 1, 45-56.

Jleli, M., KarapÄśnar, E., & Samet, B. (2013). Best proximity points for generalized-proximal contractive type mappings. *Journal of Applied Mathematics*, 2013.

Kannan, R. (1968). Some results on fixed points. *Bull. Cal. Math. Soc.*, 60, 71-76.

Kannan, R. (1969), Some result on fixed points-II, *Amer. Math. Monthly.*, 76, 405-408.

Raghuwanshi, S., Gupta, V., Ghosh, S., Bhardwaj, R., & Rai, S. (2021). Fixed point theorems for complete metric spaces. *Materials Today: Proceedings*, 47, 6996-6998.

Raj, V. S. (2011). A best proximity point theorem for weakly contractive non-self-mappings. *Nonlinear Analysis: Theory, Methods & Applications*, 74(14), 4804-4808.

Rossafi, M., & Kari, A. (2022). Best proximity point theorems for $\alpha^+ F, (\theta - \phi)$-proximal contraction. *Jurnal Matematika, Statistika dan Komputasi*, 18(2), 181-197.

Sarkar, D., Chandok, S., Konar, P., Bhardwaj, R., & Choudhary, P. R. S. (2022). Coupling, optimization, and the effect of binary relation. The *Journal of Analysis*, 1-20.

Chapter 6

Pre and Post-COVID Scenario of Fuel Economy: A Survey through Statistical Analysis

Goldina Ghosh*
Kaustav Chakraborty
Kousik Das
Pratiti Bhattacharjee
Ishita Saha
Md Anish Ahamed Molla
Department of Computer Science & Applications, Institute of Engineering and Management, Salt Lake, Kolkata, India

Abstract

The world has seen a lot of ups and downs during the COVID pandemic, which lasted for two years. During this phase, the entire economy was affected in some way or another. In some cases, the effect was either high or low. In very few cases, there might have been no change at all. To get a clear view, certain data analyses were essential. Keeping this in mind, a statistical analysis has been done in this paper. This analysis was done to determine the swing in the price of fuels during the pre-COVID and post-COVID periods. Thus, a proper interpretation of the real effect of COVID on fuel prices was obtained. Data was collected from official sources like the Indian Oil official page, Bank Bazzar, and The Economic Times for LPG, Petrol, and Diesel prices from 2017 to 2022. Both pre-

---

* Corresponding Author's Email: ghosh.goldina@gmail.com.

In: Emerging Trends in Mathematical Sciences and Computing
Editors: B. Basu Mallik, S. Ghosh, B. Kumar Pandey et al.
ISBN: 979-8-89113-751-6

COVID and post-COVID period data were collected. Several statistical methods, like mean, median, and especially standard deviation were used on the dataset to do the statistical analysis. Primarily, the dataset normalization method was applied and then divided into two parts: pre-COVID phase and post-COVID phase. A graphical representation was obtained after performing the statistical calculation. With the help of the Python programming language, a comparative study was done between the two phases. In order to understand the changes in the economical aspect, the comparison was made on several patterns like year and individual fuel price. After the final analysis, it was observed that initially the price was affected due to the volatile market, some taxation, and VAT issues. Then later, a slight effect was observed in the years 2019 and 2020, which was caused by COVID.

Keywords: pandemic, fuel economy, statistical analysis

Introduction

Due to the pandemic, many economic conditions were vulnerable. Fuel was one of the most noticeable sections affected. Fuel is an essential commodity used in every aspect of daily life. Fuel can include LPG gas, diesel, or petrol. Hence, an analysis was essential to observe the difference in price during the pandemic as well as during pre- and post-COVID scenarios in fuel consumption. In this paper statistical analysis and graphical representation have been done to determine the actual effect of COVID in fuel. At first, we compared all individual fuel prices on a yearly basis. Then compared them with each other with respect to years to get a comparable dataset and decide which fuel had a higher rate of price increase. To clearly understand the resultant values, the total dataset 2017-2022 has been divided into two parts: 2017-2019 is used as the pre-COVID dataset, and 2020-2022 is used as the post-COVID dataset. As a part of statistical analysis, mean was used to get an average for each fuel and median was used to measure the central tendency of the fuel price in pre-COVID and post-COVID scenarios Also, a standard deviation was used to measure how much data was spread out. After obtaining all the data from statistical analysis, Python programming was applied to create an interactive visualization with the help of the "matplotlib" library.

Literature Review

To continue with the research work in this paper, certain literature review analyses were essential and are discussed in this section. In the document (https://www.outlookindia.com/business/petrol-diesel-and-lpgsales-spike-due-to-festiv e-season-demand-news-230480, 2022), a report was given that states that fuel sales have been 31% higher than that of the first half of October 2020 and a change of 33.4% more during the pre-pandemic in the year 2019. Additionally, the authors noted that the sum was 1.3% higher than it was in the first half of September 2022. The report also showed that if sales and demand were considered, then with reference to the consumption rate, it goes up to 16% from October 1 to 15, 2020, and 26.6% higher compared to the pre-COVID 2019 levels.

The other article (The Hindu, 2020) shared a report for the year 2022. It has been observed that India's fuel sales were high in the first phase of October because of the economic activity that followed due to the festive season. The report also states that petrol sales have taken a rise from 22.7% to 1.28 million tons during October 2022.

From (https://www.thestatesman.com/india/despite-subsidy-lpg-cost-rose-2-5-times-8-years-1503088301.html) it has been noted that the geo-political crisis of Russia-Ukraine is one of the causes for hiking oil prices. Therefore, the price of LPG gas price has also risen in India. Rupee depreciation has also taken a major role in the price hike.

As global demand for crude oil was reduced by the coronavirus, an outbreak was created. It caused instability and resulted in a huge economic depression in the most emerging and developed countries. COVID-19 also created a supply shock, causing an oil trade conflict among major oil-producing nations like Saudi Arabia and Russia.

The epidemic of coronavirus occurred at a time when the global oil market was very weak and fuel prices were under pressure. Oil prices are not entirely decided through economic variables, but they are also affected by unexpected circumstances, which can create and lead to a state of concern and panic.

Dataset Preparation

To prepare the dataset for the experimental work, data was collected from 2017 to 2022 for LPG, Petrol, and Diesel from different official sites and sources. 2017-2019 is considered as pre-COVID period. The raw data was collected from the Indian Oil official page (https://iocl.com/indane-14Kg-nonsubsid-previous-price), Bank Bazzar (https://www.bankbazaar.com/fuel/petrol-price-kolkata.html), and The Economic Times (https://economictimes.indiatimes.com/wealth/fuel-price). The dataset is given in Table 1.

Table 1. Record of Prices of all Fuels from the year 2017 to 2022

Years	LPG	Petrol	Diesel
2017	22.89	67.48	56.31
2018	28.77	72.14	68.29
2019	23.73	75.08	67.41
2020	25.99	92.61	84.52
2021	29.05	104.8	85.78
2022	35.71	101.77	92.19

Mathematical Model

Firstly from Table 1, a testing hypothesis was derived, and the problem solving was done on the derived dataset. Here, both the null hypothesis (H_0) and the alternative hypothesis (H_a) were applied.

The derived values along with the calculations are provided as follows:

Pre-COVID Mean Results:

In general Mean can be stated as

m = Sum of the elements/number of elements (Andrew et al., 2022).

Mean value for the price of LPG is 25.13

Mean value for the price of Petrol is 71.57

Mean value for the price of Diesel is 64.003

Pre-COVID Median Results:

In general Median can be stated as

M = X[(a+1)/2] if a is odd and

(X[a/2] + X(a/2 +1)) /2 if a is even (Andrew et al., 2022).

Median value for the price of LPG is 23.73

Median value for the price of Petrol is 72.14

Median value for the price of Diesel is 67.41

Pre-COVID Standard Deviation Results:

In general, Standard Deviation can be stated as (Andrew et al., 2022).

$\boldsymbol{\sigma} = \sqrt{(\Sigma(Zi - \mu)^2)/A}$

$\boldsymbol{\sigma}$ = population standard deviation.

A = the size of the population.

Zi = each value from the population.

μ = population mean

Standard Deviation value for the price of LPG is 2.5966

Margin of error for the price of LPG is 1.4991

Standard Deviation value for the price of Petrol is 3.129

Margin of error for the price of Petrol is 1.806

Standard Deviation value for the price of Diesel is 5.45

Margin of error for the price of Diesel is 3.1502

Post-COVID Mean Results:

Mean value for the price of LPG is 30.25

Mean value for the price of Petrol is 99.48

Mean value for the price of Diesel is 87.50

Post-COVID Median Results:

Median value for the price of LPG is 29.05

Median value for the price of Petrol is 101.77

Median value for the price of Diesel is 85.78

Post-COVID Standard Deviation Results:

Standard Deviation value for the price of LPG is 4.0575

Margin of error for the price of LPG is 2.343

Standard Deviation value for the price of Petrol is 5.1820

Margin of error for the price of Petrol is 2.9918

Standard Deviation value for the price of Diesel is 3.3583

Margin of error for the price of Diesel is 1.9389

Results and Discussion

After getting the values of the mean, median, and standard deviation, the next step is to get the value of the hypothesis, which is written as,

Null Hypothesis = H_0: μl = 22.80

In the above case, the value found is the at least value, which means where the value of the price is null so that is why 22.80 is taken as the value where the value is null.

Alternative Hypothesis = H_a: μl >22.80 or 22.80 < H_a: μl < 35.71 or the value will be revolved around 25.13.

From the calculation this is clear that if the value which is found is not related with the existing data from the table then that is called as a null hypothesis and after finding that value the next step is to find the alternative which is revolving around the data set. Here μl is like a comparing value.

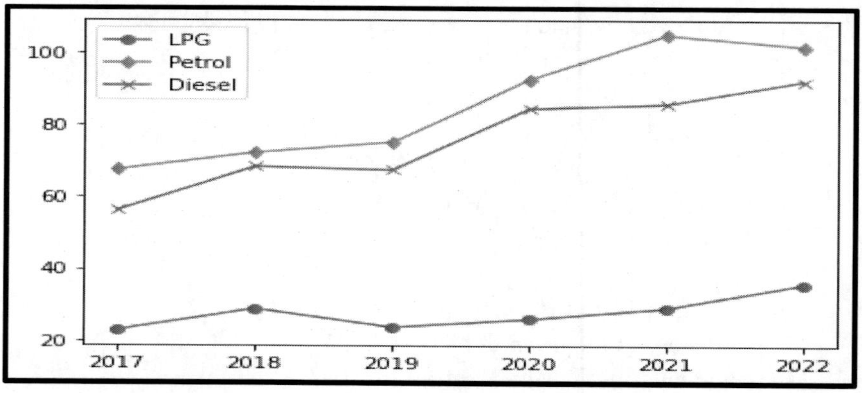

Figure 1. All Fuels Result Oriented Comparison.

After getting the mean, median, and standard deviation values, we can now create multiple datasets and implement "matplotlib" for future analysis (ML) for prediction models. As of now we will use those data to get a statistical analysis. The graphical output is given in Figure 1 for all fuels. This graph represents the result oriented value comparison of all the fuels.

Figure 2 represents the fuel price change comparison from 2017-2022.

Figure 3 represents pre and post COVID comparison mean value comparison for all fuels.

Figure 4 represents pre and post-COVID comparison median value comparison for all fuels.

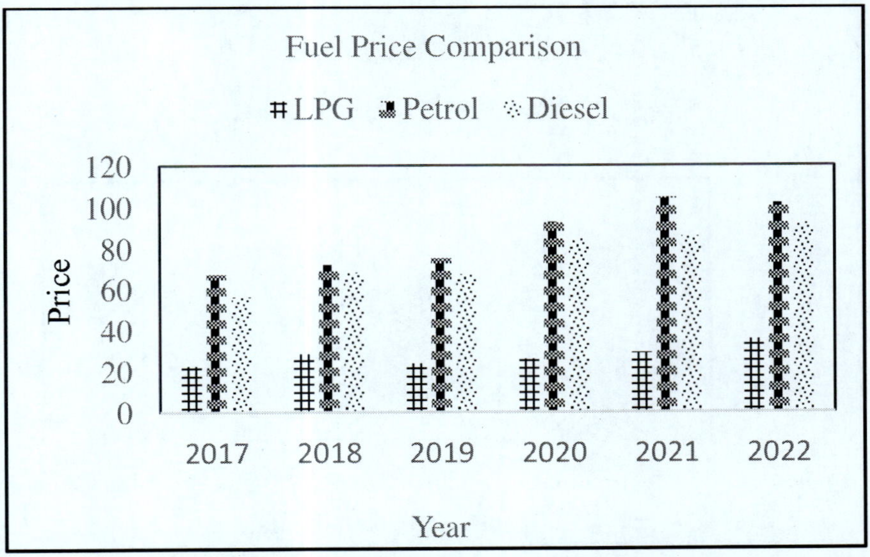

Figure 2. All Fuels Price Comparison (2017-2022).

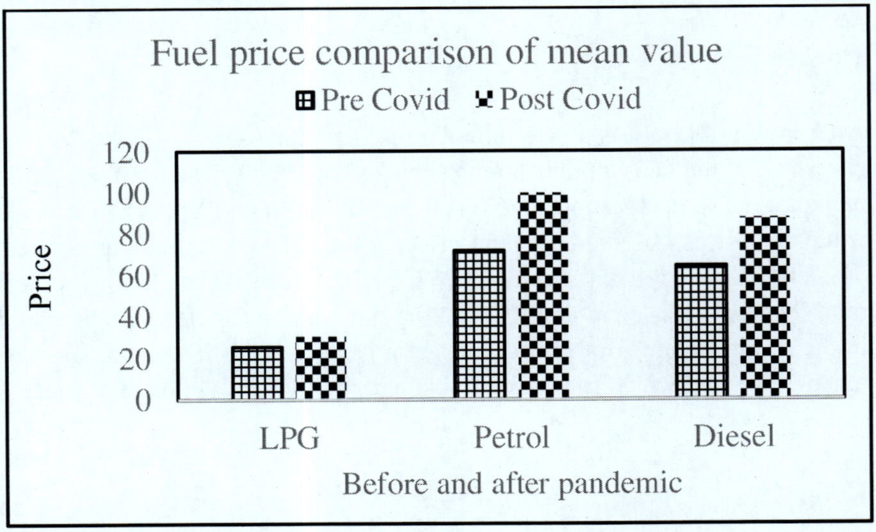

Figure 3. Pre and Post-COVID Mean Value Comparison.

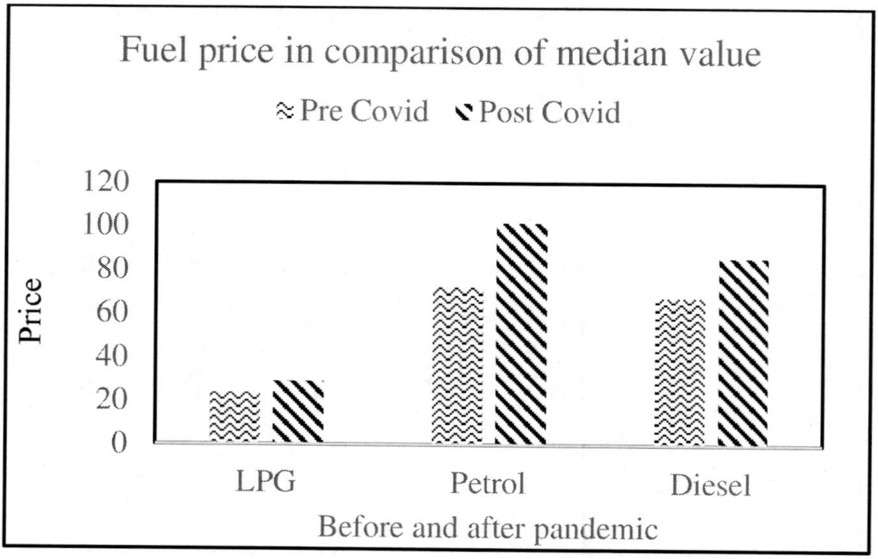

Figure 4. Pre and Post-COVID Median Value Comparison.

Conclusion

After the entire analysis, it was initially observed that COVID didn't affect the price hike of the fuels too much. The changes occurred because of the volatile market, and some taxation, and VAT and other things. But when a value comparison was observed, a slight effect from 2019 and 2020 was noticed. This time span was affected by COVID. And from the graphical representation, it is clear that COVID did not have much effect as discussed in the result section. But in order to get a clear analysis, a comparison was made year-wise, which finally leads to a clear analysis of the fuel economy.

References

Alqahtani Abdullah, Selmi Refk, Hongbing Ouyang, The financial impacts of jump processes in the crude oil price: Evidence from G20 countries in the pre- and post-COVID-19, *Resources Policy*, Volume 72, Elsevier, August 2021, 102075.

Bank Bazzar.com: https://www.bankbazaar.com/fuel/petrol-price-kolkata.html.

Bourghelle David, Jawadi Fredj, Rozin Philippe, October 2021, Oil price volatility in the context of COVID-19, *International Economics*, Volume 167, Pages 39-49 October 2021.

Data Set collected from *Indian oil* official website: https://iocl.com/indane-14Kg-nonsubsid-previous-price.

MacMillan Andrew, Preston David, Wolfe Jessica, Yu Sandy, Basic statistics- mean, median, average, standard deviation, z-scores, and p-value, *University of Michigan*, Retrieved From- https://eng.libretexts.org/@go/page/22659.pdf.

Petrol, Diesel and LPG Sales Spike Due To Festive Season Demand. (2022, October 10). Retrieved From -*Outlook.com*: https://www.outlookindia.com/business/petrol-diesel-and-lpgsales- spike-due-to-festive-season-demand-news-230480.

The Economic Times: https://economictimes.indiatimes.com/wealth/fuel-price.

The Hindu: After petrol, diesel demand returns to pre-COVID-19 levels. October 16, 2020 02:20 pm — Updated 02:24 pm IST - New Delhi.

The Statesman: https://www.thestatesman.com/india/despite-subsidy-lpg-cost-rose-2-5-times-8-years-1503088301.html.

Chapter 7

Modelling and Analysis of the Spread of Crime against Women in an Open Population

Shelly Khurana*
Sushant Shekhar
Division of Mathematics, SBAS, Galgotias University,
Greater Noida, INDIA

Abstract

India has experienced amazing progress in recent decades. Despite all progress and evolution, women continue to be victims of heinous acts. Every woman has the right to live a decent and respectable life, and so actions must be taken to safeguard women from crime. Therefore, in the present study, we propose a mathematical model and its analysis has been done for the study of the spread of crime against women by considering an open population. By open population we mean non-susceptible are increasing at a constant rate. The modelling process involves the assumptions that women become victims after their interaction with criminals and criminals influence non-susceptible to commit crimes against women. Model possible equilibria are discovered and stability analysis has been discussed in the present paper. Analysis reveals that crime-free equilibria (CFE) always exists, whereas crime exist equilibria occur only when parameters are restricted, resulting in (criminality reproduction number) $R_0 ^{c} > 1$. The local and nonlinear stability of crime exist equilibria is conditional on the fulfillment of specific requirements. Numerical simulation has been done for validation of the present model and a conclusion has been made accordingly.

Keywords: mathematical model, crime against women, epidemic approach, stability analysis, model fit

---

* Corresponding Author's Email: shellykhurana235@gmail.com.

In: Emerging Trends in Mathematical Sciences and Computing
Editors: B. Basu Mallik, S. Ghosh, B. Kumar Pandey et al.
ISBN: 979-8-89113-751-6

Introduction

Crime is the deliberate performance of an act that is generally regarded as socially destructive or dangerous and is expressly banned by, and subject to, criminal penalties. Crimes are not limited to any one group, class, society, or nation. Women in India are suffering for extended periods, not just in the modern era. Even after multiple legal changes and other government initiatives, the rate of crime against women has not decreased. Crimes have a physical and psychological impact on women, making it difficult for them to live a normal life.
The relation between crime and immigration should also be studied in [20]. Immigrants may be victims as well as criminals. Many countries have a heinous history of violence against newcomers. In recent years, more than ever, undocumented immigrants entering India have fallen victim to fraudulent and cruel smuggling, and many have died in transit before reaching the host nation. Others become slaves to "pay off" their smugglers' debts. Immigrant women are prone to criminal activities. Cross-border migrants, particularly women, are at risk of being physically abused and frequently sexually abused and some of them eventually turn to prostitution work.

However, it should not be overlooked that there is growing worried about crimes committed by immigrants, particularly unauthorized and undocumented immigrants. States in India with substantial immigrant populations, such as Assam and West Bengal, have had to commit a major percentage of their law enforcement and criminal justice budgets to examining, intercepting, and detaining immigrants to secure the safety of law-abiding residents and legitimate immigrants.

Women make up almost half of the world's population, work nearly two-thirds of the time, and earn one-tenth of the global income, according to a UN study from 1980 [16]. In India, females have traditionally and socially enjoyed a position of respect and veneration. Still, they become victim of crimes that are classified into several categories, including prostitution, unlawful detention, trafficking, dowry extortion, rape, assault, workplace harassment, gang rape, acid attack, kidnapping, and other immoral activities.

Crimes against women have become a serious problems that require their part in the national statistics collected by the NCRB [15]. According to NCRB figures, there has been an undeniable rise in crimes against women in India over the past 20 years. The count of crime cases has been up from 79,037 in 1992 to 3,71,503 in 2020. In 2021, 4,28,278 incidents of crimes against women were reported, which is 15.3% higher than the previous year. In addition, the crime rate per million women had increased to 64.5 in 2021 from 56.5 in 2020. The majority of incidents of crime against women were filed under the category of 'cruelty by husband or his relatives '(31.8%), followed by 'assault on women with intent to outrage her modesty '(20.8%), 'kidnapping and abduction of women '(17.6%), and 'rape '(7.4%).

Even in big urban regions, India is seeing an increase in violence against women, including brutal rapes that have received significant media attention. Crimes against women affect families and communities for years and promote other societal ills. Women are the true builders of our civilization, it is the need of society to take action to safeguard women from criminals. Also, there needs to be a greater understanding of the underlying causes of violence against women.

Although, there is a chance that some criminal populations may recover and abandon crimes, either temporarily or permanently, due to several factors including rehabilitation, counseling, behavioral change, police law enforcement, fear, etc. The matter is still concerning.

Many researchers have examined the dynamics of crime using various mathematical models throughout the last few decades [1, 2, 3, 4, 5, 6, 7, 8, 9, 10, 12, 13, 14, 18, 19, 21, 22, 23, 24, 25, 26, 27, 28, 29, 30, 31, 32]. To propose such crime-related models, they used multiple methodologies, including an economic approach, an epidemic approach, a predator-prey modelling approach, and a spatio-temporal approach. In particular, [5] proposed a mathematical model to investigate the impact of social interaction between susceptible, non-susceptible, and active criminals. [24] investigated the effect of technology in combating social crimes through a mathematical model that took into account the immigration and emigration of susceptible and criminals. They concluded that restricting illegal immigration would lower the crime burden. Further, [20] presented research on the relationship between immigration and crime. He demonstrated how immigrants may engage in criminal activity or fall victim to it. [3] developed a model to control corruption assuming that the non-susceptible were engaging in corruption while being influenced by the corrupt population. They concluded that corruption in society can be decreased through media, legal measures etc. Because under the effect of appropriate counseling and law enforcement, a portion of the criminally active group was giving up crime and living a regular life, [27] included a group, termed recovered people, in their model. However, because of the erratic nature of human behavior, they were returning from healthy to vulnerable.

Much effort has been made to investigate crime-related models, but as described earlier it is required to analyze crime against women individually and to build the ideal control and prevention policies.

The work being presented aims to offer a mathematical model for analyzing the dynamics of crime against women by considering an open population. By open population, we mean non-susceptible is increasing at a constant rate. It is presumable that if women connect with criminals, they become victims. Additionally, it is believed that non-susceptible people are engaging in criminal activity while under the influence of criminals. The flow of criminals to non-susceptible due to behavioral change/ laws or police is also considered. We also used the reported and convicted

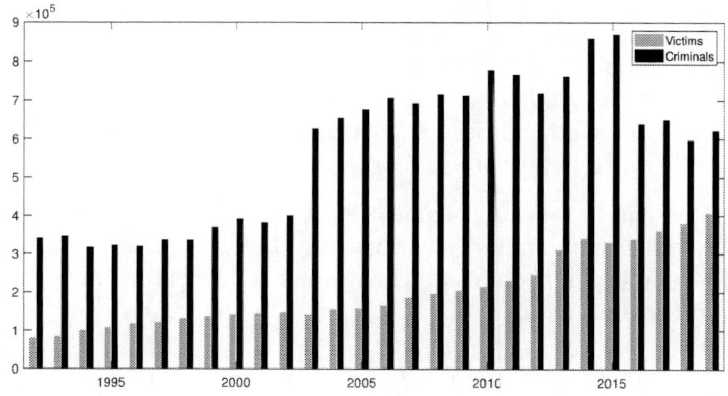

Figure 1. Reported and convicted cases in India from 1992 to 2019.

incidents in India from 1992 to 2019 (Figure 1) as inputs while parametrizing the proposed model. We employ the least square curve fitting method, which offers a good fit to the data, for parameter estimation. We may visualize our scenario using a compartmental model in light of the aforementioned survey.

The paper has 6 sections. Section 2 formulates the model to investigate the dynamics of crime against women. Section 3 discusses the proposed model's equilibria and crime reproduction number. The stability of crime-free and crime-existing equilibria is examined in Section 4. Section 5 calculates model parameters and fits models to observable data. Section 6 contains a Numerical simulation with comments that confirm the analytically determined conclusion. Section 7 concludes the study with a brief conclusion.

Formulation of Mathematical Model

Let us begin by dividing the total population $N(t)$ into four distinct compartments, namely, non-susceptible population $X(t)$, susceptible women population $Y(t)$, criminals $C(t)$ and women victims $V(t)$. Hence,

$$N(t) = X(t) + Y(t) + C(t) + V(t). \tag{1}$$

It is assumed that thewomen population is likely to become victims and hence join the susceptible class with a rate proportion to the non-susceptible population i.e., $\gamma_1 X$. Women from the susceptible class move to the victim class when they interact with criminals at a rate proportional to the density of susceptible women and the density of criminals i.e., βCY. Furthermore, it is assumed that non-susceptible commit crimes under the influence of criminals and join the criminal class with a rate proportional to both the density of non-susceptible and the density of criminals i.e., $\gamma_2 XC$. Also, there is a possibility of criminals giving up crime and moving to non-susceptible class with a rate proportional to the criminal population i.e., $\gamma_3 C$. Lastly, the natural death rate μ of all classes is considered to be proportional to their respective class density.

Considering all the above mentioned assumptions, the following mathematical model is proposed:

$$\begin{aligned}
\frac{dX}{dt} &= A - \gamma_1 X - \gamma_2 XC + \gamma_3 C - \mu X, \\
\frac{dY}{dt} &= \gamma_1 X - \beta CY - \mu Y, \\
\frac{dC}{dt} &= \gamma_2 XC - \gamma_3 C - \mu C, \\
\frac{dV}{dt} &= \beta CY - (\mu + \alpha)V,
\end{aligned} \tag{2}$$

where $X(0) > 0$, $Y(0) \geq 0$, $C(0) \geq 0$, $V(0) \geq 0$.
In the above model system, A is the immigration rate, parameter γ_1 measures the rate of flow from non-susceptible to susceptible, γ_2 is the crime committing rate of non-susceptible, γ_3 is the conversion rate of criminals to non-susceptible, β is the rate at which susceptible are getting victimized under the influence of criminals, α is the death rate of victims and μ is the natural death rate.

Since $N = X + Y + C + V$, rewriting the above model:

$$\begin{aligned}
\frac{dN}{dt} &= A - \mu N - \alpha V, \\
\frac{dY}{dt} &= \gamma_1 (N - Y - C - V) - \beta CY - \mu Y, \\
\frac{dC}{dt} &= \gamma_2 (N - Y - C - V)C - \gamma_3 C - \mu C, \\
\frac{dV}{dt} &= \beta CY - (\mu + \alpha)V.
\end{aligned} \tag{3}$$

It suffices to study the above model. For the solutions of model (3), the region of attraction [25] is given by the set:

$$\Omega = \Big\{(N,Y,C,V) \in \mathbb{R}^4_+ \ : \ 0 \le Y \le N \le \frac{A}{\mu}, 0 \le C \le \frac{A}{\mu}(\frac{\gamma_2}{\gamma_3+\mu}) = C_r,$$
$$0 \le V \le \frac{\beta C_r A}{\mu(\mu+\alpha)}\Big\}. \tag{4}$$

Equilibrium Analysis

The two non-negative equilibria of the above model system (3) are:
(i) Crime free equilibrium (CFE) $E_0(\frac{A}{\mu}, \frac{\gamma_1 A}{\mu(\mu+\gamma_1)}, 0, 0)$ always exists.
(ii) Crime exists equilibrium $E^*(N^*, Y^*, C^*, V^*)$ exists provided

$$R_0^c > 1, \tag{5}$$

where R_0^C is defined as criminality reproduction number (CRN).

Existence of Equilibria

It is straightforward to find the crime-free equilibrium E_0. Next, for crime exist equilibrium put the model system (3) equals to zero:

$$A - \mu N - \alpha V = 0, \tag{6}$$

$$\gamma_1(N - Y - C - V) - \beta CY - \mu Y = 0, \tag{7}$$

$$\gamma_2(N - Y - C - V)C - \gamma_3 C - \mu C = 0, \tag{8}$$

$$\beta CY - (\mu+\alpha)V = 0. \tag{9}$$

From (6) and (9) we get

$$N = \frac{A - \alpha V}{\mu}, \tag{10}$$

$$V = \frac{\beta CY}{(\mu+\alpha)}. \tag{11}$$

Equation (8) gives

$$N - Y - C - V = \frac{\gamma_3 + \mu}{\gamma_2}. \tag{12}$$

Using (12) in (8), we get

$$\gamma_1 (\frac{\gamma_3 + \mu}{\gamma_2}) - \beta CY - \mu Y = 0, \tag{13}$$

which implies

$$Y = \frac{\gamma_1(\gamma_3 + \mu)}{\gamma_2(\beta C + \mu)} = g(C). \tag{14}$$

Using (10), (11) and (14) in (12), we get

$$F(c) = \frac{A}{\mu} - \frac{\alpha\beta C g(C)}{\mu(\mu+\alpha)} - g(C) - C - \frac{\beta C g(C)}{\mu+\alpha} \frac{\gamma_3 + \mu}{\gamma_2} = 0. \tag{15}$$

It can be easilty noted from equation (15) that
(i) $F(0) = \frac{A}{\mu} - \frac{(\gamma_3+\mu)(\gamma_1+\mu)}{\gamma_2\mu} > 0(say)$,
(ii) $F(\frac{A}{\mu}) = -\frac{\alpha\beta\frac{A}{\mu}g(\frac{A}{\mu})}{\mu(\mu+\alpha)} - g(\frac{A}{\mu}) - \frac{A}{\mu} - \frac{\beta\frac{A}{\mu}g(C)}{\mu+\alpha}\frac{\gamma_3+\mu}{\gamma_2} < 0.$

Thus, $F(C^*) = 0$ for a unique C^* in $(0, C_r)$ provided $\frac{A\gamma_2}{(\gamma_1+\mu)(\gamma_3+\mu)} > 1$. Hence, equilibrium $E^*(N^*, Y^*, C^*, V^*)$ exists, whenever condition (5) is satisfied.

Stability Analysis

Here, we will talk about stability analysis of crime free equilibrium E_0 and crime exist equilibrium E^*. Local stability conditions of both equilibria E_0 and E^* is given by Theorem 1. Theorem 2 discusses about global stability properties of crime exist equilibrium E^*.

Local Stability

Theorem 1. *(i) The crime free equilibrium (CFE) E_0 always exists and is unstable if* $\frac{A\gamma_2}{(\gamma_1+\mu)(\gamma_3+\mu)} > 1$.
(ii) The crime exist equilibrium E^* whenever exists, is stable if Routh-Hurwitz criteria is satisfied.

Proof. The Jacobian matrix J for the model system (3) is calculated as follows:

$$J = \begin{pmatrix} -\mu & 0 & 0 & -\alpha \\ \gamma_1 & -\gamma_1 - \beta C - \mu & -\gamma_1 - \beta Y & -\gamma_1 \\ \gamma_2 C & -\gamma_2 C & \gamma_2(N-Y-V) - 2\gamma_2 C - \gamma_3 - \mu & -\gamma_2 C \\ 0 & \beta C & \beta Y & -(\mu+\alpha) \end{pmatrix}.$$

Let the matrix J at E_0 and E^* be defined as J_0 and J^*. Then, J_0 is given by

$$J_0 = \begin{pmatrix} -\mu & 0 & 0 & -\alpha \\ \gamma_1 & -\gamma_1 - \mu & -\gamma_1 - \beta(\frac{\gamma_1 A}{\mu(\mu+\gamma_1)}) & -\gamma_1 \\ 0 & 0 & \gamma_2(\frac{A}{\mu} - (\frac{\gamma_1 A}{\mu(\mu+\gamma_1)})) - \gamma_3 - \mu & 0 \\ 0 & 0 & \beta(\frac{\gamma_1 A}{\mu(\mu+\gamma_1)}) & -(\mu+\alpha) \end{pmatrix}.$$

Two eigen values of the above matrix are $-(\gamma_1 + \mu) and - \mu$. The other two eigen values can be obtained from the submatrix

$$\begin{pmatrix} \gamma_2(\frac{A}{\mu} - (\frac{\gamma_1 A}{\mu(\mu+\gamma_1)})) - \gamma_3 - \mu & 0 \\ \beta(\frac{\gamma_1 A}{\mu(\mu+\gamma_1)}) & -(\mu+\alpha) \end{pmatrix}.$$

Clearly, third eigen value is $-(\mu+\alpha)$and the last eigen value is positive if $R_0^c > 1$.

Further, J^* is given by

$$J^* = \begin{pmatrix} -\mu & 0 & 0 & -\alpha \\ \gamma_1 & a_{11}^* & a_{12}^* & -\gamma_1 \\ \gamma_2 C^* & -\gamma_2 C^* & -\gamma_2 C^* & -\gamma_2 C^* \\ 0 & \beta C^* & \beta Y^* & a_{34}^* \end{pmatrix},$$

where $a_{11}^* = -\gamma_1 - \beta C^* - \mu, a_{12}^* = -\gamma_1 - \beta Y^*$ and $a_{34}^* = -(\mu+\alpha)$.
The characteristic polynomial of J^* is given by

$$P(\lambda) = \lambda^4 + A_1\lambda^3 + A_2\lambda^2 + A_3\lambda + A_4 = 0, \tag{16}$$

where

$$\begin{aligned}
A_1 &= 3\mu + \gamma_1 + \beta C^* + \gamma_2 C^* + \alpha,\\
A_2 &= -\mu a_{11}^* + \mu\gamma_2 C^* - (a_{11}^* - a_{12}^*)\gamma_2 C^* - (\mu - a_{11}^*)a_{34}^* + \gamma_2\beta C^*\\
&\quad -\gamma_2 C^* a_{34}^* - \gamma_2\beta C^* Y^*,\\
A_3 &= a_{11}^* a_{34}^*\mu + \gamma_2\beta(C^*)^2(a_{12}^* + \gamma_1) + (a_{11}^* - a_{12}^*)(a_{34}^*\gamma_2 C^* - \mu\gamma_2 C^*)\\
&\quad -\mu\gamma_2 C^* a_{34}^* + \gamma_1\beta C^*(\mu+\alpha) - \gamma_2\beta C^* Y^*(a_{11}^* - \mu\alpha + \gamma_1),\\
A_4 &= a_{34}^*\mu\gamma_2 C^*(a_{11}^* - a_{12}^*) + (\mu+\alpha)[\gamma_2\beta(C^*)^2(a_{12}^* + \gamma_1)\\
&\quad -\gamma_2\beta C^* Y^*(a_{11}^* + \alpha)].
\end{aligned}$$

According to R.H criteria, E^* is locally stable if $A_1 > 0, A_4 > 0, A_1A_2 - A_3 > 0$ and $A_1A_2A_3 - A_3^3 - A_4A_1^2 > 0$.

□

Global Stability

Theorem 2. *The crime exist equilibrium E^* exists whenever $R_0^c > 1$ and is non-linearly asymptotically stable if the following conditions are fulfilled:*

$$max\{A,B\} < min\{C,D,E\}, \tag{17}$$

$$max\{G,H\} < \frac{1}{3}\frac{\mu(\mu+\alpha)^3}{\alpha^2}, \tag{18}$$

$$36\beta^2(Y^*)^2 < (\mu+\alpha)^2, \tag{19}$$

where
$A = \frac{9\gamma_2}{\gamma_1+\mu}, B = \frac{216\beta^4(y^*)^2}{(\gamma_1+\mu)(\mu+\alpha)}, C = \frac{1}{9}\frac{\gamma_2(\gamma_1+\mu)}{\gamma_1^2}, D = \frac{1}{9}\frac{\gamma_2(\gamma_1+\mu)}{\beta^2(y^*)^2},$
$E = \frac{1}{6}\frac{(\gamma_1+\mu)(\mu+\alpha)^3}{\gamma_1^2}, G = \frac{9}{2}\frac{\gamma_2}{\mu}, H = \frac{9}{2}\frac{\gamma_1^2 max(A,B)}{\mu(\gamma_1+\mu)}$

Proof. To establish the global stability of crime exist equilibrium E^*, consider a positive definite function:

$$W = \frac{m_1}{2}(N-N^*)^2 + \frac{m_2}{2}(Y-Y^*)^2 + \left((C-C^*) - C^* log\frac{C}{C^*}\right) + \frac{m_3}{2}(V-V^*)^2,$$

where m_1, m_2 and m_3 are positive constants to be determined. On differentiating W w.r.t t along the solutions of model system (3), we get

$$\begin{aligned}
\frac{dW}{dt} &= -m_1\mu(N-N^*)^2 - m_2(\gamma_1+\mu+\beta C)(Y-Y^*)^2 \\
&\quad -\left(\frac{\gamma_2(C+C^*-N^*+Y^*+V^*)+\gamma_3+\mu}{C}\right)(C-C^*)^2 \\
&\quad -m_3(\mu+\alpha)(V-V^*)^2 + m_2\gamma_1(N-N^*)(Y-Y^*) \\
&\quad +\gamma_2(N-N^*)(C-C^*) - m_1\alpha(N-N^*)(V-V^*) - \\
&\quad -\gamma_1 m_2(Y-Y^*)(C-C^*) - \gamma_2(Y-Y^*)(C-C^*) \\
&\quad -\beta Y^* m_2(Y-Y^*)(C-C^*) - \gamma_1 m_2(Y-Y^*)(V-V^*) \\
&\quad +\beta m_3 C(Y-Y^*)(V-V^*) - \gamma_2(V-V^*)(C-C^*) \\
&\quad +Y^* m_3(V-V^*)(C-C^*).
\end{aligned}$$

Now, $\frac{dW}{dt}$ is negative definite provided m_1, m_2 and m_3 satisfy the following inequalities:

$$\gamma_1^2 m_2 < \frac{4}{18} m_1\mu(\gamma_1+\mu), \tag{20}$$

$$\gamma_2 < \frac{4}{18} m_1\mu, \tag{21}$$

$$m_1\alpha^2 < \frac{4}{12} m_3\mu(\mu+\alpha), \tag{22}$$

$$
\begin{aligned}
m_2\gamma_1^2 &< \frac{4}{36}(\gamma_1+\mu)\gamma_2, & (23)\\
m_2(Y^*)^2\beta^2 &< \frac{4}{36}\gamma_2(\gamma_1+\mu), & (24)\\
\gamma_2 &< \frac{4}{36}m_2(\gamma_1+\mu), & (25)\\
\gamma_1^2 m_2 &< \frac{4}{24}m_3(\gamma_1+\mu)(\mu+\alpha), & (26)\\
\beta^2 m_3 C^2 &< \frac{4}{24}m_2(\gamma_1+\mu)(\mu+\alpha), & (27)\\
\gamma_2 &< \frac{4}{24}m_3(\mu+\alpha), & (28)\\
m_3(Y^*)^2\beta^2 &< \frac{4}{64}\gamma_2(\mu+\alpha). & (29)
\end{aligned}
$$

From inequalities (28) and (29), we may easily choose positive m_2 given by (19). Now using this value of m_3 and inequalities (23-27), we may choose $m_2 > 0$ provided condition (17) is satisfied. Similarly, using the value of m_2 and inequalities (20-22), we may choose $m_1 > 0$ provided condition (18) is satisfied. □

Model Simulation and Parameter Estimation

This section deals with fitting data to the proposed model for verifying the reported criminals and victims in India. We use real incidences recorded by NCRB between 1992 and 2019 to determine suitable parameters and forecast crime cases against women in India. To parametrize the model, we must first determine some of the model's parameters, such as the natural death and immigration rate of the population. The average life span in India is 69.89 years [17], therefore $\mu = 0.0153$ per year. For immigration rate, we consider the total population of India in 1992 to be $N(0) = 909,307,017$, thus, $A = \mu N(0) = 13011000$. The remaining parameters were acquired by the best fit of the model system with the recorded cases of criminals and victims using the technique of non-linear least square curve fitting

Table 1. Fitted or estimated parameters for present model

Parameters	Description	Baseline value (per year)	Source
A	Immigration Rate	13011000	Estimated
γ_1	Rate of flow from X to Y	0.2	Fitted
γ_2	Crime committing rate of X	0.00000000132	Fitted
γ_3	Rate of flow from C to X	0.0115	Fitted
β	Rate at which Y are getting victimised under the influence of criminals	0.000000000240112	Fitted
α	Death rate of victims	0.00005	Fitted
μ	Natural death rate	0.0153	Estimated

[11], and the results are given in Table 1. The figure 2 demonstrates how closely the model simulation coincides with the actual data. Furthermore, the figure shows that if no preventative measures are implemented, the number of offenders and victims would grow with time. The resultant parameter values have been used to visualise the model solution.

Numerical Simulation and Discussion

In this part, we use the data-fitted parameter values to simulate the model system (3). The values for these parameters are listed in table 1. We use the MATLAB tool to explain the numerical solution of the model and exhibit the graphical results. The resulting set of parameters guarantees the existence and non-linear stability of equilibria E^*. The equilibrium values of coordinates of E^* are $N^* = 908991506$, $Y^* = 24065199$, $C^* = 616951684$ and $V^* = 248429167$. The numerically determined eigenvalues of the Jacobian matrix corresponding to the crime exist equilibria E^* for the aforementioned set of parameters are -0.16243, -0.01435, -0.0172, and -0.01144. As all of the eigenvalues are negative, the Routh Hurwitz criteria indicates that crime occurs and that the equilibrium E^* is locally asymptotically stable.

Furthermore, graphs of susceptible women $'Y(t)'$ vs. criminals $'C(t)'$ and criminals $'C(t)'$ vs. victims $'V(t)'$ with various initial values are presented in Figure 3, using

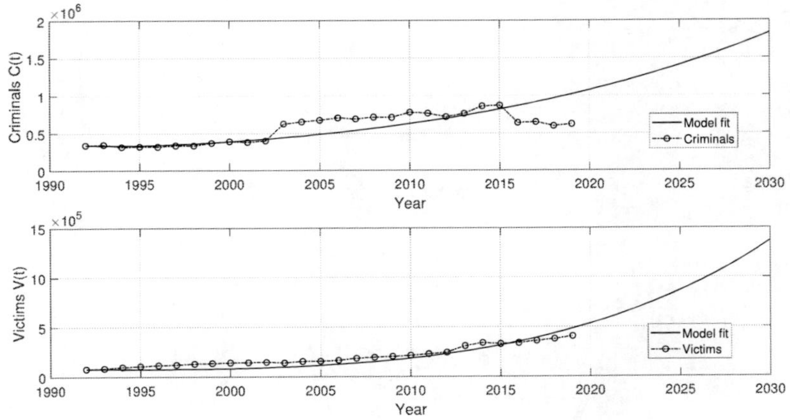

Figure 2. Solution of model system (3) vs the no. of criminals and victims reported in NCRB.

the aforementioned set of parameter values.

Figure 4 showed how susceptible women $Y(t)$ and victims $V(t)$ behaved in relation to time $'t'$ for various values of γ_1. The graph demonstrated that the number of susceptible women and victims rises as γ_1 grows in value.
The variation of criminals $C(t)$ and victims $V(t)$ with respect to time $'t'$ for different values of γ_2 is shown in Figure 5. This graph makes it clear that as the value of γ_2 increases, criminals increases but victims decreases.
Figure 6 depicted the fluctuation of criminals $C(t)$ and susceptible women $Y(t)$ over time $'t'$ for various values of γ_3. According to the graph, criminals decreases as γ_3 decreases, whereas susceptible women increases with increase in γ_3 .

The behavior of susceptible women $Y(t)$ and victims $V(t)$ with respect to time $'t'$ for various values of β is illustrated in Figure 7. It is evident from the figure that susceptible women $Y(t)$ decreases while Victims $V(t)$ increases with an increase in β.

Conclusion

The dynamics of crime against women in India have been studied using a nonlinear mathematical model with the consideration of an open population. We hypothesized that the population is split into four groups: susceptible women, non-

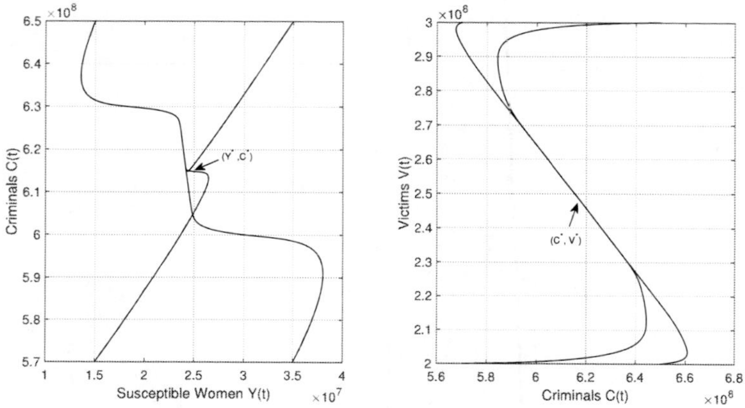

Figure 3. Nonlinear stability of (Y^*, C^*) in the Y-C plane and (C^*, V^*) in the C-V plane.

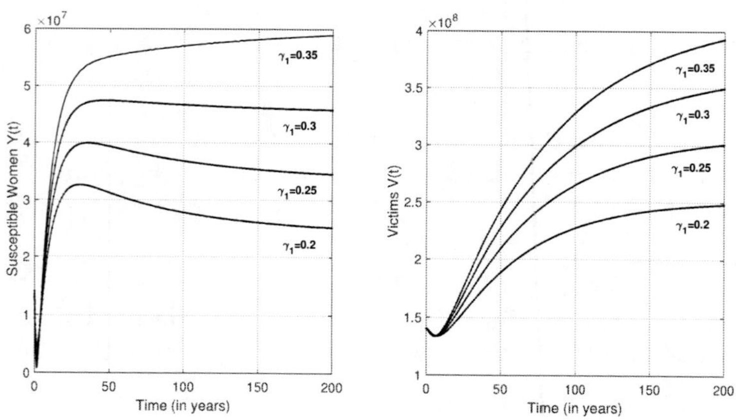

Figure 4. Variation in susceptible women population Y(t) and victims V(t) population with variation in γ_1.

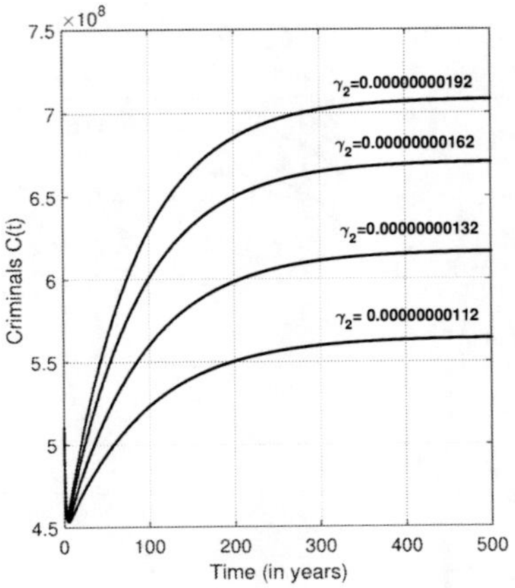

Figure 5. Variation in criminals C(t) and victims V(t) with variation in γ_2.

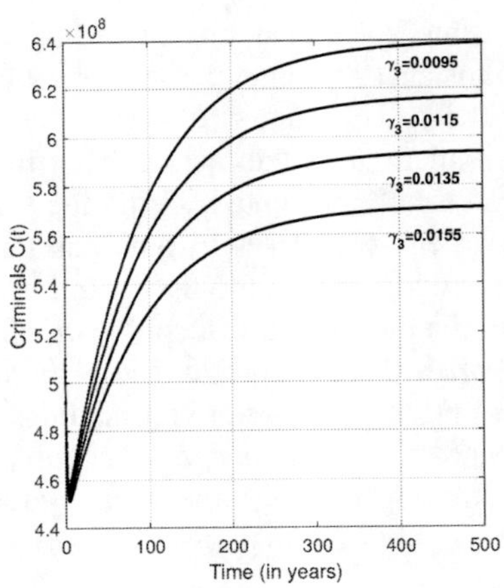

Figure 6. Variation in criminals C(t) and susceptible women population Y(t) population with variation in γ_3.

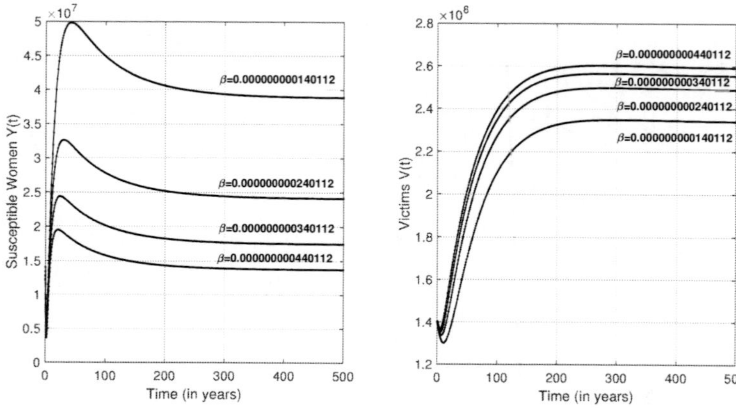

Figure 7. Variation in susceptible women population Y(t) and victims V(t) population with variation in β.

susceptible women, criminals, and women victims. Additionally, it has been presumed that when the susceptible come into contact with criminals, they become victims. The crime-free equilibria (CFE) and the crime-existing equilibria are the two non-negative equilibria of the model. Stability analysis revealed that crime-free equilibrium E_0 always exists but it is unstable if $\frac{A\gamma_2}{(\gamma_1+\mu)(\gamma_3+\mu)} > 1$ (i.e. $R_0^c > 1$). While crime exists equilibria E^* exist any time, E_0 is unstable and is both locally and non-linearly stable under certain circumstances. To get parameter values, the least square curve fitting method was utilized. The numerical results were then shown in graphical form. We performed simulations of the factors that effectively lessen victimization, and the findings were visually presented. Using the statistics and their comparison, we concluded that when crime rises in India, so does the number of victims. Furthermore, the study found that as the flow rate from non-susceptible to susceptible increased, so did the number of susceptible women and victims. Additionally, it was shown that when the crime rate of non-susceptible people rises, the number of criminals rises and the number of victims falls. Similarly, as criminals stop committing crimes and move into the non-susceptible class, the number of victims rises. Lastly, susceptible women become victims more frequently when the rate at which they are targeted by criminals rises.

As a result of the preceding debate, it is possible to conclude that the number of criminals may be decreased by informing them of the outcomes of their actions. Behavioral changes, counseling, and rehabilitation are also important in reducing the number of criminals. Furthermore, imposing security can limit the number of victims by minimizing the contact between criminals and susceptible. Furthermore, it might be reduced by conducting an awareness campaign for susceptible women about the possible location/area/spots of their connection with criminals. Criminals' capability to engage with the susceptible is likewise limited by technology. To the best of our knowledge and belief, the above issue has not yet been investigated to curb crime against women, which leaves room for future research.

References

[1] S. Abbas, J. P. Tripathi, and A. A. Neha. Dynamical analysis of a model of social behavior: Criminal vs non-criminal population. *Chaos Solitons Fractals*, 98:121–129, 2017.

[2] J. O. Akanni, F. O. Akinpelu, S. Olaniyi, A. T. Oladipo, and A. W. Ogunsola. Modelling financial crime population dynamics: optimal control and cost-effectiveness analysis. *International Journal of Dynamics and Control*, 8:531–544, 2019.

[3] S. Athithan, M. Ghosh, and X. Z. Li. Mathematical modelling and optimal control of corruption dynamics. *Asian Eur J Math*, 11(6):1850090, 2018.

[4] G. S. Becker. Crime and punishment: An economic approach. *Journal of Political Economy*, 76(2):169–217, 1968.

[5] M. Campbell and P. Ormerod. Social interactions and the dynamics of crime. *Tech. Rep., Volterra Consulting*, (1), 1998.

[6] W. H. Chiu and P. Madden. Burglary and income inequality. *Journal of Public Economics*, 69(1):123–141, 1998.

[7] J. P. Curtis, F. T. Smith, and X. Ye. Modelling burglaries in streets. *Mathematics in Industry*, 15(3):777–783, 2010.

[8] E. L. Glaeser, B. Sacerdote, and J. A. Scheinkman. Crime and social interactions. *Quarterly Journal of Economics*, 111(2):507–548, 1996.

[9] G. Gonzlez-Parra, B. Chen-Charpentier, and H. V. Kojouharov. Mathematical modelling of crime as a social epidemic. *Journal of Interdisciplinary Mathematics*, 21(3):623–643, 2018.

[10] S. Khurana and S. Shekhar. Mathematical models studying crime dynamics: A review on adopted approaches. *Indian J Forensic Med Pathol.*, 14(3 Special):223–230, 2022.

[11] M. R. Kristensen. Parameter estimation in nonlinear dynamical systems. *Chem Eng*, page 139, 2004.

[12] D. McMillon, C. P. Simon, and J. Morenoff. Modeling the underlying dynamics of the spread of crime. *PLoS ONE*, 9(4):e88923, 2014.

[13] F. Mohammad and U. A. M. Roslan. Analysis on the crime model using dynamical approach. *AIP Conference Proceedings*, 1870(1):040067, 2017.

[14] J. C. Nuno, M. A. Herrero, and M. Primicerio. A triangle model of criminality. *Physica A: Statistical Mechanics and its Applications*, 387(12):2926–2936, 2008.

[15] Report. National crime records bureau. `https://ncrb.gov.in/en`, 1992.

[16] Report. `https://www.legalserviceindia.com/legal/article-3393-crimes-against-women.html`, 2019.

[17] Report. Ministry of health and family welfare. `https://pib.gov.in/PressReleseDetail.aspx?PRID=1606209`, 2019.

[18] USGPO Report. Commission on law enforcement and administration of justice, 'the challenge of crime in a free society'. *United States Government Printing Office*, 1967.

[19] M. Rivera-Castro, P. Padmanabhan, C. Caiseda, P. Seshaiyer, and C. BoriaGuanill. Mathematical modelling, analysis and simulation of the spread of gangs in interacting youth and adult populations. *Letters in Biomathematics*, 6(2):1–19, 2019.

[20] P. Saikia. Study on rise of crime rate with population growth in assam (india) with special reference to illegal migrants. *International Research Journal of Social Sciences*, 4(1):9–15, 2015.

[21] M. B. Short, P. J. Brantingham, A. L. Bertozzi, and G. E. Tita. Dissipation and displacement of hotspots in reaction-diffusion models of crime. *PNAS*, 107(9):3961–3965, 2010.

[22] M. B. Short, M. R. D'orsogna, P. J. Brantingham, and G. E. Tita. Measuring and modeling repeat and near-repeat burglary effects. *Journal of Quantitative Criminology*, 25:325–339, 2008.

[23] M. B. Short, M. R. D'orsogna, V. B. Pasour, G. E. Tita, P. J. Brantingham, A. L. Bertozzi, and L. B. Chayes. A statistical model of criminal behaviour. *Mathematical Models and Methods in Applied Sciences*, 18(1):1249–1267, 2008.

[24] J. B. Shukla, A. Goyal, K. Agrawal, and H. Kushwa. Role of technology in combating social crimes: A modeling study. *European Journal of Applied Mathematics*, 24(4):501–514, 2013.

[25] J. B. Shukla, V. Singh, and A. K. Misra. Modeling the spread of an infectious disease with bacteria and carriers in the environment. *Nonlinear Anal. RWA*, 12:2541–2551, 2011.

[26] J. Sooknanan, B. Bhatt, and D. M. G. Comissiong. A modified predator prey model for the interaction of police and gangs. *Royal Society Open Science*, 3(9), 2016.

[27] A. K. Srivastav, M. Ghosh, and P. Chandra. Modeling dynamics of the spread of crime in a society. *Stochastic Analysis and Applications*, 37(6):991–1011, 2019.

[28] C. H. Ugwuishiwu, D. S. Sarki, and G. C. E. Mbah. Nonlinear analysis of the dynamics of criminality and victimisation: A mathematical model with case generation and forwarding. *Journal of Applied Mathematics*, 11:1–17, 2019.

[29] W. Zengli and Z. Hong. Construction, detection, and interpretation of crime patterns over space and time. *ISPRS International Journal of Geo-information*, 9(6):339–349, 2020.

[30] W. Zengli, L. Lin, Z. Hanlin, and L. Minxuan. How is the confidentiality of crime locations affected by parameters in kernel density estimation? *ISPRS International Journal of Geo-Information*, 8(12):544–555, 2019.

[31] W. Zengli and L. Xuejun. Analysis of burglary hot spots and near-repeat victimization in a large chinese city. *ISPRS International Journal of Geo-Information*, 6(5):148–161, 2017.

[32] H. Zhao, Z. Feng, and C. C. Chavez. The dynamics of poverty and crime. *Journal of Shanghai Normal University*, 43(5):486–495, 2015.

Chapter 8

Boundedness Characterization of Pseudo-differential Operators on $W_M(R^n)$

Anuj Kumar[1,*]
Hemendra Kumar Patel[2,†]
Jitendra Kumar Dubey[3,‡]
[1]Department of Mathematics, Chandigarh University
Mohali, Punjab (India)
[2]Department of Mathematics, Ujjain Engineering College,
Ujjain (India)
[3]Department of Applied Sciences and Humanities, United College of Engineering and Research, Prayagraj (India)

Abstract

In this article, boundedness characteristics of infinite order pseudo-differential operators using fractional Fourier transform on WM (Rn)-space have been studied.

Keywords: pseudo-differential operator, fractional Fourier transform, Gelfand-Shilov spaces

AMS subject classification 2020: 35S05, 46F12, 46E35

---

* Corresponding Author's Email: nujk743@gmail.com.
† Corresponding Author's Email: hemendra.iitkgp@gmail.com.
‡ Corresponding Author's Email: jitendradubey1989@gmail.com.

In: Emerging Trends in Mathematical Sciences and Computing
Editors: B. Basu Mallik, S. Ghosh, B. Kumar Pandey et al.
ISBN: 979-8-89113-751-6

Introduction

Pseudo-differential operators (pdo's) of infinite order have been investigated by several authors with the Fourier transform (Boutet de Monvel, 1972; Zanghirati, 1985; Cappieello, 2003; Upadhyay et al., 2012). Thereupon, infinite order pseudo-differential operators using fractional Fourier transform were explored on Gelfand-Shilov spaces of types $W_M(\mathbb{R}^n)$ and $W_M^\Omega(\mathbb{C}^n)$ (Upadhyay et al., 2014; Upadhyay and Dubey, 2015) and Wong (2014) discussed the L^p-boundedness of pseudo-differential operators on Schwartz space. Motivated by the above work, we have investigated various important results of boundedness and mainly L^p-boundedness of infinite order pseudo-differential operators with symbol $\theta(x, \zeta)$, where $\zeta = u + it$, involving fractional Fourier transform on $W_M(\mathbb{R}^n)$ type space.

Definitions and Notations: (Wong, 2014; Friedman, 1963; Gel'fand and Shilov, 1967) The inner product of $\xi, \eta \in \mathbb{R}^n$ is $\langle \xi, \eta \rangle = \sum_{j=1}^{n} \xi_j . \eta_j$ and norm of ξ is,

$$|\xi| = \left(\sum_{j=1}^{n} \xi_j^2 \right)^{\frac{1}{2}} = \left(\xi_1^2 + \cdots + \xi_n^2 \right)^{\frac{1}{2}}.$$

The continuous fractional Fourier transform (De Bie and De Schepper, 2012; Upadhyay et al., 2014) of $\phi(x) \in W_M(\mathbb{R}^n)$ is denoted by $(F_\sigma \phi)(u) = \hat{\phi}_\sigma(u)$ and given by

$$\hat{\phi}_\sigma(u) = (F_\sigma \phi)(u) = \int_{\mathbb{R}^n} K_\sigma(x, u) \phi(x) dx, \quad u \in \mathbb{R}^n, \tag{1}$$

where, the kernel

$$K_\sigma(x, u) = \begin{cases} C_\sigma e^{\frac{i(|x|^2+|u|^2)\cot\sigma}{2} - i\langle x, u \rangle \csc\sigma} & \text{if } \sigma \neq n\pi \\ \frac{1}{(2\pi)^{\frac{n}{2}}} e^{-i\langle x, u \rangle} & \text{if } \sigma = \frac{\pi}{2}, \end{cases} \qquad \forall n \in \mathbb{Z},$$

and

$$C_\sigma = (2\pi i \sin\sigma)^{-\frac{n}{2}} e^{\frac{in\sigma}{2}}.$$

Its inverse is given as follows,

$$\phi(x) = \int_{\mathbb{R}^n} \overline{K_\sigma(x, u)} \, \hat{\phi}_\sigma(u) \, du, \quad x \in \mathbb{R}^n, \tag{2}$$

where

$$\overline{K_\sigma(x, u)} = C'_\sigma e^{\frac{-i(|x|^2+|u|^2)\cot\theta}{2} + i\langle x, u \rangle \csc\sigma},$$

and

$$C'_\sigma = \frac{(2\pi i \sin\sigma)^{\frac{n}{2}}}{(2\pi \sin\sigma)^n} e^{-\frac{in\sigma}{2}}. \tag{3}$$

Let $\mu_v(\zeta_v)$ and $w_v(\eta_v)$ be continuous function and increasing on $[0, \infty)$ for $v = 1, ..., n$, with $\mu_v(0) = 0 = w_v(0)$ and $\mu_v(\infty) = w_v(\infty) \to \infty$.
Assuming,

$$M_v(x_v) = \int_0^{x_v} \mu_v(\zeta_v) d\zeta_v, \qquad x_v \geq 0 \tag{4}$$

$$\Omega_v(y_v) = \int_0^{y_v} w_v(\eta_v) d\eta_v, \qquad y_v \geq 0 \tag{5}$$

where $v = 1, ..., n$. Therefore, $M_v(x_v)$ and $\Omega_v(y_v)$ are continuous, convex and increasing functions having $M_v(0) = \Omega_v(0) = 0$ and $M_v(\infty) = \Omega_v(\infty) \to \infty$, we get

$$M_v(-x_v) = M_v(x_v), \qquad M_v(x_v) + M_v(x'_v) \leq M_v(x_v + x'_v), \tag{6}$$

$$\Omega_v(-y_v) = \Omega_v(y_v), \qquad \Omega_v(y_v) + \Omega_v(y'_v) \leq \Omega_v(y_v + y'_v). \tag{7}$$

$W_M(\mathbb{R}^n)$ is the space of all infinitely differentiable functions $\phi(x)$ on $\mathbb{R}^n$ which satisfy the inequality

$$\left| D_x^k \phi(x) \right| \leq C_k \, e^{[-M(ax)]}, \tag{8}$$

for some $a \in \mathbb{R}_+^n$, where $e^{[-M(ax)]} = e^{[-M_1(a_1 x_1) - \cdots - M_n(a_n x_n)]}$,

$D_x^k = D_{x_1}^{k_1} \cdots D_{x_n}^{k_n}$ and $C_k, a_i > 0, i = 1, 2, ...n$ are constants depending on the function $\phi(x)$.

If the functions $M_v(x_v)$ and $\Omega_v(y_v)$ defined by (4) and (5) are mutually inverse, that is $\mu_v(w_v(\eta_v)) = \eta_v$ and $w_v(\mu_v(\zeta_v)) = \zeta_v$, then the related functions $M_v(x_v)$ and $\Omega_v(y_v)$ are dual in the sense of Young. In this situation, the Young inequality

$$x_v y_v \leq M_v(x_v) + \Omega_v(y_v), \tag{9}$$

applies for any $x_v \geq 0$, $y_v \geq 0$ and equality holds only for $y_v = \mu_v(x_v)$, then inequality (9) turns into equality.

Definition 1 (Upadhyay et al., 2014) Symbol class $U^m(\mathbb{R}^n \times \mathbb{C}^n)$ where $m \in \mathbb{R}$, is the space of all entire functions $\theta(x, \zeta) \in C^\infty(\mathbb{R}^n \times \mathbb{C}^n)$ in ζ where $\zeta = u + it$, such that

$$\left| (D_\zeta^q D_x^r \theta)(x, \zeta) \right| \leq C_{q,r} (1 + |\zeta|)^{m - |q|} \, e^{[\Omega(a_0 t)]}, \; \forall x \in \mathbb{R}^n, \tag{10}$$

satisfies for $q, r \in \mathbb{N}_0^n$ where $C_{q,r} > 0$ is a constant.
In the case of $t = 0$ the class $U^m(\mathbb{R}^n \times \mathbb{C}^n)$ converts into the symbol class $S^m(\mathbb{R}^n \times \mathbb{R}^n)$ (Wong, 2014).
Let $\theta(x, \zeta) \in U^0$, then for any two multi-indices q and r, we define

$$\left|(D_\zeta^q D_x^r \theta)(x, \zeta)\right| \leq C_{q,r}(1 + |\zeta|)^{-|q|}\, e^{[\Omega(a_0 t)]}. \tag{11}$$

Definition 2 (Upadhyay et al., 2014) If the symbol $\theta(x, \zeta) \in U^m(\mathbb{R}^n \times \mathbb{C}^n)$, then the pdo A_θ^σ associated with $\theta(x, \zeta)$ is defined by

$$(A_\theta^\sigma \phi)(x) = \int_{\mathbb{R}^n} \overline{K_\sigma(x, \zeta)}\ \theta(x, \zeta)\hat{\phi}_\sigma(\zeta)\, d\zeta, \ \ \phi \in W_M(\mathbb{R}^n) \tag{12}$$

where $\hat{\phi}_\sigma(\zeta)$ represents the fractional Fourier transform of $\phi(\zeta)$.

Example 1 Let $L = \sum_{j=1}^{n} \Delta_{x_j}^2$, for $j = 1, 2, 3 \cdots n$ be an operator, where

$$\Delta_{x_j} = \left(\frac{\partial}{\partial x_j} + i x_j \cot \sigma\right)$$

Then $\Delta_{x_j} \overline{K_\sigma(x, \zeta)} = (i\zeta_j \csc \sigma)\overline{K_\sigma(x, \zeta)}$ and $\Delta_{x_j}^2 \overline{K_\sigma(x, \zeta)} = (i\zeta_j \csc \sigma)^2 \overline{K_\sigma(x, \zeta)}$

Therefore, $L\overline{K_\sigma(x, \zeta)} = -|\zeta \csc \sigma|^2 \overline{K_\sigma(x, \zeta)}$.
The symbol of L is $-|\zeta \csc \sigma|^2$, which is an element of $U^2(\mathbb{R}^n \times \mathbb{C}^n)$ and from the arguments of Ruzhansky and Turunen (p. 261, 2010), we can denote the operator $(1 - L)^{m/2}$ as a pdo with symbol $(1 + |\zeta \csc \sigma|^2)^{m/2} \in U^m(\mathbb{R}^n \times \mathbb{C}^n)$.

Important Results:

In this part, some boundedness results of pdo's using fractional Fourier transform are obtained on $W_M(\mathbb{R}^n)$-space.

Theorem 1 Let $\theta(x, \zeta) \in U^m$, where $m \in \mathbb{R}$. Then A_θ^σ is a continuous map from $W_M(\mathbb{R}^n)$ space into itself.

Proof. Proof of this theorem has been discussed by Upadhyay et al., (2014).

Theorem 2 Let $a(\zeta) \in C^k(\mathbb{C}^n)$, $k > \frac{n}{2}$, there is a constant $C > 0$, depends on n and q such that

$$|(D_\zeta^q a)(\zeta)| \leq C(1 + |\zeta|)^{-|q|} \exp[\Omega(a_0 t)], \ \ \zeta \in \mathbb{C}^n \tag{13}$$

for the multi indices q having $|q| \leq k$. Then for the $1 \leq p < \infty$, we have

$$\|(A_a^\sigma \phi)(x)\|_p \leq D\|\phi(x)\|_p \ \forall \phi(x) \in W_M(\mathbb{R}^n), \tag{14}$$

where

$$(A_a^\sigma \phi)(x) = C'_\sigma \int_{\mathbb{R}^n} e^{\frac{-i(|x|^2+|\zeta|^2)\cot\sigma}{2} + i\langle x,\zeta\rangle \csc\sigma} a(\zeta)\hat{\phi}_\sigma(\zeta)d\zeta \tag{15}$$

and D is a positive constant depending on σ, q and n.

Proof. Pseudo-differential operator defined by (15), can be written as

$$(A_a^\sigma \phi)(x) = F_\sigma^{-1}[a(\zeta)\hat{\phi}_\sigma(\zeta)](x). \tag{16}$$

Now we consider that

$$F_\sigma^{-1}[a(\zeta)\hat{\phi}_\sigma(\zeta)](x) = (g\Theta h)(x),$$

where, Θ is the notation of weighted convolution of g and h, for fractional Fourier transform defined by Singh and Saxena (p. 193, 2012) Then,

$$\begin{aligned} a(\zeta)\hat{\phi}_\sigma(\zeta) &= F_\sigma[(g\Theta h)(x)](\zeta), \\ &= C_\sigma \int_{\mathbb{R}^n} e^{\frac{i(|x|^2+|\zeta|^2)\cot\sigma}{2} - i\langle x,\zeta\rangle \csc\sigma}(g\Theta h)(x)dx. \end{aligned}$$

From the arguments of Upadhyay and Dubey (p. 121-122, 2015), then (16) can be written as

$$(A_a^\sigma \phi)(x) = (C_\sigma F_\sigma^{-1}[e^{\frac{i|\zeta|^2\cot\sigma}{2}} a(\zeta)]\Theta\phi)(x) \tag{17}$$

From the arguments of Wong (p.9, 2014), it is clear that, $\|g\Theta\phi\|_p \leq \|g\|_1\|\phi\|_p$ for $g \in L^1(\mathbb{R}^n)$ and $\phi \in L^p(\mathbb{R}^n)$, so we have

$$\begin{aligned} \|(A_a^\sigma \phi)(x)\|_p &= \|C_\sigma F_\sigma^{-1}[e^{\frac{i|\zeta|^2\cot\sigma}{2}} a(\zeta)]\Theta\phi)(x)\|_p \\ &\leq \|C_\sigma F_\sigma^{-1}[e^{\frac{i|\zeta|^2\cot\sigma}{2}} a(\zeta)](x)\|_1\|\phi(x)\|_p. \end{aligned} \tag{18}$$

Now, we show that

$$F_\sigma^{-1}(e^{\frac{i|\zeta|^2\cot\sigma}{2}} a(\zeta))(x) \in L^1(\mathbb{R}^n), \ \forall \zeta \in \mathbb{C}^n. \tag{19}$$

Therefore,

$$|x^q F_\sigma^{-1}(e^{\frac{i|\zeta|^2\cot\sigma}{2}} \theta(\zeta))(x)| \leq |C'_\sigma(\csc\sigma)^{-|q|}| \int_{\mathbb{R}^n} |e^{i\langle x,\zeta\rangle\csc\sigma}||(D_\zeta^q a)(\zeta)|d\zeta.$$

Using (13), we have

$$|x^q F_\sigma^{-1}(e^{\frac{i|\zeta|^2 \cot\sigma}{2}}\theta(\zeta))(x)| \leq |C'_\sigma(\csc\sigma)^{-|q|}|C\int_{\mathbb{R}^n}|e^{-\langle x,t\rangle\csc\sigma}|(1+|\zeta|)^{-|q|}\exp[\Omega(a_0 t)]d\zeta.$$

Now, from the facts of Gel'fand-Shilov (p. 19, 1967) and (9), we get

$$|x^q F_\sigma^{-1}(e^{\frac{i|\zeta|^2 \cot\sigma}{2}}a(\zeta))(x)| \leq |C'_\sigma(\csc\sigma)^{-|q|}|Ce^{-M(\frac{x\csc\sigma}{a_0})}\int_{\mathbb{R}^n}(1+|\zeta|)^{-|q|}d\zeta.$$

Thus, for the sufficiently large value of q the above integral is converges, then

$$|x^q F_\sigma^{-1}(e^{\frac{i|\zeta|^2 \cot\sigma}{2}}a(\zeta))(x)| \leq |C'_\sigma(\csc\sigma)^{-|q|}|C_q e^{-M(\frac{x\csc\sigma}{a_0})}.$$

Hence, we have

$$|F_\sigma^{-1}(e^{\frac{i|\zeta|^2 \cot\sigma}{2}}a(\zeta))(x)| \leq C_{q,\sigma}(1+|x|)^{-q}e^{-M(\frac{x\csc\sigma}{a_0})}.$$

Then

$$\begin{aligned}\|F_\sigma^{-1}(e^{\frac{i|\zeta|^2 \cot\sigma}{2}}a(\zeta))(x)\|_1 &\leq C_{q,\sigma}\|(1+|x|)^{-|q|}e^{-M(\frac{x\csc\sigma}{a_0})}\|_1, \\ &< \infty.\end{aligned}$$

Therefore,

$$F_\sigma^{-1}(e^{\frac{i|\zeta|^2 \cot\sigma}{2}}a(\zeta))(x) \in L^1(\mathbb{R}^n).$$

From (18), we get

$$\begin{aligned}\|(A_a^\sigma\phi)(x)\|_p &= C_{q,\sigma}|C_\sigma|\|(1+|x|)^{-|q|}e^{-M(\frac{x\csc\sigma}{a_0})}\|_1\|\phi(x)\|_p \\ &\leq D\|\phi(x)\|_p, \text{ for } \phi(x)\in W_M(\mathbb{R}^n).\end{aligned}$$

Lemma 1 If $\theta_m(x,\zeta)$ is a symbol with compact support in x, then for $\phi \in W_M(\mathbb{R}^n)$,

$$(A_{\theta_m}^\sigma\phi)(x) = \int_{\mathbb{R}^n}\overline{K_\sigma(x,\lambda)}\left(\int_{\mathbb{R}^n}\overline{K_\sigma(x,\zeta)}\hat{\theta}_{m,\sigma}(\lambda,\zeta)\hat{\phi}_\sigma(\zeta)d\zeta\right)d\lambda,$$

where $\lambda \in \mathbb{R}^n$, $\zeta \in \mathbb{C}^n$ and

$$\hat{\theta}_{m,\sigma}(\lambda,\zeta) = \int_{\mathbb{R}^n}K_\sigma(x,\lambda)\theta_m(x,\zeta)dx, \;\; \forall\, x\in\mathbb{R}^n. \tag{20}$$

Proof. We know that

$$(A_{\theta_m}^\sigma\phi)(x) = C'_\sigma\int_{\mathbb{R}^n}e^{\frac{-i(|x|^2+|\zeta|^2)\cot\sigma}{2}+i\langle x,\zeta\rangle\csc\sigma}\theta_m(x,\zeta)\hat{\phi}_\sigma(\zeta)d\zeta. \tag{21}$$

Using the inversion formula of the fractional Fourier transform, we have

$$(A^{\sigma}_{\theta_m}\phi)(x) = \int_{\mathbb{R}^n} \overline{K_\sigma(x,\zeta)} \left\{ \int_{\mathbb{R}^n} \overline{K_\sigma(x,\lambda)} \hat{\theta}_{m,\sigma}(\lambda,\zeta) d\lambda \right\} \hat{\phi}_\sigma(\zeta) d\zeta. \quad (22)$$

From Fubini's theorem, we get

$$(A^{\sigma}_{\theta_m}\phi)(x) = \int_{\mathbb{R}^n} \overline{K_\sigma(x,\lambda)} \left(\int_{\mathbb{R}^n} \overline{K_\sigma(x,\zeta)} \hat{\theta}_{m,\sigma}(\lambda,\zeta) \hat{\phi}_\sigma(\zeta) d\zeta \right) d\lambda.$$

Lemma 2 For the all multi-indices q and γ, there exists a constant $C_{q,\gamma} > 0$, depends on q and γ, so that

$$|(D^q_\zeta \hat{\theta}_{m,\sigma})(\lambda,\zeta)| \leq C_{q,\gamma}(1+|\zeta|)^{-|q|}(1+|\lambda \csc\sigma|^{|\gamma|})^{-1} \exp[\Omega(a_0 t)], \quad (23)$$

where $\zeta = u + it$ and $\hat{\theta}_{m,\sigma}(\lambda,\zeta)$ is defined by (20).

Proof. Let $\mathbb{R}^n = \cup_{m\in\mathbb{Z}^n} Q_m$, where Q_m be the cube with edges of length one and centre at $m \in \mathbb{Z}^n$. Let $\eta(x) \in \mathbb{C}_0^\infty$ such that $\eta(x) = 1$ for $x \in Q_0$. Let for $\theta \in U^0$, we have $\theta_m(x,\zeta) = \eta(x-m)\theta(x,\zeta)$, so that

$$\begin{aligned}
&(-i\lambda\csc\sigma)^\gamma (D^q_\zeta \hat{\theta}_{m,\sigma})(\lambda,\zeta) \\
= \quad & C'_\sigma(-i\lambda\csc\sigma)^\gamma D^q_\zeta \int_{\mathbb{R}^n} e^{\frac{i(|x|^2+|\lambda|^2)\cot\sigma}{2} - i\langle x,\lambda\rangle\csc\sigma} \theta_m(x,\zeta)dx. \\
= \quad & C'_\sigma(-i\lambda\csc\sigma)^\gamma D^q_\zeta \int_{\mathbb{R}^n} e^{\frac{i(|x|^2+|\lambda|^2)\cot\sigma}{2} - i\langle x,\lambda\rangle\csc\sigma} \eta(x-m)\theta(x,\zeta)dx. \\
= \quad & C'_\sigma D^q_\zeta \int_{\mathbb{R}^n} \left(D^\gamma_x e^{-i\langle x,\lambda\rangle\csc\sigma}\right) e^{\frac{i(|x|^2+|\lambda|^2)\cot\sigma}{2}} \eta(x-m)\theta(x,\zeta)dx. \\
= \quad & C'_\sigma(-1)^{|q|} \int_{\mathbb{R}^n} e^{-i\langle x,\lambda\rangle\csc\sigma} D^\gamma_x [e^{\frac{i(|x|^2+|\lambda|^2)\cot\sigma}{2}} \eta(x-m) D^q_\zeta\theta(x,\zeta)]dx. \\
= \quad & C'_\sigma(-1)^{|q|} \sum_{\gamma\leq s} \binom{\gamma}{s} \int_{\mathbb{R}^n} e^{-i\langle x,\lambda\rangle\csc\sigma} (D^s_x e^{\frac{i(|x|^2+|\lambda|^2)\cot\sigma}{2}}) D^{\gamma-s}_x [\eta(x-m) D^\beta_\zeta \theta(x,\zeta)]dx. \\
= \quad & C'_\sigma(-1)^{|q|} \sum_{\gamma\leq s} \binom{\gamma}{s} \sum_{\delta\leq\gamma-s} \binom{\gamma-s}{\delta} \sum_{s'\leq s} b_{s'}(\cot\sigma) \int_{\mathbb{R}^n} e^{-i\langle x,\lambda\rangle\csc\sigma} e^{\frac{i(|x|^2+|\lambda|^2)\cot\sigma}{2}} \\
\times \quad & [x^{s'} D^\delta_x \eta(x-m)][D^{\gamma-s-\delta}_x D^q_\zeta \theta(x,\zeta)]dx.
\end{aligned}$$

Now, using the property of the function $\eta(x-m)$ and the facts of $\theta \in U^0$, there exists a constant $C_{q,\gamma} > 0$, such that

$$|(-i\lambda\csc\sigma)^\gamma (D^q_\zeta \hat{\theta}_{m,\sigma})(\lambda,\zeta)| \leq C_{q,\gamma}(1+|\zeta|)^{-|q|} \exp[\Omega(a_0 t)] \quad (24)$$

This gives

$$|(D^q_\zeta \hat{\theta}_{m,\sigma})(\lambda,\zeta)| \leq C_{q,\gamma}(1+|\zeta|)^{-|q|}(1+|\lambda\csc\sigma|^{|\gamma|})^{-1} \exp[\Omega(a_0 t)] \quad (25)$$

where $\lambda \in \mathbb{R}^n$ and $\zeta \in \mathbb{C}^n$.

Kernel representation of pdo's:
From (12), we have

$$\begin{aligned}
A_\theta^\sigma(x) &= \int_{\mathbb{R}^n} \overline{K_\sigma(x,\zeta)}\, \theta(x,\zeta)\hat{\phi}_\sigma(\zeta)d\zeta, \quad \phi \in W_M(\mathbb{R}^n) \\
&= \int_{\mathbb{R}^n} \overline{K_\sigma(x,\zeta)}\, \theta(x,\zeta) \left(\int_{\mathbb{R}^n} K_\sigma(y,\zeta)\phi(y)dy \right) d\zeta \\
&= C_\sigma C'_\sigma \int_{\mathbb{R}^n}\int_{\mathbb{R}^n} e^{\frac{-i(|x|^2+|\zeta|^2)\cot\sigma}{2}+i\langle x,\zeta\rangle \csc\sigma}\theta(x,\zeta) * \\
&\quad * e^{\frac{i(|y|^2+|\zeta|^2)\cot\sigma}{2}-i\langle y,\zeta\rangle\csc\sigma}\phi(y)\; dy\; d\zeta.
\end{aligned} \tag{26}$$

Substituting $x - y = z$ and using the arguments of Prasad and Praveen (p. 119, 2016), we get

$$\begin{aligned}
A_\theta^\sigma(x) &= (2\pi\sin\sigma)^{-n} \int_{\mathbb{R}^n}\int_{\mathbb{R}^n} e^{\frac{i(|z|^2-2<x,z>)\cot\sigma}{2}+i\langle z,\zeta\rangle\csc\sigma}\theta(x,\zeta) * \\
&\quad * \phi(x-z)dz\; d\zeta \\
&= (2\pi\sin\sigma)^{-n} \int_{\mathbb{R}^n} K(x,z)\phi(x-z)dz
\end{aligned}$$

where,

$$K(x,z) = \int_{\mathbb{R}^n} e^{\frac{i(|z|^2-2<x,z>)\cot\sigma}{2}+i\langle z,\zeta\rangle\csc\sigma}\theta(x,\zeta)d\zeta, \;\; \zeta = u + it. \tag{27}$$

Lemma 3 If the function $K(x,z) = \int_{\mathbb{R}^n} e^{\frac{i(|z|^2-2<x,z>)\cot\sigma}{2}+i\langle z,\zeta\rangle\csc\sigma}\theta(x,\zeta)d\zeta$, for $x, z \in \mathbb{R}^n$ is given in the sense of distribution. Then
(i) $K(x,.)$ is a function defined on $\mathbb{R}^n - \{0\}$ for each fixed $x \in \mathbb{R}^n$,.
(ii) for each sufficiently large integer $N > 0$, there exists a constant C'_N such that

$$|K(x,z)| \le C'_N |z\csc\sigma|^{-N} e^{-M\left[\frac{z\csc\sigma}{a_0}\right]}, \quad z \ne 0.$$

(iii) for each fixed $x \in \mathbb{R}^n$, $\phi \in W_M(\mathbb{R}^n)$ vanishes in a neighbourhood of x, we get

$$(A_\theta^\sigma\phi)(x) = (2\pi\sin\sigma)^{-n} \int_{\mathbb{R}^n} K(x, x-z)\phi(z)dz.$$

Proof. From (27), we have

$$K(x,z) = e^{\frac{i(|z|^2-2<x,z>)\cot\sigma}{2}} \int_{\mathbb{R}^n} e^{i\langle z,\zeta\rangle \csc\sigma}\theta(x,\zeta)d\zeta \tag{28}$$

Therefore,

$$(-iz\csc\sigma)^q K(x,z) \quad = \quad e^{\frac{-i(|x|^2-|y|^2)\cot\sigma}{2}} \int_{\mathbb{R}^n} e^{i<x-y,\zeta>\csc\sigma} \left(D_\zeta^q\theta(x,\zeta)\right) d\zeta.$$

This implies,

$$\begin{aligned} |(-iz\csc\sigma)^q K(x,z)| &\leq \int_{\mathbb{R}^n} \left|e^{i<z,\zeta>\csc\sigma}\right| \times |D_\zeta^q\theta(x,\zeta)|d\zeta \\ &= \int_{\mathbb{R}^n} e^{-<z,t>\csc\sigma}|D_\zeta^q\theta(x,\zeta)|d\zeta \\ &\leq \int_{\mathbb{R}^n} e^{-<z,t>\csc\sigma}e^{\Omega(a_0t)}(1+|\zeta|)^{-q}d\zeta. \end{aligned} \tag{29}$$

Using the equality, $|z\csc\sigma||t| = M\left(\frac{z\csc\sigma}{a_0}\right) + \Omega(a_0t)$, then the exponent in (29) becomes

$$\begin{aligned} -<x-y,t>\csc\sigma + \Omega(a_0t) &= -M\left[\frac{z\csc\sigma}{a_0}\right] - \Omega(a_0t) + \Omega(a_0t) \\ &= -M\left[\frac{z\csc\sigma}{a_0}\right]. \end{aligned}$$

Hence (29) gives,

$$|(-iz\csc\sigma)^q K(x,z)| \leq e^{-M\left[\frac{z\csc\sigma}{a_0}\right]} \times \int_{\mathbb{R}^n} (1+|\zeta|)^{-|q|}d\zeta$$

i.e.,

$$|K(x,z)| \leq C'_N \; |z\csc\sigma|^{-N} e^{-M\left[\frac{z\csc\sigma}{a_0}\right]}.$$

Hence the results (i) and (ii) follow immediately and part (iii) can be proved by using the arguments of Upadhyay and Dubey (pp. 129-132, 2015).

Theorem 3 Let $\theta(x,\zeta) \in U^0(\mathbb{R}^n \times \mathbb{C}^n)$, given by the (11) then the pseudo-differential operator A_θ^σ is a bounded linear operator from $L^p(\mathbb{R}^n)$ into $L^p(\mathbb{R}^n)$ where $1 < p < \infty$.

Proof. Let $\theta_m(x,\zeta) = \eta(x-m)\theta(x,\zeta)$, where $x \in \mathbb{R}^n$and $\zeta \in \mathbb{C}^n$.
From Lemma 1 and Lemma 2, it is clear that $A^\sigma_{\theta_m} = \eta(x-m)A^\sigma_\theta$ and

$$\int_{Q_m} |(A^\sigma_\theta \phi)(x)|^p dx \leq \int_{\mathbb{R}^n} |(A^\sigma_{\theta_m}\phi)(x)|^p dx, \ \forall \phi \in W_M(\mathbb{R}^n). \tag{30}$$

Now, we have

$$\begin{aligned}
&(A^\sigma_{\theta_m}\phi)(x) \\
&= \int_{\mathbb{R}^n} \overline{K_\sigma(x,\zeta)}\, \theta_m(x,\zeta)\, \hat{\phi}_\sigma(\zeta)\, d\zeta \\
&= \int_{\mathbb{R}^n} \overline{K_\sigma(x,\zeta)} \left(\int_{\mathbb{R}^n} \overline{K_\sigma(x,\lambda)} \hat{\theta}_{m,\sigma}(\lambda,\zeta) d\lambda \right) \hat{\phi}_\sigma(\zeta) d\zeta \\
&= \int_{\mathbb{R}^n} \overline{K_\sigma(x,\lambda)} \left(\int_{\mathbb{R}^n} \overline{K_\sigma(x,\zeta)} \hat{\theta}_{m,\sigma}(\lambda,\zeta) \hat{\phi}_\sigma(\zeta) d\zeta \right) d\lambda
\end{aligned} \tag{31}$$

where,

$$\hat{\theta}_{m,\sigma}(\lambda,\zeta) = \int_{\mathbb{R}^n} K_\sigma(x,\lambda)\theta_m(x,\zeta) dx$$

From the Lemma 2, we have

$$|\hat{\theta}_{m,\sigma}(\lambda,\zeta)| \leq C_{0,\gamma}\ (1 + |\lambda \csc \sigma|^{|\gamma|})^{-1} \exp[\Omega(a_0 t)]\ \ \forall \phi \in W_M(\mathbb{R}^n)$$

From the Lemma 2 and Theorem 2, implies that $\phi \to S^\sigma_\lambda \phi$ defined on $W_M(\mathbb{R}^n)$, then

$$(S^\sigma_\lambda \phi)(x) = \int_{\mathbb{R}^n} \overline{K_\sigma(x,\zeta)} \hat{\theta}_{m,\sigma}(\lambda,\zeta) \hat{\phi}_\sigma(\zeta) d\zeta, \tag{32}$$

and it can be defined on L^p-norm as given below

$$\| (S^\sigma_\lambda \phi)(x) \|_p \ \leq \ C'_q (1 + |\lambda \csc \sigma|^{|\gamma|})^{-1} \| \phi(x) \|_p \, . \tag{33}$$

Using Minkowski's inequality in integral form (31), (32) and (33), we get

$$\begin{aligned} \| (A^{\sigma}_{\theta_m}\phi)(x) \|_p &= \left(\int_{\mathbb{R}^n} \left| \int_{\mathbb{R}^n} \overline{K_\sigma(x,\lambda)}(S^\sigma_\lambda \phi)(x) d\lambda \right|^p dx \right)^{1/p} \\ &\leq \left(\int_{\mathbb{R}^n} \int_{\mathbb{R}^n} \left| \overline{K_\sigma(x,\lambda)}(S^\sigma_\lambda \phi)(x) dx \right|^p \right)^{1/p} d\lambda \\ &\leq \left(\int_{\mathbb{R}^n} \int_{\mathbb{R}^n} |(S^\sigma_\lambda \phi)(x) dx|^p \right)^{1/p} d\lambda \\ &= \int_{\mathbb{R}^n} \| S^\sigma_\lambda \phi \|_p \, d\lambda \\ &\leq C'_q \| \phi \|_p \int_{\mathbb{R}^n} (1 + |\lambda \csc\sigma|^{|\gamma|})^{-1} d\lambda. \end{aligned}$$

By choosing $|\gamma| = N$, we have

$$\| (A^{\sigma}_{\theta_m}\phi)(x) \|_p \leq C_N \| \phi \|_p, \ \forall \ \phi \in W_M(\mathbb{R}^n) \tag{34}$$

From (30) and (34), we can write

$$\int_{Q_m} |(A^\sigma_\theta \phi)(x)|^p dx \leq C^p_N \| \phi \|^p_p, \ \forall \ \phi(x) \in W_M(\mathbb{R}^n). \tag{35}$$

Conclusion

Using the Lemma 3, Theorem 3 and facts of Wong (pp. 79-83, 2014), it is clear that A^σ_θ is a bounded linear operator on $L^p(\mathbb{R}^n)$.

Example 2 Consider the equation is

$$(1 - L)\phi = f \in C^\infty_0$$

Applying Fractional Fourier transform on both sides, we get

$$(1 + |\zeta \csc\sigma|^2)\hat{\phi}_\sigma(\zeta) = \hat{f}_\sigma(\zeta)$$

This implies that,

$$\hat{\phi}_\sigma(\zeta) = \frac{\hat{f}_\sigma(\zeta)}{(1 + |\zeta \csc\sigma|^2)}$$

or

$$\phi = P^\sigma_\theta f = \int_{\mathbb{R}^n} \overline{K_\sigma(x,\zeta)} \frac{1}{(1 + |\zeta \csc\sigma|^2)} \hat{f}(\zeta) d\zeta$$

This shows that P_θ^σ is the inverse operator of the pseudo-differential operator $(1-L)$. In this way, we can generalize the technique of pseudo-differential operator. Thus, the pseudo-differential operator employing fractional Fourier transform is also a convenient tool to solve partial differential equations. A similar motivation has been discussed by Esposito and Napolitano (2015) by using the Fourier transform.

References

[1] Boutet de Monvel, L.: Operateurs pseudo-differentiels analytiques et operateurs d'ordre infini. *Annales de I'Institut Fourier* (1972) 22: 229-268.

[2] Cappiello, M.: Pseudodifferential parametrices of infinite order for SG-hyperbolic problems. *Rend. Sem. Mat. Univ. Pol. Torino* (2003) 61(4): 411-441.

[3] De Bie, H., De Schepper, N.: Fractional Fourier transforms of hypercomplex signals. *SIVip* (2012) 6: 381-388.

[4] Esposito, G., Napolitano, G. M.: Geometry and physics of pseudodifferential operators on manifolds. *IL NUOVO CIMENTO* (2015) 38C: 158-172.

[5] Friedman, A.: Generalized Functions and Partial Differential Equations. *Prentice Hall, Englewood Cliffs, N.J.*; 1963.

[6] Gel'fand, I. M. and Shilov, G. E.: Generalized functions, Theory of Differential Equations. *Vol.3, Academic Press, Newyork*; 1967.

[7] Prasad, A., Praveen, K.: Pseudo-differential operator with the fractional Fourier transform. *Mathematical Communications* (2016) 21: 115-126.

[8] Ruzhansky, M., Turunen, V.: Pseudo-differential operators and symmetries, Background Analysis and Advanced Topics. *Birkhauser, Basel*; 2010.

[9] Singh, A. K., Saxena, R.: On convolution and product theorems for FRFT. *Wireless Personal Communications* (2012) 65: 189-201.

[10] Upadhyay, S. K., Dubey, J. K.: Pseudo-differential operators of infinite order on $W_M^\Omega(\mathbb{C}^n)$-space involving fractional Fourier transform. *J. Pseudo-Differ. Oper. Appl.* (2015) 6: 113-133.

[11] Upadhyay, S. K., Kumar, A. and Dubey, J. K., Characterization of spaces of type W and pseudo-differential operators of infinite order involving fractional Fourier transform. *J. Pseudo-Differ. Oper. Appl.* (2014) 5(2): 215-230.

[12] Upadhyay, S. K., Yadav, R. N., Debnath, L.: Infinite pseudo-differential operators on $W_M(R^n)$ space. *Analysis* (2012) 32: 163-178.

[13] Wong, M. W.: An introduction to pseudo-differential operators. *3rd edn. World Scientific Publishing, Singapore*; 2014.

[14] Zanghirati, L.: Pseudodifferential operators of infinite order and Gevrey classes. *Ann. Univ. Ferrara, Sez. VII, Sc. Mat.* (1985) 31: 197-219.

Chapter 9

Study of a *GI/M/1/N* Queue Including Negative Consumers, Disasters and Working Vacations

K. Jyothsnar[1,*]
P. Vijaya Kumar[2]
P. Vijaya Laxmi[3]
[1]Department of Mathematics, GSS, GITAM (Deemed to be University), Visakhapatnam, Andhra Pradesh, India
[2]Department of Mathematics, GITAM (Deemed to be University), Visakhapatnam, Andhra Pradesh, India
[3]Department of Applied Mathematics, Andhra University, Visakhapatnam, Andhra Pradesh, India

Abstract

Negative arrivals, which occur outside of the actual service process and result in the cancellation of consumers, are a common problem in real-world queuing systems.

When a hostile virus attacks a computer network or telecommunication system, it can result in the deletion of some or all of the system's data files. Many authors have previously suggested numerous lethal methods in this direction. This research unifies a large number of killing tactics for the classic single-server queue, wherein arrivals occur as a general process with exponential service time distribution. As early as the service facility realises that the system is dormant, he will go on a working vacation and the service will be delivered at a reduced rate. The model is analysed at steady-state with the help of supplementary variable and iterative techniques. The probability distribution of the count of consumers who are currently using the system prior to the arrival of consumers as well as at random epochs are calculated. In addition, research is done to determine how the functionality of the system is affected by different parameters.

* Corresponding Author's Email: mail2jyothsnak@yahoo.co.in

In: Emerging Trends in Mathematical Sciences and Computing
Editors: B. Basu Mallik, S. Ghosh, B. Kumar Pandey et al.
ISBN: 979-8-89113-751-6

Keywords: probability and stochastic processes

PACS 2.30.Hq, 2.50.-r, 2.50.Ga.

Introduction

The conceptualization of negative arrivals, originally presented by Gelenbe (1989), has received a lot of attention in queueing literature. The word "G-queues" is widely used to characterise queues that encounter some kind of negative arrivals and it was coined in the 1980s. Positive consumers (abbreviated as PC) behave like regular consumers and seek services whereas negative arrivals result in the eradication of positive consumers. Two different forms of negative arrivals exist: a disaster, which completely wipes out all of the current consumers from the system at once and a negative consumer (NC), which destroys one PC from the system. It's possible for NC and disasters to originate from the same origin as PC or they can originate from an origin unrelated to the arrival and service processes. Two distinct killing disciplines are possible for a NC. One is removing consumers at the beginning of the queue (RCH) and the other one is removing consumers at the back of the queue (RCE).

Due to the practical uses of queues with negative arrivals and disasters in computer networks, neural networks, etc., they have been thoroughly investigated during the past few decades. Harrison and Pitel (1993) explored an exponential queue with Poisson arrivals of NC and in their findings the Laplace transforms of the waiting duration was derived. Additional generalisations of the work that was done in Harrison and Pitel (1993) have been made for the general service queuing system with negative consumers by Harrison and Pitel (1996), for the general service queuing system including disasters by Jain and Sigman (1996) and by Yang and Chae (2001) for the general input queuing model involving negative consumers and disasters. Vladimir and Jesus (2001) have conducted research on the investigation of retrial queues with multi servers and negative arrivals. Retrial queues with multiple servers and negative arrivals has been considered by Yang Woo Shin (2007) . Lee et al. (2015) estimated the generating function of the queue size and the active duration for the general service queueing model, taking into account both negative arrivals and disasters. Koh et al. (2018) made the assumption of Poisson arrival of negative consumers and a uniform rate for the distribution of service duration. Using these two assumptions, they were able to derive the count of consumers in the model for a general service queue at steady state. It is essential to emphasise that the occurrence of a negative consumer or a disaster does not have any relevance to the procedures involved in the service and arrival processes in any of the research that was presented earlier in this section.

In recent years, working vacation (WV) queues have reaped enormous benefits as a direct result of the widespread implementation of these models across a variety of systems, including electronic networks, telecommunication systems, production systems and many others. Working vacations are a form vacation policy in which the service facility is permitted to continue running at somewhat a lesser rate rather than suspending all the operations totally while it is on vacation. This is in contrast to traditional vacations, which completely halts all activities. This form of WV scheme was initially developed by Servi and Finn (2002) in an exponential queue. The generalization of the $M/M/1$ queue including WVs has been done by Baba (2005) to a steady-state general arrival and multiple working vacations (MWVs) queueing model. He established the queue size distribution at different time epochs. Generalizing Servi and Finn's (2002) exponential queue, Wu and Takagi (2006) came up with a general service queue with WV. For further information about WVs queues, one may explore the works of Liu et al. (2007), Zhang and Hou (2011), Yue et al. (2012), and the references contained therein. An exponential retrial queue with WVs and negative arrivals has been explored by Tian Van Do et al. (2014). A fluid model regulated by an exponential working vacations queue with negative arrivals was researched by Xu et al. (2018). Gopinath and Goswami (2022) have found the equilibrium joining approaches of positive consumers in an exponential queue subject to negative arrivals and working vacations.

Negative consumers frequently enter the system from the same origin as positive consumers do when they arrive to obtain service in a wide range of everyday settings including those involving industrial and processing networks, data transmission and communications. Disasters can also have an impact on the system by way of a power outage, server crash, machine malfunction or virus attack regardless of the service and arrival processes. The assumption that the source of both positive and negative arrivals is same makes it challenging to analyse the system. Further, there is no research work that studies a limited buffer queue with negative consumers and disasters together with working vacations under renewal input process. Because of this, we were inspired to carry out the analysis of a limited buffer queue that includes negative consumers, disasters and working vacations under renewal input process.

This article examines a limited buffer queue with negative consumers, disasters and WVs under renewal input and exponential service. The time between successive arrivals of consumers are presumed to follow arbitrary distribution. It is considered that the distribution of vacation periods and service times throughout ordinary service, WV is exponential. Supplementary variable and recursive methods are the two techniques that have been utilized in this article to compute the probabilities of the system lengths at various epochs. Finally, numerical findings are presented as tables and graphs that illustrate how model parameters affect the performance indices.

The remaining sections of the article are organised in the following fashion. In the next section, we will provide an overview of the model followed by the investigation of the queueing model at steady state. Performance metrics and sensitivity analysis are the topics of discussion in the following sections, respectively. The paper is brought to a conclusion in the last section.

Overview of the Model

Taken into consideration a queueing system with single server that includes negative consumers, disasters and MWVs. It is supposed that the system is of maximum capacity L. The time between two successive arrivals (IAT) are taken to be generally distributed, independent and identical random variables (r.v.s). It is assumed that the times between arrivals are r.v.s with a general distribution $A(y)(y \geq 0)$, pdf $a(y)(y \geq 0)$, Laplace-Stieltjes transform (LST) $\hat{a}(s)$ and mean $1/\lambda = -\hat{a}^{(1)}(0)$.

There are three different outcomes that might occur when a consumer arrives: enters the system as a positive consumer (PC) with a probability p^+ and joins the queue (or the server, if it is empty); kills an existing consumer who is getting service (also known as RCH killing discipline) with p^- probability as a negative consumer (NC); or turns out be an internal disaster with probability p^d and empties the system. Further, $p^+ + p^- + p^d = 1$.

Additionally, a disaster from outside termed as external disaster arises, following Poisson process with rate δ, that wipes out the entire system's PC. The process of an external disaster occurrence has absolutely no effect on the arrival and service procedures. While the queueing model is empty, neither the NC nor the disasters has no impact.

Single service facility offers service on the FCFS queue discipline to the waiting consumers. If there are no consumers to be served, the server will leave for a WV. In contrast to the traditional vacation queueing approach, the service facility offers service to the waiting consumers at a lower speed during WVs. When it comes out of a WV and discovers that the queue isn't empty it changes to the ordinary service period and starts providing service with ordinary service rate; if there is no consumer waiting, a new WV will begin and it will continue until there is at least one consumer waiting when the vacation ends. We have made an assumption that the service durations that occur during the ordinary service and during WVs are both r.v.s following an exponential distribution with rates, respectively, μ and η. In addition to this, the vacation times are distributed exponentially with a rate of γ.

The below three r.v.s describe the model at time t:

- $C(t)$ = the total count of consumers who are currently logged into the system,
- $Y(t)$ = the residual IAT for the subsequent consumer,
- $\xi(t) = \begin{cases} 0, & \text{when the service facility is operating in WV,} \\ 1, & \text{when the service facility is operating normally throughout the ordinary service period.} \end{cases}$

Let's start by defining the combined probability as

$$\begin{aligned} \pi_l(y,t)dy &= P\Big\{C(t) = l, y \le Y(t) \le y + dy,\ \xi(t) = 0\Big\},\ 0 \le l \le N,\ y \ge 0, \\ \omega_l(y,t)dy &= P\Big\{C(t) = l,\ y \le Y(t) \le y + dy,\ \xi(t) = 1\Big\},\ 1 \le l \le L, y \ge 0. \end{aligned}$$

Let $\pi_l(y) = \lim_{t\to\infty} \pi_l(y,t)$ and $\omega_l(y) = \lim_{t\to\infty} \omega_l(y,t)$.

The following are the Laplace-Stieltjes transformations defined in this article.

$$\hat{\pi}_l(s) = \int_0^\infty e^{-sy}\pi_l(y)dy, 0 \le l \le L;\ \hat{\omega}_l(s) = \int_0^\infty e^{-sy}\omega_l(y)dy, 1 \le l \le L.$$

Let the probability for the being of l consumers in the queueing model with the service facility in WV and in ordinary service, respectively, at any given epoch be represented by $\pi_l \equiv \hat{\pi}_l(0), 0 \le n \le L$ and $\omega_l \equiv \hat{\omega}_l(0), 1 \le l \le L$, respectively.

Steady-state Analysis

Using the supplementary variable approach, the differential difference equations are obtained by contrasting the system state at two separate time instants in succession, denoted by t and $t + dt$, respectively. The differential difference equations that are valid at steady-state may be written as

$$\begin{aligned} -\pi_0^{(1)}(y) &= -\delta\pi_0(y) + \eta\pi_1(y) + \delta\left(\textstyle\sum_{l=0}^{L}\pi_l(y) + \sum_{l=1}^{L}\omega_l(y)\right) + a(y)\Bigg(p^-\left(\pi_1(0)\right. \\ &\quad \left.+\pi_0(0)\right) + p^d\left(\textstyle\sum_{l=0}^{L}\pi_l(0) + \sum_{l=1}^{L}\omega_l(0)\right) + p^-\omega_1(0)\Bigg) + \mu\omega_1(y), \\ -\pi_l^{(1)}(y) &= -\left(\eta+\gamma+\delta\right)\pi_l(y) + \eta\pi_{l+1}(y) + a(y)\left(p^+\pi_{l-1}(0) + p^-\pi_{l+1}(0)\right), \\ &\quad 1 \le l \le L-1, \\ -\pi_L^{(1)}(y) &= -\left(\eta+\gamma+\delta\right)\pi_L(y) + a(y)p^+\left(\pi_{L-1}(0) + \pi_L(0)\right), \\ -\omega_1^{(1)}(y) &= -\left(\mu+\delta\right)\omega_1(y) + \gamma\pi_1(y) + \mu\omega_2(y) + a(y)p^-\omega_2(0), \\ -\omega_l^{(1)}(y) &= -\left(\mu+\delta\right)\omega_l(y) + \gamma\pi_l(y) + \mu\omega_{l+1}(y) + a(y)\left(p^+\omega_{l-1}(0) + p^-\omega_{l+1}(0)\right), \\ &\quad 2 \le l \le L-1, \\ -\omega_L^{(1)}(y) &= -\left(\mu+\delta\right)\omega_L(y) + \gamma\pi_L(y) + a(y)p^+\left(\omega_{L-1}(0) + \omega_L(0)\right). \end{aligned}$$

The resultant set of equations after multiplying the preceding equations with e^{-su} and integrating over s between 0 and ∞ is

$$
\begin{aligned}
(\delta - s)\,\hat{\pi}_0(s) &= -\pi_0(0) + \eta\hat{\pi}_1(s) + \delta\left(\sum_{l=0}^{L}\hat{\pi}_l(s) + \sum_{l=1}^{L}\hat{\omega}_l(s)\right) \\
&\quad + \hat{a}(s)\left(p^-\left(\pi_1(0)+\pi_0(0)\right) + p^d\Big(\sum_{l=0}^{L}\pi_l(0) + \sum_{l=1}^{L}\omega_l(0)\Big)\right. \\
&\quad \left. + p^-\omega_1(0)\right) + \mu\hat{\omega}_1(s), \qquad (1) \\
(\eta+\gamma+\delta-s)\hat{\pi}_l(s) &= -\pi_l(0) + \hat{a}(s)\left(p^+\pi_{l-1}(0) + p^-\pi_{l+1}(0)\right) + \eta\hat{\pi}_{l+1}(s), \\
&\quad 1 \le l \le L-1, \qquad (2) \\
(\eta+\gamma+\delta-s)\hat{\pi}_L(s) &= -\pi_L(0) + \hat{a}(s)p^+\left(\pi_{L-1}(0) + \pi_L(0)\right), \qquad (3) \\
(\mu+\delta-s)\hat{\omega}_1(s) &= -\omega_1(0) + \hat{a}(s)p^-\omega_2(0) + \mu\hat{\omega}_2(s) + \gamma\hat{\pi}_1(s), \qquad (4) \\
(\mu+\delta-s)\hat{\omega}_l(s) &= -\omega_l(0) + \hat{a}(s)\left(p^+\omega_{l-1}(0) + p^-\omega_{l+1}(0)\right) + \mu\hat{\pi}_{l+1}(s) \\
&\quad + \gamma\hat{\pi}_l(s), 2 \le l \le L-1, \qquad (5) \\
(\mu+\delta-s)\hat{\omega}_L(s) &= -\omega_L(0) + \hat{a}(s)p^+\left(\omega_{L-1}(0) + \omega_L(0)\right) + \gamma\hat{\pi}_L(s). \qquad (6)
\end{aligned}
$$

By summing the previously given equations, setting the limit as $s \to 0$ and implementing the normalising condition: $\sum_{l=0}^{L}\pi_l + \sum_{l=1}^{L}\omega_l = 1$ we get $\sum_{l=0}^{L}\pi_l(0) + \sum_{l=1}^{L}\omega_l(0) = \lambda$.

Let $c_1 = \eta + \gamma + \delta$ and $c_2 = \mu + \delta$. By applying the recursive solution method to the preceding system of equations, we obtain

$$
\begin{aligned}
\pi_l(0) &= \psi(l)\pi_L(0), 1 \le l \le L \\
\hat{\pi}_l(s) &= \Psi(l,s)\pi_L(0), 1 \le l \le L, \\
\omega_l(0) &= \theta(l)\pi_L(0) + \phi(l)\omega_L(0), 1 \le l \le L,
\end{aligned}
$$

$$
\hat{\omega}_l(s) = \Theta(l,s)\pi_L(0) + \Phi(l,s)\omega_L(0), 1 \le l \le L,
$$

where

$$\begin{aligned}
\psi(L) &= 1,\\
\psi(L-1) &= \frac{1-p^+\hat{a}(c_1)}{p^+\hat{a}(c_1)},\\
\Psi(L,s) &= \begin{cases} \dfrac{\hat{a}(s)p^+\psi(L-1)+\left(\hat{a}(s)p^+-1\right)\psi(L)}{c_1-s}, \text{ when } s\neq c_1,\\ -\hat{a}^{(1)}(s)p^+\left(\psi(L-1)+\psi(L)\right), \text{ when } s=c_1, \end{cases}\\
\Psi^{(n)}(L,s) &= \begin{cases} \dfrac{\hat{a}^{(n)}(s)p^+\left(\psi(L-1)+\psi(L)\right)+n\Psi^{(n-1)}(L,s)}{c_1-s}, \text{ when } s\neq c_1,\\ -\dfrac{\hat{a}^{(n+1)}(s)p^+\left(\psi(L-1)+\psi(L)\right)}{n+1}, \text{ when } s=c_1, \end{cases}\\
\psi(l) &= \frac{\psi(l)-\eta\Psi(l+1,c_1)-\hat{a}(c_1)p^-\psi_{l+1}}{p^+\hat{a}(c_1)}, l=L-2,\ldots,0.
\end{aligned}$$

For $l=L-1,L-2,\ldots,1$, we have

$$\begin{aligned}
\Psi(l,s) &= \begin{cases} \dfrac{\hat{a}(s)\left(p^+\psi(l-1)+p^-\psi(l+1)\right)+\eta\Psi(l+1,s)-\psi(l)}{c_1-s}, \text{ when } s\neq c_1,\\ -\hat{a}^{(1)}(s)\left(p^+\psi(l-1)+p^-\psi(l+1)\right)+\eta\Psi^{(1)}(l+1,s), \text{ when } s=c_1, \end{cases}\\
\Psi^{(n)}(l,s) &= \begin{cases} \dfrac{\hat{a}^{(n)}(s)\left(p^+\psi(l-1)+p^-\psi(l+1)\right)+\eta\Psi^{(n)}(l+1,s)+n\Psi^{(n-1)}(l,s)}{c_1-s},\\ \qquad \text{when } s\neq c_1,\\ -\dfrac{\hat{a}^{(n+1)}(s)\left(p^+\psi(l-1)+p^-\psi(l+1)\right)+\eta\Psi^{(n+1)}(l+1,s)}{n+1}, \text{ when } s=c_1. \end{cases}
\end{aligned}$$

Further,

$$\begin{aligned}
\theta(L) &= 0,\\
\theta(L-1) &= -\frac{\gamma\Psi(L,c_2)}{\hat{a}(c_2)p^+},\\
\phi(L) &= 1,\\
\phi(L-1) &= \frac{1-\hat{a}(c_2)p^+}{\hat{a}(c_2)p^+},\\
\Theta(L,s) &= \begin{cases} \dfrac{\hat{a}(s)p^+\theta(L-1)+\gamma\Psi(L,s)}{c_2-s}, \text{ when } s\neq c_2,\\ -\left(\hat{a}^{(1)}(s)p^+\theta(L-1)+\gamma\Psi^{(1)}(L,s)\right), \text{ when } s=c_2, \end{cases}\\
\Theta^{(n)}(L,s) &= \begin{cases} \dfrac{\hat{a}^{(n)}(s)p^+\theta(L-1)+\gamma\Psi^{(n)}(L,s)+n\Theta^{(n-1)}(L,s)}{c_2-s}, \text{ when } s\neq c_2,\\ -\dfrac{\hat{a}^{(n+1)}(s)\,p^+\theta(L-1)+\gamma\Psi^{(n+1)}(L,s)}{n+1}, \text{ when } s=c_2, \end{cases}\\
\Phi(L,s) &= \begin{cases} \dfrac{\hat{a}(s)p^+\left(\phi(L-1)+\phi(L)\right)-\phi(L)}{c_2-s}, \text{ when } s\neq c_2,\\ -\hat{a}^{(1)}(s)p^+\left(\phi(L-1)+\phi(L)\right), \text{ when } s=c_2, \end{cases}
\end{aligned}$$

$$\Phi^{(n)}(L,s) = \begin{cases} \dfrac{\hat{a}^{(n)}(s)p^{+}\left(\phi(L-1)+\phi(N)\right)+n\Phi^{(n-1)}(L,s)}{c_2-s}, & \text{when } s\neq c_2, \\ -\dfrac{\hat{a}^{(n+1)}(s)p^{+}\left(\phi(L-1)+\phi(L)\right)}{n+1}, & \text{when } s=c_2, \end{cases}$$

$$\theta(l) = \frac{\theta(l)-\mu\Theta(l+1,c_2)-\hat{a}(c_2)p^{-}\theta(l+1)-\gamma\Psi(l,c_2)}{\hat{a}(c_2)p^{+}}, l=L-2,\ldots,1,$$

$$\phi(l) = \frac{\phi(l)-\mu\Phi(l+1,c_2)-\hat{a}(c_2)p^{-}\phi(l+1)}{\hat{a}(c_2)p^{+}}, l=L-2,\ldots,1,$$

For, $l=L-1,L-2,\ldots,1$, we have

$$\Theta(l,s) = \begin{cases} \dfrac{\hat{a}(s)\left(p^{-}\theta(l+1)+p^{+}\theta(l-1)\right)+\mu\Theta(l+1,s)+\gamma\Psi(l,s)-\theta(l)}{c_2-s}, \\ \quad \text{when } s\neq c_2, \\ -\left(\hat{a}^{(1)}(s)\left(p^{-}\theta(l+1)+p^{+}\theta(l-1)\right)+\mu\Theta^{(1)}(l+1,s)+\gamma\Psi^{(1)}(l,s)\right), \\ \quad \text{when } s=c_2, \end{cases}$$

$$\Theta^{(n)}(l,s) = \begin{cases} \dfrac{\hat{a}^{(n)}(s)\left(p^{-}\theta(l+1)+p^{+}\theta(l-1)\right)+\mu\Theta^{(n)}(l+1,s)+\gamma\Psi^{(n)}(l,s)+n\Theta^{(n-1)}(l,s)}{c_2-s}, \\ \quad \text{when } s\neq c_2, \\ -\left(\dfrac{\hat{a}^{(n+1)}(s)\left(p^{-}\theta(l+1)+p^{+}\theta(l-1)\right)+\mu\Theta^{(n+1)}(l+1,s)+\gamma\Psi^{(n+1)}(l,s)}{n+1}\right), \\ \quad \text{when } s=c_2, \end{cases}$$

$$\Phi(l,s) = \begin{cases} \dfrac{\hat{a}(s)\left(p^{-}\phi(l+1)+p^{+}\phi(l-1)\right)+\mu\Phi(l+1,s)-\phi(l)}{c_2-s}, & \text{when } s\neq c_2, \\ -\left(\hat{a}^{(1)}(s)\left(p^{-}\phi(l+1)+p^{+}\phi(l-1)\right)+\mu\Phi^{(1)}(l+1,s)\right), & \text{when } s=c_2, \end{cases}$$

$$\Phi^{(n)}(l,s) = \begin{cases} \dfrac{\hat{a}^{(n)}(s)\left(p^{-}\phi(l+1)+p^{+}\phi(l-1)\right)+\mu\Phi^{(n)}(l+1,s)+n\Phi^{(n-1)}(l,s)}{c_2-s}, & \text{when } s\neq c_2, \\ -\left(\dfrac{\hat{a}^{(n+1)}(s)\left(p^{-}\phi(l+1)+p^{+}\phi(l-1)\right)+\mu\Phi^{(n+1)}(l+1,s)}{n+1}\right), & \text{when } s=c_2, \end{cases}$$

and

$$\omega_L(0) = k\pi_L(0),$$

where

$$k = \frac{\theta(1)-\mu\Theta(2,c_2)-\hat{a}(c_2)p^{-}\theta(2)-\gamma\Psi(1,c_2)}{\hat{a}(c_2)p^{-}\phi(2)+\mu\Phi(2,c_2)-\phi(1)}.$$

Pre-arrival Instant Probabilities

Let us make the assumption that the probability for the presence of l consumers in the queueing model at the pre-arrival instant with the service facility operating in WV is represented by $\pi_l^{-}, 0\leq l\leq L$ and that $\omega_l^{-}, 1\leq l\leq L$ is the probability of there being l consumers in the model at the pre-arrival instant when the service facility is in ordinary service phase. With the help of Bayes' theorem, we have

$$\pi_l^- = \frac{1}{\lambda}\pi_l(0); 0 \le l \le L, \tag{7}$$

$$\omega_l^- = \frac{1}{\lambda}\omega_l(0), 1 \le l \le L. \tag{8}$$

To obtain π_l^- and ω_l^- we need $\pi_l(0)$ and $\omega_l(0)$ which are obtained in the previous section.

Arbitrary Instant Probabilities

In this subsection, the probabilities at arbitrary epochs π_l and ω_l are derived from the probabilities at pre-arrival epochs π_l^- and ω_l^-. Setting $s = 0$ in (2) to (6) and using (7), (8) the probabilities π_l and ω_l are obtained as below.

$$\pi_L = \frac{\lambda p^+}{c_1}\pi_{L-1}^- + \frac{\lambda(p^+ - 1)}{c_1}\pi_L^-,$$

$$\pi_l = \frac{\eta}{c_1}\pi_{l+1} + \frac{\lambda p^+}{c_1}\pi_{l-1}^- + \frac{\lambda p^-}{c_1}\pi_{l+1}^- - \frac{\lambda}{c_1}\pi_l^-, 1 \le l \le L-1,$$

$$\omega_L = \frac{\gamma}{c_2}\pi_L + \frac{\lambda(p^+ - 1)}{c_2}\omega_L^- + \frac{\lambda p^+}{c_2}\omega_{L-1},$$

$$\omega_l = \frac{\mu}{c_2}\omega_{l+1} + \frac{\gamma}{c_2}\pi_l + \frac{\lambda p^-}{c_2}\omega_{l+1}^- + \frac{\lambda p^+}{c_2}\omega_{l-1} - \frac{\lambda}{c_2}\omega_l^-, 2 \le l \le L-1,$$

$$\omega_1 = \frac{\mu}{c_2}\omega_2 + \frac{\lambda p^-}{c_2}\omega_2^- + \frac{\gamma}{c_2}\pi_1^- - \frac{\lambda}{c_2}\omega_1^-.$$

At last, π_0, the sole unknown is calculated from the normalization condition as $\pi_0 = 1 - \sum_{l=1}^{L}(\pi_l + \omega_l)$.

Performance Metrics

Performance metrics are one of the many queueing system aspects that are crucial since they show how effective the system is.

- *Expected system length:* The expected length of the system, denoted by L_s, at any given arbitrary epoch may be calculated as follows

$$L_s = \sum_{l=1}^{L} l(\pi_l + \omega_l)$$

Table 1. Various instant probabilities for exponential and Erlang-5 IAT distributions

	Exponential				Erlang-5			
l	π_l^-	ω_l^-	π_l	ω_l	π_l^-	ω_l^-	π_l	ω_l
0	0.83367	–	0.83367	–	0.91909	–	0.80767	–
1	0.09598	0.04302	0.09598	0.04302	0.03245	0.04222	0.12223	0.05492
2	0.01105	0.01182	0.01105	0.01182	0.00115	0.00463	0.00432	0.00970
3	0.00127	0.00246	0.00127	0.00246	0.00004	0.00040	0.00015	0.00092
4	0.00015	0.00046	0.00015	0.00046	0.00000	0.00003	0.00000	0.00008
5	0.00002	0.00008	0.00002	0.00008	0.00000	0.00000	0.00000	0.00000

- *Busy period probabilities:* The equations below provide the server's busy probabilities in WV and during an ordinary service period, respectively.

$$P_v = \sum_{l=0}^{L} \pi_l, \; P_b = \sum_{l=1}^{L} \omega_l.$$

- *Expected rate of negative consumers:* The formula for calculating the expected rate of negative consumers (E_{NC}) is given by

$$E_{NC} = \sum_{l=1}^{L} \lambda p^- \left(\pi_l + \omega_l\right).$$

Sensitivity Analysis

A few numerical results have been displayed as tables and graphs to demonstrate the reliability of the formulas found in the prior sections. The model's inputs are considered to be $L = 10,\ \lambda = 2.0, \mu = 3.4,\ \gamma = 2.6,\ \eta = 3.0,\ \delta = 1.5,\ p^+ = 0.5,\ p^- = 0.3,\ p^d = 0.2$. For HE_2 IAT distribution, we have chosen $\rho_1 = 0.149883, \rho_2 = 0.850117, \varsigma_1 = 0.484237$ and $\varsigma_2 = 2.380330$.

Tables 1 and 2 present the probabilities prior to an arrival and at random instants for different IAT distributions. Due to the memoryless quality of the exponential IAT distribution, one can see from the table that the probabilities at pre-arrival instant and the probabilities at arbitrary instant are equal. The numerical values of the performance metrics for various IAT distributions under consideration are displayed in Table 3.

The consequence of the rate of arrival (λ) on the expected system length for distinct values of δ is depicted in Figure 1 when the time between successive arrivals follow

Table 2. Various instant probabilities for HE_2 and deterministic IAT distributions

	HE_2				Deterministic			
l	π_l^-	ω_l^-	π_l	ω_l	π_l^-	ω_l^-	π_l	ω_l
0	0.82498	–	0.83636	–	0.94771	–	0.79927	–
1	0.10082	0.04393	0.09367	0.04166	0.01392	0.03585	0.13039	0.06020
2	0.01232	0.01276	0.01145	0.01199	0.00020	0.00223	0.00191	0.00775
3	0.00151	0.00280	0.00140	0.00263	0.00000	0.00011	0.00003	0.00043
4	0.00018	0.00055	0.00017	0.00052	0.00000	0.00000	0.00000	0.00002
5	0.00002	0.00010	0.00002	0.00010	0.00000	0.00000	0.00000	0.00000

Table 3. Numerical values of performance metrics for different IAT

	Exponential	Erlang-5	HE_2	Deterministic
L_s	0.19898	0.20876	0.19779	0.21139
P_v	0.94214	0.93437	0.94308	0.93160
P_b	0.05786	0.06563	0.05692	0.06840
E_{NC}	0.09980	0.11540	0.09818	0.12044

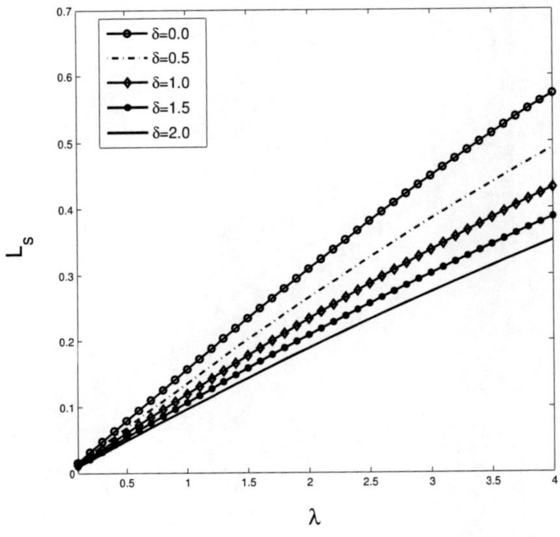

Figure 1. The repercussion of λ on L_s

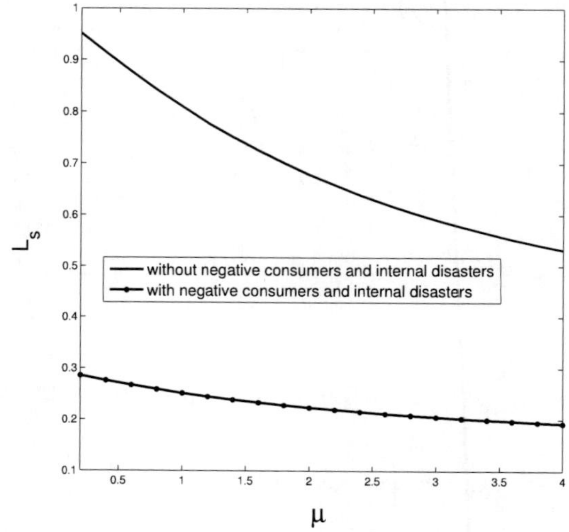

Figure 2. Effect of μ on L_s with and without negative consumers and disasters

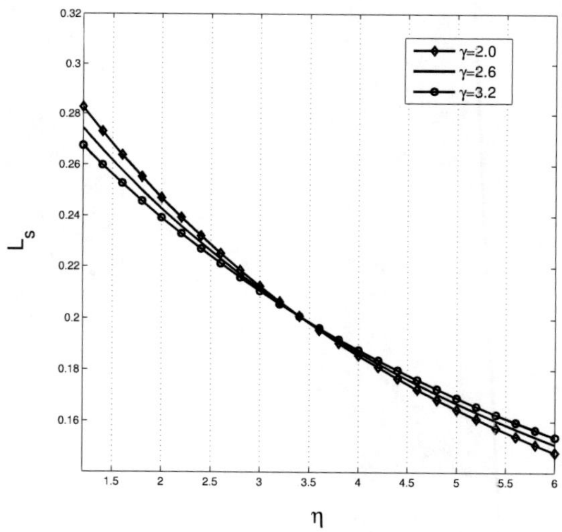

Figure 3. Consequences of η on L_s for different γ

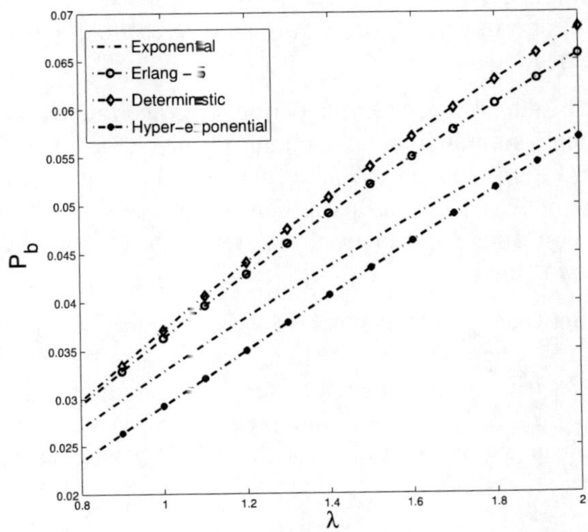

Figure 4. Role of λ on P_b

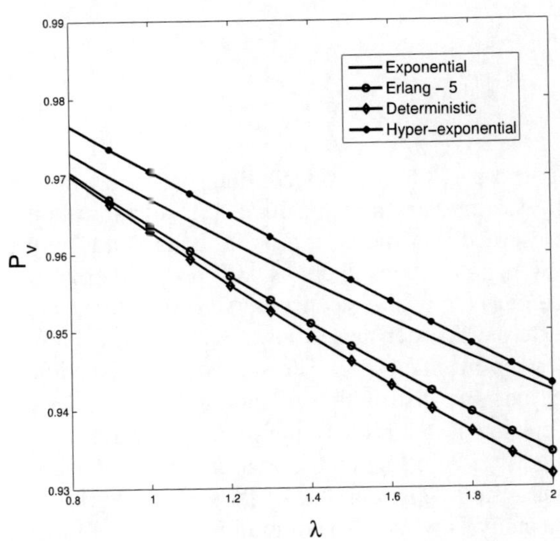

Figure 5. Role of λ on P_v

Erlang-5 distribution. L_s grows as a result of an increase in λ regardless of the value of δ. In addition, for a given value of λ, an increase in δ reduces the expected system length of the model (L_s).

The repercussion of the ordinary service period's service rate on the expected system length in models including and excluding negative consumers, internal disasters is depicted in Figure 2 when the times between the arrivals are exponentially distributed. As μ increases, L_s drops in both the models. Furthermore, models without negative consumers and internal disasters have a longer system size than models with these features.

The relationship between η and the expected system length (L_s) for varying values of vacation rates (γ) when inter-arrival times follow deterministic distribution is shown in Figure 3. It is obvious that for every γ, L_s reduces as η increases. In addition, for $\eta < \mu$, L_s drops as the vacation rate (γ) rises, although this tendency got reversed when η crossed μ. Our decision that η being less than μ is strengthened by this.

Figures 4 and 5 present the role of λ on P_b and P_v, respectively, when inter-arrival times follow various distributions. One may observe that for any IAT distribution as λ rises the server's busy probability during ordinary service increases as shown in Figure 4 while the server's busy probability in WV reduces with the increase of λ as displayed in Figure 5. This is a result of the fact that when λ increases, the number of consumers participating in the model increases, which causes an increase in P_b and a decline in P_v.

Conclusion

This research incorporates three distinct killing processes into the general input queue along with working vacations, positive consumers, negative consumers and disasters. It is presumed that the system is influenced not only by positive consumers but also by negative consumers as well as by internal disasters that arise from the exact origin as the positive consumers. The system can also be negatively impacted by an external disaster that follows Poisson distribution and is unrelated to the input or service mechanisms. The steady-state behaviour of the queueing model is analysed and the distribution of the model's positive consumers is calculated for each epoch. In addition, some numerical information is provided for the aim of investigating the effect that model parameters have on the characteristics of the queuing system. The purpose of the current work is to give a new way for conducting the analysis while also combining various killing rules and working vacations into a single model. In conclusion, it is anticipated that the model that is currently under consideration will be helpful for academics as well as industry professionals who are working to understand systems that have negative consumers in the fields of data transmissions, communication systems and other related fields.

References

Baba, Y. 2005. "Analysis of $GI/M/1$ queue with multiple working vacations". *Operations Research Letters* 33(2):201–209.

Gelenbe, E. 1989. "Random neural networks with negative and positive signals and product form solution". *Neural Computing* 1(4):502–510.

Gopinath P. and Veena Goswami. 2022. "Equilibrium joining strategies of positive customers in a Markovian queue with negative arrivals and working vacations". *Methodology and Computing in Applied Probability* 24:1439–1466.

Harrison, P. G. and Pitel, E. 1993. "Sojourn times in single-server queues by negative customers". *Journal of Applied Probability* 30(4):943–963.

Harrison, P. G. and Pitel, E. 1996. "The $M/G/1$ queue with negative customers". *Advances in Applied Probability* 28(2):540–566.

Jain, G. and Sigman, K. 1996. "A Pollaczek-Khintchine formula for $M/G/1$ queues with disasters'. *Journal of Applied Probability* 33(4):1191–1200.

Koh, S., Chin, C., Tan, Y., Teoh, L., Pooi, A. and Goh, Y. 2018. *Stationary queue length of a single-server queue with negative arrivals and non exponential service time distributions.* In: MATEC Web of Conferences, 189:02006. EDP Sciences.

Lee, D. H., Park, H. M. and Lim, D. E. 2015. "Queue length and busy period analysis for the $M/G/1$ queue with negative arrivals". *Indian Journal of Science and Technology* 8(34):1–7.

Liu, W., Xu, X. and Tian, N. 2007. "Stochastic decomposition in the $M/M/1$ queue with working vacations". *Operations Research Letters* 35(5):595–600.

Servi, L. D. and Finn, S. G. 2002. "$M/M/1$ queue with working vacations ($M/M/1/WV$)". *Performance Evaluation* 50(1):41–52.

Tien Van Do, Denes Papp, Ram Chakka, Janos Sztrik and Jinting Wang. 2014. "$M/M/1$ retrial queue with working vacations and negative customer arrivals". *International Journal of Advanced Intelligence Paradigms* 6(1):52–65.

Vladimir V. Anisimov and Jesus R. Artalejo. 2001. "Analysis of Markov multiserver retrial queues with negative arrivals". *Queueing Systems* 39:157–182.

Wu, D. and Takagi, H. 2006. "$M/G/1$ queue with multiple working vacations". *Performance Evaluation* 63(7):654–681.

Xiu-li Xu, Xian-ying Wang, Xiao-feng Song and Xiao-qing Li. 2018. "Fluid model modulated by an $M/M/1$ working vacation queue with negative customer". *Acta Mathematicae Applicatae Sinica, English Series* 34:404–415.

Yang Woo Shin. 2007. "Multi-server retrial queue with negative customers and disasters". *Queueing Systems* 55:223–237.

Yang, W. S. and Chae, K. C. 2001. "A note on the $GI/M/1$ queue with Poisson negative arrivals". *Journal of Applied Probability* 38(4):1081–1085.

Yue, D., Yue, W. and Xu, G. 2012. "Analysis of customers' impatience in an $M/M/1$ queue with working vacations". *Journal of Industrial and Management Optimization* 8(4):895–908.

Zhang, M. and Hou, Z. 2011. "Steady state analysis of the $GI/M/1/N$ queue with a variant of multiple working vacations". *Computers & Industrial Engineering* 61(4):1296–1301.

Chapter 10

Provable Secure Proxy Signature Scheme over Elliptic Curves Using Chaotic Map

Namita Tiwari[1,*], **PhD**
Navaneet Ojha[2,†], **PhD**
Shiv Gulam[1,‡], **MSc**
[1]Department of Mathematics, School of Basic Sciences, C.S.J.M. University, Kanpur, Uttar Pradesh, India
[2]Department of Mathematics, School of Sciences, I.F.T.M. University, Muradabad,
Uttar Pradesh, India

Abstract

Proxy signature is a good alternative for signing documents digitally in the absence of the original signer. Since security and efficiency are the main concerns in the digital world, we have proposed a new digital proxy signature scheme (PSS) using Chaotic maps (CMs) over elliptic curves. Security of our PSS relies on "elliptic curve discrete logarithm (ECDL) and integer factorization (FAC) problems." Implementation of it requires only low-complexity computation, which increases efficiency. Moreover, it is the first PSS in such a security setting and can also be assumed to be secure in the post-quantum cryptographic world. Our proposed PSS is provable. It can be used digitally in a pandemic time like COVID-19.

---

* Corresponding Author's Email: namita.mnnit@gmail.com.
† Corresponding Author's Email: navaneet15@gmail.com.
‡ Corresponding Author's Email: shivgulam93@gmail.com.

In: Emerging Trends in Mathematical Sciences and Computing
Editors: B. Basu Mallik, S. Ghosh, B. Kumar Pandey et al.
ISBN: 979-8-89113-751-6

Keywords: proxy signature, ID-based public key cryptography, chaotic maps, elliptic curve cryptography

Introduction

Digitization has attracted the world to collect increasing data. Data authenticity is a big problem in the digital world. Digital signature scheme has been used to provide the authenticity of a digital message/data. These digital signatures have been used for software distribution, data authenticity, e-commerce, e-voting, e-transactions on computer networks, detection of forgery, or tampering etc. As per the situation, different kinds of digital signatures like proxy, blind, ring, threshold, and designated verifier signatures have been proposed in the existing literature. Consider the scenario, if the head of an institution goes on vacation or he/she is not able to be present in his/her working place for some serious reasons. Then, how is it possible to authenticate the data /message in his/her absence? The solution is PSS (Mambo et al. 1996). Therefore, if the actual signer is unavailable for a day, the proxy signature may be used as a substitute. In addition, PSS is applicable in electronic transactions and mobile agent environments (Kim, 2001). Covid-19 and its variants are currently causing a lot of people to experience PSS, which is attracting a lot of attention from researchers.

Literature

There is a lot of literature on proxy signature schemes based on different mathematical assumptions and computationally hard problems. Using the bi-linear pairing concepts, authors proposed many such PSS (Wang et al.., 2010; Ji et al., 2009; Gu et al., 2008; Zhu et. al, 2008, Wu et al., 2007; Gu et al. 2005). These schemes are based on bi-linear pairings, which are very expensive cryptography primitives. Since bi-linear pairing is one of the most expensive cryptography-primitive, the computing cost of one pairing is ten times more than one scalar multiplication (He 2011; Granger 2006). There are many PSS without bi-linear pairings (Padhye and Tiwari 2011; He et al. 2011; Yoon and Jeon, 2011), over the mathematics of elliptic curves. On the other hand, in 2018, Liu et al. demonstrated one security attack and then proposed a strong ID-based PSS (Liu. 2018). The authors (Chen et al. 2020) proposed a PSS based on multivariate public key cryptography (PKC). Recently, many PSS (Wang et al. 2022; Alamlou et al. 2016; Granger et al. 2006) have been proposed using the concept of multivariate PKC and lattice-based cryptography, which are the most promising candidates to post-quantum cryptography.

Motivation

Literature analysis shows that many PSS have common cryptography features like single cryptography assumptions, e.g., Diffe and Hellman, discrete logarithm, or factoring a large composite integer problem (FAC). In the future, the security of PSS based on the above problems will become a serious issue. To improve the security as well as efficiency of a PSS whose security is based on solving two difficult mathematical problems simultaneously, would be more attractive. 160-bits non-super singular elliptic curves are often used for obtaining 1024-bit RSA standard security. Thus, use of elliptic curves, reduces the computational complexity of PSS. With the motivation of improving the security as well as efficiency of PSS, we propose a new PSS using chaotic map with security based on ECDL and FAC. Implementation of it requires low-complexity computation, which increases efficiency. Moreover, it is the first PSS in such a security setting and can also be assumed to be secure in the post-quantum cryptographic world. Our proposed PSS is provable and secure against "adaptive-chosen –message attack." It can be used digitally in a pandemic situation like COVID-19.

Mathematical Foundation

Brief Mathematics of "Group over Elliptic Curve" (Tiwari et al. 2011)

Let F_q be a prime field, and the symbol 'EC/F_q' refer to an "elliptic curve EC over a finite field F_q" such that $z^2 = y^3 + ay + b, a, b \in F_q$, and $discriminant = 4a^3 + 27b^2 \neq 0$. The set of points of EC/F_q with (point at infinity ∞) is a group $G' = \{(y, z): y, z \in F_q, EC(y, z) = 0\} \cup \{\infty\}$ under point addition "+ ". Find the cyclic subgroup G of G'. Let n be the order of G with P as generator of group G such that. n is a large prime.

Complexity (ECDLP)

"For any Q and generator P in elliptic curve group G such that $Q = xP$, to find $x \in Z^*{}_n$ is computationally intractable in polynomial time."

Chebyshev-chaotic maps (Tahat and Shatnawi, 2022; Chain and Kuo, 2007; Yoon and Jeon, 2011)

We describe here the Chebyshev-Chaotic Maps (CCMs) and related hard problems.

Definition 1. The "Chebyshev polynomial" is $T_k(x) = \cos(k\cos^{-1} x)$, $k \in N$, $x \in [-1,1]$,

Its Recurrence relation is as follows;

$$T_k(x) = 2xT_{k-1}(x) - T_{k-2}(x) \quad k \geq 2\,;\ T_0(x) = 1 \text{ and } T_1(x) = x$$

Properties of Chaotic Maps (C map)

If p is a large prime and $k \geq 2$, $x \in [-1,1]$, then C map satisfies commutative property under composition i.e., Tu(Tv(x)) = Tv(Tu(x)) = Tuv(x) (mod p).

Discrete Logarithm under Chaotic Maps

Given two elements a, b, to find s such that $T_s(a) = b$ is known as the discrete logarithm under chaotic map.

Diffe-Hellman under Chaotic Maps

Given three elements x; $T_a(x)$, $T_b(x)$, to compute $T_{ab}(x)$ is called Diffe-Hellman problem.

Definition 2. [9] Suppose an adversary T takes security parameter k and performs an experiment $Exp(PSS\_T)$ as following:

Setup: Challenger C runs it to obtain a private-public key pair (sk, pk) and gives pk to T.

Queries: T proceeds adaptively and requests signatures for at most qs-messages of its own choice, say, $M_1, M_{2,} ...., M_{qs} \in \{0,1\}^*$. C responds with $z\_i = Sign(sk, M_i)$ as a signature to adversary T.

Output: T outputs a message-signature pair (m, z) on target message and so wins.

Thus experiment $Exp(PSS\_T)$ gives yes if

Message m does not belong to the set $\{M_1, M_{2,} ...., M_{qs}\} \in \{0,1\}^*$ and

$VERIFICATION\ (PK, m, z) = valid$.

Otherwise it returns No.

Definition 3. (Padhye and Tiwari 2011) A PSS is said to be "Existential-Delegation- Signature-Unforgeable against Adaptive-Chosen-Message Attacks" if probability $\Pr[Exp(PSS\_T)(k)]$ for any "polynomial-time -adversary" T is negligible

Proposed scheme (PSS)

We have proposed a new PSS over elliptic curves factoring problem using chaotic map.

Setup (System Parameters)

a. Choose two hash functions $H_1 : \{0,1\}^* \rightarrow Z^*{}_n$, $H_2 : \{0,1\}^* \times G' \rightarrow Z^*{}_n$ for security reasons. Set output bit length as 128 bit and n is large prime. Choose a prime p (large enough) and a modulus m = p` q` and m is a factor of p-1.
b. Define a finite field Fp with p elements and pick a generator $P \neq \infty$ with order n in G such that. $nP = \infty$, here p' , q' are to be kept secret.

Key Generation (Key Generating Center (KGC))

a. Picks an integer $x \in_R Z^*_m$ s.t. gcd (e, m) = 1.
b. Computes a secret key d such that $ed \equiv 1 \bmod m$.
c. Selects $sk_i \in_R Z^*_n$ and computes $pk_i = sk_i P, i = O, P$.

Hence public keys are (n, P, p, PKi) and secret keys are (d, ski, p', q').

Delegation Generation

It takes sko and warrant message m_w.

a. Chooses randomly $a \in Z^*_n$.
b. Finds K = aP = (x_1, x_2).
c. Choose μ = x_1 mod n.
d. Calculates $h_1 = H_2(m_w, PK_p)$.
e. $\beta =$ sko h_1 + μ a mod n.
f. Computes $\sigma = T_d(\beta)$ mod p.
g. Original signer sends the delegation (K, σ) as delegation on message warrant m_w.

Delegation Verification

Proxy Signer Computes

a. $h_1 = H_2(m_w, PK_p)$.
b. $w = T_e(\sigma)$ mod p and verify that $w \in Z^*_n$.
c. $W_1 = wP$.

d. Calculates $W_2 = pk_O h_1 + \mu K$.

e. Accepts the delegation if $W_1 = W_2$.

Correctness Proof

$W_1 = wP = T_e(\sigma)P = T_e(T_d(\beta))P = T_{ed}(\beta)P = T_1(\beta)P$

$= (\beta)P$ = (h_1 sko + a μ mod n) P = h_1 (sko P) + a μP = h_1 PKo + μ K = W_2 .

Since $W_1 = W_2$, hence delegation is verified.

Proxy-Key Extraction

After validating the delegation, proxy signer creates the proxy key as: $sk_{pr} = sk_p + T_e(\sigma)h_2 \bmod n$ where $h_2 = H_2(m_w, pk_p)$.

Proxy-Signature Generation Algorithm

Given proxy key sk_{pr} , a message m, it runs as:

a. Randomly picks $b \in Z^*_n$.

b. R = h (bP) = (x_3, x_4), where h = $H_1(m)$.

c. Computes η = x_3 mod n.

d. Computes δ = sk_{pr} + bη h mod n.

e. Computes s = Td(δ).

f. Proxy signature is (PKo, PK_p , K, R, m_w , m, s).

Proxy Signature Verification Algorithm

Verifier does as follows:

a. Computes h = $H_1(m)$.

b. Computes z = Te(s).

c. Computes z_1 = zP.

d. Computes $z_2 = (h_1$ PKo + μ K$)h_2$ + PK P + η R,

e. and accepts the proxy-signature iff $z_1 = z_2$.

Security Analysis (Padhye and Tiwari 2011)

Let us assume that an adversary *T* can break the proposed PSS. Now construct a polynomial-time-algorithm *F* which solves the ECDLP when it simulates C and interacts with *T*.

Theorem. "Consider Adaptively-Chosen-Message Attack against PSS. If there exist an adversary T to break PSS with, at most, q-Hash queries and qs signature queries within time bound t and non-negligible-probability ", then ECDLP can be solved with non-negligible probability.

Proof. Suppose T performs adaptively chosen-message attack and breaks PSS, then $\Pr[Exp(PSS\_T)(k) = yes]$ is non-negligible. Now using the power of T, we can construct the algorithm F to solve ECDLP. To do so, F sets $\{F_p, G, P, H_1, H_2, H_3, k, n\}$ as system parameters and outputs T's queries accordingly as follows.

Setup:

Algorithm *F* obtains a public key pk and a private key sk. The adversary *T* is given pk.

PSS-query:

T is allowed to query the PSS oracle for m_w, PK_o, PK_p . There is a simulator *S* that chooses $t_1 \in Z_n^*$ at random and $Kh_2 + PK_p + R = t_1(PK_o - PK),\ h_1h_2 = -t_1 \bmod n,\ z = h_1h_2SK,$.

Then (z, m_w) satisfies

$$zP = h_1h_2SK\ P = h_1h_2PK = -t_1PK = Kh_2 + PK_p + R - t_1PK_O = PK_p + R + (h_1PK_O + K)h_2.$$

Output:

If T forges a valid (z, m_w) with probability $\Pr[Exp(PSS\_T)(k) = yes] = \varepsilon \geq 10(q_H + 1)(q_H + q_s)/2^k$, where m_w has never been queried to the PSS oracle, then *F* replays with the same random choices but different hash H_2 and outputs two valid $(PK_O, PK_P, m_w, m, K, R, h_1, h_2, z)$ and $(PK_O, PK_P, m_w, m, K, R, h_1^{'}, h_2, z^{'})$.

Thus, we have,

$$zP = PK_p + R + (h_1 PK_O + K)h_2, \quad and \quad z^{'}P = PK_p + R + (h_1^{'} PK_O + K)h_2$$

Now, subtracting we have, $(z - z^{'})P = (h_1 h_2 - h_1^{'} h_2)PK_O$.

Consider $f = (z - z^{'})$, $g = (h_1 h_2 - h_1^{'} h_2)^{-1}$, so that $sk_O = fg \bmod n$.

Therefore, Lemma 4 of [26] concludes that the ECDLP is solvable with probability $\varepsilon' \geq \frac{1}{9}$ and time $t' \leq 23 q_H t / \varepsilon$. Besides the above demonstration, our proposed PSS also satisfies all the following security requirements.

Distinguishability

Proposed proxy (PKo, PKp, K, R, m_w, m, s) contains warrant m_w while it is not in the Normal-signature. Thus, both the signatures are different. In addition, if we see the verification equation, the public keys PKo, PKp and m_w have been used, so the normal signature and proxy signature can be distinguished easily.

Verifiability

Anyone can verify that the PS by checking the equation $z_2 = (h_1$ PKo + μ K)h_2 + PK_p + ηR= z_1 Furthermore, the above equation involves PKo and

m_w so that anyone could be convinced about theagreement of the original signer.

Unforgeability

Designated proxy signer can only make sign on message m, since $sk_{pr} = T_e(\sigma)h_2 + sk_p \bmod n$ involves skp. Computing skp is as hard as solving ECDLP.

Non-Repudiation

Verification equation requires warrant m_w PKo, PKp. In addition, proxy signature generation algorithm needs sko, skp, respectively. So, neither the original signer nor the proxysigner can repudiate about their signing roles.

Identifiability

In the equation $z_2 = (h_1 \mathrm{PKo} + \mu \mathrm{K})h_2 + PK_p + \eta \mathrm{R} = z_1$. Since PKo, PKp are asymmetric in position, if one interchanges the position at the time of input, verification equation does not hold true.

Prevention of Misuse

Original signer delegates (pko, m_w, K, η) to Proxy signer. Proxy signer cannot transfer on computer network his/her proxy signing rights to third party until he/she gives proxy private key skpr. In addition, m_w has the limit of delegation. So the proxy signer cannot misuse the delegation rights.

Application

The proposed "Proxy Signature Scheme" PSS can be used for delegating signing power to the third party for desired short periods. PSS has been highly used in e-Governance, mobile agents (Kim et al. 2001), electronic commerce (Neuman, 1993), distributed computing (Calvelli and Varadharajan, 1992) and grid computing, Internet of things (IoT) (Castiglione et al. 2017). During pandemic like COVID-19, if there is a lockdown period, people would need to sign the documents digitally. Suppose the government orders for fifty percent attendance and the original signer is absent/ill, then he/she can designate any other person to sign the documents for short/limited periods. If implemented, our proposed PSS "Proxy signature" is much feasible in such situation.

Conclusion

We propose a "new PSS based on ECDL and FAC problems using chaotic maps (CMs)." It contains all the requirements of an ideal "proxy signature scheme." Due to use of non super-singular elliptic curves and calculations made at 160 bit parameters, it requires only low-complexity computation, which increases the efficiency. It is the first such "PSS" using CMs based on ECDL and FAC problems. It can be assumed to be secure in the "post - quantum cryptographic world." It can be highly used in pandemic period like COVID-19. In the future, we would prove its security in "Random Oracle Model."

References

Alamélou, Q., Blazy, O., Cauchie, S., Gaborit, P. (2016). A Practical Group Signature Scheme Based on Rank Metric. In: Duquesne, S., Petkova-Nikova, S. (eds) *Arithmetic of Finite Fields.* WAIFI 2016. Lecture Notes in Computer Science, vol 10064. Springer, Cham. https://doi.org/10.1007/978-3-319-55227-9_18.

Calvelli, C., and Varadharajan, V. (1992). An analysis of some delegation protocols for distributed systems. *[1992] Proceedings The Computer Security Foundations Workshop V*, 92-110.

Chen, J. and Ling, J. (2020) "Post quantum proxy signature scheme based on the multivariate public key cryptographic signature," *International Journal of Distributed Sensor Networks*, Vol. 16, No 4, doi:10.1177/1550147720914775.

Castiglione A., Choo R., Nappi M. and Ricciardi, S. (2017) "Context Aware Ubiquitous Biometrics in Edge of Military Things," in *IEEE Cloud Computing*, Vol. 4, no. 6, pp. 16-20, doi: 10.1109/MCC.2018.1081072.

Chain, K., and Kuo, WC. (2013). A new digital signature scheme based on chaotic maps. *Nonlinear Dyn* 74, 1003–1012.

Debnath, S. K., Choudhury, T., Stănică, P., Dey, K., and Kundu, N. (2023). Delegating signing rights in a multivariate proxy signature scheme. *Adv. Math. Commun., 17*, 681-696.

Gu, C., Zhu, Y. (2008). An Efficient ID-Based Proxy Signature Scheme from Pairings. In: Pei, D., Yung, M., Lin, D., Wu, C. (eds) *Information Security and Cryptology. Inscrypt* 2007. Lecture Notes in Computer Science, vol 4990. Springer, Berlin, Heidelberg. https://doi.org/10.1007/978-3-540-79499-8_5.

Gu, C., Zhu, Y. (2005). Provable Security of ID-Based Proxy Signature Schemes. In: Lu, X., Zhao, W. (eds) *Networking and Mobile Computing*. ICCNMC 2005. Lecture Notes in Computer Science, vol 3619. Springer, Berlin, Heidelberg. https://doi.org/10.1007/11534310_134.

Granger, R., Page, D., Smart, N.P. (2006). High Security Pairing-Based Cryptography Revisited. In: Hess, F., Pauli, S., Pohst, M. (eds) *Algorithmic Number Theory*. ANTS 2006. Lecture Notes in Computer Science, vol 4076. Springer, Berlin, Heidelberg. https://doi.org/10.1007/11792086_34.

He, D., and Chen, J. (2011). "An ID-Based proxy signature schemes without bi-linear pairings." *Annalas of Telecommunication*, Vol. 66, pp. 657–662, doi:10.1007/s12243-011-0244-0 2011.

Ji, H., Han, W., Han W., Lang, Z. (2009). "An identity-based proxy signature from bi-linear pairings," *International Conference on Information Engineering* 2009 WASE, pp. 14-17.

Kim, H., and Baek, J. (2001). "Secret computation with secrets for mobile agent using one-time proxy signature," In: *Cryptog. and Infor. Secur.*, Canada, pp. 307-312.

Lee, B., Kim, H., & Kim, K. (2002). Strong Proxy Signature and its Applications, in *Proceedings of the SCIS*, Vol. 1, pp. 603-608.

Liu, W., Mu, Y., Yang, G. and Tian Y. (2018). "Strong Identity Based Proxy Signature Schemes, Revisited." *Wireless Communications and Mobile Computing*, Vol. 2018, Article ID 6925019, 11 pages, https://doi.org/10.1155/2018/6925019, 2018.

Mambo, M., Usuda, K., and Okamoto E. (1996). "Proxy signatures: Delegation of the power to sign message." *IEICE Transactions Fundamentals*, Vol. 79, No. 9, pp. 1338-1353.

Neuman, B. (1993). "Proxy-based authorization and accounting for distributed systems", in *Proceedings of the the 13th International Conference on Distributed Computing Systems*, Pittsburgh, PA, USA, pp. 283-291.

Padhye, S., and Tiwari, N. (2011). "Provable secure proxy signature scheme without bi-linear pairings." *International Journal of Communication System*, Wiley, doi:10.1002/dac.1367 , 2011.

Tahat, N. and Shatnawi, S. (2022). "New Signature Scheme Based on Elliptic Curve and Factoring Problems Using Chaotic Map," *Journal of Applied Security Research*, 2022, doi: 10.1080/19361610.2022.2041157, 2022.

Tay, C., Quan, J. and Chain W. (2010). "Color image encryption based on interference and virtual optics." *Optics and Laser Technology,* Vol. 42 No. 2, pp. 409-415, https://doi.org/10.1016/j.optlastec.2009.08.016, 2010.

Wang, A., Li, J. & Wang, Z. (2010). A provably secure proxy signature scheme from bilinear pairings. *J. Electron.* (China) 27, 298–304. https://doi.org/10.1007/s11767-010-0334-6.

Wang, L., Huang, C. & Cheng, H. (2023). Novel proxy signature from lattice for the post-quantum internet of things. *J Ambient Intell Human Comput* 14, 9939–9946. https://doi.org/10.1007/s12652-021-03661-4.

Wu, W., Mu, Y., Susilo, W., Seberry, J., Huang, X. (2007). Identity-Based Proxy Signature from Pairings. In: Xiao, B., Yang, L. T., Ma, J., Muller-Schloer, C., Hua, Y. (eds) *Autonomic and Trusted Computing*. ATC 2007. Lecture Notes in Computer Science, vol 4610. Springer, Berlin, Heidelberg. https://doi.org/10.1007/978-3-540-73547-2_5.

Yoon, E., and Jeon, J. (2011) "An efficient and secure Diffe-Hellman key agreement protocol based on Chebyshev chaotic map." *Communications in Nonlinear Science and Numerical Simulation,* Vol. 16, No. 6, pp. 2383-2389. https://doi.org/10.1016/j.cnsns.2010.09.021, 2011.

Zhang, J., Zou, W. (2007) Another ID-based proxy signature scheme and its extension. *Wuhan Univ. J. of Nat. Sci*. 12, 33–36. https://doi.org/10.1007/s11859-006-0162-6.

Chapter 11

Numerical Modelling of Dispersion of Suspended Particles in a Turbulent Open Channel Flow: A Fitted Operator Approach

Naresh M. Chadha[1,*]
Nanda Poddar[2,4,†]
Niall Madden[3,‡]
Kajal Kumar Mondal[2,§]
[1]School of Physical Sciences, DIT University, Uttarakhand, India
[2]Department of Mathematics, Cooch Behar Panchanan Barma University, Cooch Behar, India
[3]School of Mathematics, Statistics and Applied Mathematics, NUI, Galway, Ireland
[4]Department of Environmental Physics, BIDR, Ben-Gurion University of the Negev, Sde Boker, Israel

Abstract

In this article, a mathematical model based on convection-diffusion equation with the Dirichlet boundary conditions has been simulated to study the process of longitudinal spreading of the particles with suspension and settling velocity into turbulent shear flows over a uneven bottom surface. The tracers are discharging from a continual elevated point-source. The computed solution exhibits adumbration of settling of particles as the equi-concentration contour plots. At the free surface, the eddy diffusivity tends to zero. Consequently, the convection-diffusion problem becomes convection dominated.

* Email: nareshmchadha@gmail.com.
† Email: nandapoddarcr7@gmail.com.
‡ Email: Niall.Madden@NUIGalway.ie.
§ Corresponding Author Email: kkmondol@yahoo.co.in.

In: Emerging Trends in Mathematical Sciences and Computing
Editors: B. Basu Mallik, S. Ghosh, B. Kumar Pandey et al.
ISBN: 979-8-89113-751-6

Typically, the result for these type of models demonstrate sharp layer phenomenon which demands for a special numerical treatment. Conventional numerical methods fail to produce acceptable computational results on a uniform mesh. The numerical scheme considered here is based on two-dimensional fitted operator on a uniform mesh. The scheme successfully captures the layer phenomenon depicted by suspended particles at various locations. The numerical results are in good agreement with the experimental data available in the previous literature.

Keywords: dispersion, open channel flow, settling velocity, fitted operator, spurious oscillations

Introduction

Longitudinal transport of contaminants emitted from sources in turbulent flow is an active area of research for its applications in various environmental related issues. Most commonly, these type of problems appear while dealing with hazardous waste that is being dumped into the water bodies by various sources; very often being piped directly into the flow below the surface. The introduction of these contaminants in a water body may have serious consequences. For instance, it may affect the biodiversity, the structure of the food chain, and may kill certain habitats in a water body. Numerous theoretical and experimental investigations have been conducted on dispersion processes of particles deposited deposited in streams of various geometries, including bodies of water, see e.g., (Taylor (1954), Aris (1960), Yasuda (1984), Nezu and Nakagawa (1983), Mazumder and Dalal (2000), Mazumder and Bandyopadhyay (2001), Islam et al. (2017)).

The main goal of this paper is to investigate the dispersion of inert suspended particle being injected from an elevated continual point-source into a turbulent flow using an efficient and easy to implement numerical scheme which can be extended to deal with more complex problems. Similar problems have been studied in Mondal and Mazumder (Mondal and Mazumder (2006), Mondal and Mazumder (2008)) where the authors studied transport of suspended particles with sediment velocity in a shearing turbulent flow over a rough bottom surface, the discharged particles are injected from a continual elevated line-source. They used the finite-difference scheme which combines a central difference operator with four-point upwind operator to obtain the solution of the turbulent steady convective-diffusion equation. In the present study, the particles are discharged from a continual elevated point-source for which the governing equation is convection dominated convection diffusion problem which exhibit sharp layer phenomenon. To compute accurate numerical approximations, a finite difference technique on the basis of a fitted operator, applied on a uniform grid is used.

Fitted operator method used here was introduced by Il'in (1969), and have been successfully used to for various types of *singularly perturbed differential equations*, see e.g., Miller et al. (1996), Roos et al. (2008) and Munyakazi et al. (2018). Note that convection dominated dispersion problems belong to the class of *singularly perturbed differential equations* and require special consideration. One of the ways to address these problems is to design special layer adapted meshes which require some prior knowledge of an exact solution that is rarely available; or one may use finite difference operators such as upwinding for convection term(s) which would produce qualitatively better solution but at the cost of compromising with the accuracy. The accuracy of the computed solution can be improved by using higher order finite-difference operators for upwinding (as done in Mondal and Mazumder (2008)) but this would result in a finite difference scheme with a wider stencil, and it may further complicate the implementation issues. In general, a fitted operator method employs an exponential fitting factor which introduces an artificial viscosity in the diffusion term to track the rapid increase or decrease of the numerical results in the layer areas. These methods can be applied in conjunction with a uniform grid. Thus, the sophistications of setting specialized layer adapted meshes can be omitted. For convection term, contrary to using first order upwind operator, the standard central difference operator, which is second order accurate, can be used in a fitted operator method. Furthermore, theoretical results are available in the literature to suggest that the fitted operator method leads to stable and convergent finite difference schemes yielding sufficiently accurate computed solution, see e.g, (Doolan et al. (1980), Roos et al. (2008)). For our problem, we look for a method which can be extended to dealing with more complex problems with more sophisticated boundary conditions related to the study of settling particles with suspension in a turbulent shear current. The fitted operator method seems to offer all these desired properties. Thus, the fitted operator method was a natural choice for the problem considered in this article.

The computed solution produced by the numerical scheme presented hers is based on the fitted operator method. The scheme produce more stable solution which is free from spurious oscillations in both physical and computational domain. By the physical domain, we mean that on which the original problem is posed (here, an infinite domain), while the computational domain is an artificially chosen (finite) domain onto which the original problem is mapped. The results show how the tracer particles spread with the current along various downstream distances and how transport of particles are affected with the joint activity of turbulent shear flow, sediment velocity, eddy diffusivity and other factors over the rough-surface. Furthermore, the numerical results for zero settling velocity are validated against the experimental outcomes of Raupach and Legg (1983), and the numerical solutions by Sullivan and Yip (1987) at four distinct downstream stations. It is shown that the layer phenomenon could be captured by the two dimensional fitted operator approach and depicted at all down stream stations.

Particularly, at the closest down-stream location where a peaked interior thickness appears because of the flow nature, the numerical solutions presented here are well agreed with the results of (Raupach and Legg (1983), Sullivan and Yip (1987)). In previous attempts, in the closest distance, the concentration profile for steady dispersion could not be matched perfectly with these solutions, see for example, (Mazumder and Dalal (2000), Mondal and Mazumder (2008), Madden and Mondal (2011)). In recent days, Mondal et al. (2020), Poddar et al. (2021), Poddar et al. (2021) and Dhar et al. (2021) have shown their interest to study the transport process of solute to tackle the problem arises in wetland, sewage treatment and annulus flow. They considered numerical approach with layer adopted mesh and it is interesting to notice that the outcomes of their studies exactly matched with the existing experimental work of Raupach and Legg (1983).

This chapter is organized as follows: On the basis of steady state convection-diffusion problem, the sketch of the flow geometry, the model is explained, and the problem is formulated. In order to obtain a numerical solution The problem is mapped onto an artificially chosen computational domain using an artanh transformation, with the boundary conditions adapted appropriately for the new finite computational domain for the numerical solution of the model. The application of fitted operator for a model singularly perturbed problem is discussed before implementing onto the convection-diffusion problem which is a governing equation for stream-wise dispersion of inert suspended particles is solved using fitted approach in both physical and computational domains, theoretical results have been substantiated by numerical experiments. We conclude the chapter with summary of our main results and some real world applications of the present work.

Mathematical Formulation

The Figure 1 is a schematic diagram of the flow geometry of infinitely long stream of a turbulent flow of finite depth D. Here, a model for the spreading of suspended fine particles that settle towards the bed of the water body has been considered in two-dimension. For the Cartesian system of coordinates considered here x^*-axis towards the direction of the flow velocity and z^*-axis is along the perpendicular direction of the stream. It has been assumed that the stream is homogeneous through out the longitudinal direction, the velocity is changing along the vertical z^*-axis and the turbulent eddy diffusivity is varying only in the vertical coordinate direction. The uneven bed surface is situated at $z = z_0 > 0$, the other surface which is considered to be a free surface is situated at $z = 1$. The tracers are discharged in the stream from a continual elevated point-source situated at that point $x = 0$, $z = z_p$. Then, the concentration of these particles satisfy following time-independent di-

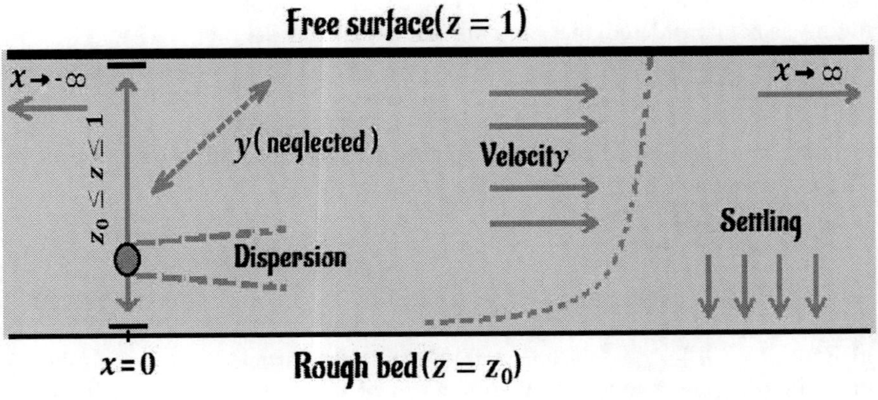

Figure 1. Sketch of the geometry of an open channel flow

mensionless convection-diffusion equation given by

$$-k_x(z)\frac{\partial^2 C}{\partial x^2} - \frac{\partial}{\partial z}\left(k_z(z)\frac{\partial C}{\partial z}\right) + u(z)\frac{\partial C}{\partial x} - \omega_s\frac{\partial C}{\partial z} = f(x,z), \quad (1a)$$

on $(-\infty,\infty)\times(z_0,1)$, under the condition of associated boundary conditions

$$C(-\infty,z) = C(\infty,z) = 0; \quad C(x,z_0) = C(x,1) = 0 \quad (1b)$$

Here, the model is expressed in terms of non-dimensional variables as follows:

$$x = \frac{x^*}{D}, \quad z = \frac{z^*}{D}, \quad t = \frac{t^* u_*}{D}, \quad u = \frac{u^*}{u_*}, \quad \omega_s = \frac{\omega_s^*}{u_*},$$

$$k_x(z) = \frac{k_x^*}{u_* D}, \quad k_z(z) = \frac{k_z^*}{u_* D},$$

here u_* be abrasion velocity (considered as characteristic velocity) and D be the ravine of the bearer stream and z_0 be the boundary roughness height. We set $f(x,z) = \delta(x)\delta(z - z_p)$, that is an elevated continual source at the point $(x,z) = (0,z_p)$.

Velocity Distribution and Eddy Diffusivity

We apply the normal 'log-wake-law', which is a multitude of 'log-law' Coles (1956) & wake function and it is utilized for the homogeneous and fairly developed turbulent flow. In this research work, the impact of in-homogeneous turbulent fluidity is not considered, therefore the velocity profile is

$$u(z) = \frac{1}{\kappa} \ln\left(\frac{z}{z_0}\right) + W(z),$$

κ, z_0 are known as von-*Kármán* constant and the equipotential roughness of bed. The Wake function $W(z)$ is assumed as in Coles (1956):

$$W(z) = \frac{2\Pi}{\kappa} \sin^2\left(\frac{\pi}{2} z\right),$$

here the wake strength parameter is denoted by Π. In view of decomposition by Reynolds, for the laminar convective-diffusion one can decompose the flow velocity of fluid $u = \overline{u} + u'$, and the concentration of tracer particle $C = \overline{C} + C'$ as the summation of their average and oscillating terms. The expression $\partial(\overline{u'C'})/\partial x_j$ denotes the dispersion of the solute concentration C for the turbulent pulsations. In general, the molecular diffusion coefficient (k_m) is too small, i.e., $\overline{u'C'} \gg k_m \partial C/\partial x_j$. Thus, usually it is ignored considering more dominating effects due to the turbulence, see e.g., in (Mazumder and Dalal (2000), Sullivan and Yip (1987)). However, in the present model, molecular diffusion plays an important role at the smallest scales which suggests following diffusivity profile

$$k_x(z) = k_\mathrm{m} + k_\mathrm{e}(z),$$

where k_m be the molecular diffusivity and $k_\mathrm{e}(z)$ be the eddy-diffusivity (Nezu and Rodi (1986)):

$$k_\mathrm{e}(z) = \kappa(1-z)\left[\frac{1}{z} + \Pi\pi\sin(\pi z)\right]^{-1}.$$

In the next section, the numerical scheme is developed and implemented onto the problem Equation 1.

Numerical Solution of the Model

For an efficient implementation of a numerical scheme to deal with a complex problem with boundary conditions defined at infinity such as for a problem defined in Equation 1, it is desired to convert an infinite domain into a finite domain using an appropriate transformation. Here, an *artanh* transformation have been used to map an infinite domain (which is a physical domain where the original problem is posed) $(x,z) \in (-\infty,\infty) \times [z_0, 1])$ into a finite domain (commonly, referred to as a computational domain, generally chosen artificially) $(\chi, z) \in (-1,1) \times [z_0, 1]$. The *artanh* transformation is:

$$x = \frac{1}{2\beta} \log\left(\frac{1+\chi}{1-\chi}\right), \tag{2}$$

here β is a stretching factor which may be tuned depending on exactly which region of the physical domain is of most interest in the simulation. In view of transformation given by Equation 2, the problem given by Equation 1 is transformed to the following equation

$$-\beta^2 k_\chi(z)(1-\chi^2)\left[(1-\chi^2)\frac{\partial^2 C}{\partial \chi^2} - 2\chi\frac{\partial C}{\partial \chi}\right] - \frac{\partial}{\partial z}\left(k_z(z)\frac{\partial C}{\partial z}\right)$$
$$+u(z)\beta(1-\chi^2)\frac{\partial C}{\partial \chi} - \omega_s\frac{\partial C}{\partial z} = \delta(\chi)\delta(z-z_p) \qquad \text{(3a)}$$

along with following boundary conditions

$$C(-1,z) = C(1-\gamma,z) = 0, \qquad C(\chi,z_0) = C(\chi,1) = 0 \qquad \text{(3b)}$$

In order to deal with a possible singularity at $\chi = 1$ due to the *artanh* transformation, a small parameter γ ($\approx O(10^{-4})$) has been introduced into the boundary condition in χ- direction. The diffusion along downstream of the tracers is much smaller than the convection along χ direction as the flow velocity is fully developed and turbulent, the convection is much larger than the diffusion of the particles along downstream direction. Thus, the fine tracers released from the source of line $\chi = 0$ will only reach to the positive side i.e. downstream direction due to the effect of the convection dominance. Hence, the tracer concentration for $-1 \le \chi < 0$ may be assumed to zero.

The Numerical Method

In order to derive fitted operator technique for the present model in Equation 3, let us consider a problem which is a singularly perturbed boundary value problem

$$-\mu u''(x) + m(x)u'(x) + n(x)u(x) = g(x), u(0) = 0, u(1) = 0, x \in \Omega = [0,1]. \quad (4)$$

Here, the coefficients $m(x)$, $n(x)$ and $g(x)$ are considered as sufficiently smooth functions and such that the problem does not exhibit any turning point phenomenon over the domain $[0,1]$.

For numerical solution of Equation 4, the difference operators are defined as

$$D^- w_j = \frac{w_j - w_{j-1}}{h}, \quad D^+ w_j = \frac{w_{j+1} - w_j}{h},$$
$$D^0 = \frac{w_{j+1} - w_{j-1}}{2h}, \quad D^+D^- w_j = \frac{w_{j-1} - 2w_j + w_{j+1}}{h^2}. \qquad (5)$$

on a uniform grid $0 = x_0 < x_1 < \ldots < x_N = 1$, with grid length $h = 1/N$. In view of operators given in Equation 5, we have the following numerical scheme

$$-\mu D^+D^- u_j + m_j D^0 u_j + n_j u_j = g_j \text{ for } j = 2, \cdots, N, \quad \text{with } u_1 = 0, u_{N+1} = 0. \qquad (6)$$

In a case when $\mu \ll 1$, the problem becomes convection dominated, and the solutions of such problems given by Equation 4 may exhibit sharp layers. The scheme in Equation 6 applied on a uniform mesh may yield a computed solution which is dominated by spurious oscillations, and thus is not acceptable. One of the possible means to solve these type of problems in an efficient way is to employ specialized non-uniform grids which are smooth in the layered areas and coarse otherwise. Shishkin and Bakhvalov meshes are the exceptional examples of those kind of meshes, refer Roos et al. (2008) for additional information. However, all these meshes involve a transition point which works as a separator between fine and coarse part of the mesh, and to determine this point, one must have *a prior* data concerning the precise solution and its derivatives. In many practical situations this becomes very restrictive to construct a layer adapt mesh for solving a complicated problem such as ours. An alternative way to compute solutions free of such spurious oscillations is to use an upwind operator for the convection term in place of the central difference operator. The corresponding difference scheme is as follows

$$-\mu D^+D^-u_j + m_j D^+ u_j + n_j u_j = g_j \text{ for } j = 2, \cdots, N, \quad \text{with } u_1 = 0, u_{N+1} = 0. \tag{7}$$

This scheme given by Equation 7 yields qualitative better solution but the cost of compromising with the accuracy in the computed solution. Note that upwind operator is first order accurate while central difference operator offers second order accuracy. Thus, using an upwind operator for the convection term may not yield an optimal solution.

For the model problem Equation 4, a fitted operator approach proposed by Il'in-Allen-Southwell (Il'in (1969), De et al. (1955)) is employed which leads to the following difference scheme:

$$-\mu\sigma([q(x_j)])D^+D^-u_j + m_j D^0 u_j + n_j u_j = g_j \text{ for } j = 2, \cdots, N,$$
$$u_1 = 0,\ u_{N+1} = 0. \tag{8}$$

Here, $\sigma[q(x)] = q(x)\coth q(x)$ and $q(x) = \frac{m(x)h}{2\mu}$.

It may be interesting to compare to compare difference schemes given by Equation 7 and Equation 8. In fact, the difference scheme involving upwind operator Equation 7 can be rewritten as

$$-\left(\mu + \frac{m_j h}{2}\right) D^+D^-u_j + m_j D^0 u_j + n_j u_j = g_j \text{ for } j = 2, \cdots, N,$$
$$\text{with } u_1 = 0, u_{N+1} = 0. \tag{9}$$

Note that the finite difference scheme given by Equation 9 is equivalent to using central difference operator for the convection term. However, the coefficient of diffusion is changed from μ to $\left(\mu + \frac{m_j h}{2}\right)$. This implies that induction of certain amount of artificial diffusion may be helpful to curb the spurious oscillations due to central differencing term for the convection term, and brings more stability in the computed solution. This is the main motivation for us to use this fitted operator approach for our problem formulated in Equation 1. Moreover, the fitted operator approach can be used in conjunction with a uniform mesh which is an additional advantage. The effort towards setting a transition point to design a layer adapted mesh is no more required.

As a way to solve the Equation 3a under the boundary conditions given by Equation 3b, a two-dimensional fitted operator approach has been followed that is defined below. Let $C(i,j)$ denote the concentration value C at i-th mesh point towards the χ-axis and the j-th mesh point towards the z-axis and the operators are defined as follows

$$\left.\frac{\partial C}{\partial \chi}\right|_{i,j} = \frac{1}{2h_1}[C(i+1,j) - C(i-1,j)] + O(h_1{}^2),$$
$$\left.\frac{\partial^2 C}{\partial \chi^2}\right|_{i,j} = \frac{1}{h_1{}^2}[C(i+1,j) - 2C(i,j) + C(i-1,j)] + O(h_1{}^2),$$

where, $h_1 = \frac{1}{M}$ is the mesh interval along the χ axis;

$$\left.\frac{\partial C}{\partial z}\right|_{i,j} = \frac{1}{2h_2}[C(i,j+1) - C(i,j-1)] + O(h_2{}^2),$$
$$\left.\frac{\partial^2 C}{\partial z^2}\right|_{i,j} = \frac{1}{h_2{}^2}[C(i,j+1) - 2C(i,j) + C(i,j-1)] + O(h_2{}^2),$$

where $h_2 = \frac{1}{N}$ is the grid spacing along z axis; M and N denote the highest grid interval number on a uniform mesh, respectively along χ and z directions. Here $i = 1, i = M+1$ relates to $\chi = 0, \chi = 1 - \gamma$, in some respects and $j = 1, j = N+1$ relates to $z = z_0$, $z = 1$, respectively. The grid point, for the injection of particles, is located at $(1, j_p)$, where $j = j_p$ corresponds to $z = z_p$. For convection terms, the standard central difference operators have been used, and for the diffusion terms $-\beta^2 k_\chi(z)(1-\chi^2)^2 \frac{\partial^2 C}{\partial \chi^2}$ and $-k_z(z)\frac{\partial^2 C}{\partial z^2}$ along χ direction (i.e. along flow direction) and z direction (i.e., along normal direction to bed of the stream) respectively, fitted operators have been used which are defined at (i,j)-th grid point. This leads to following difference scheme

$$
\begin{aligned}
&-\beta^2 k_\chi(z)(1-\chi^2)^2\sigma_1[q_1(\chi)]\left.\frac{\partial^2 C}{\partial\chi^2}\right|_{i,j}+u(z)\beta(1-\chi^2)\left.\frac{\partial C}{\partial\chi}\right|_{i,j}\\
&-k_z(z)\sigma_2[q_2(z)]\left.\frac{\partial^2 C}{\partial z^2}\right|_{i,j}-\omega_s\left.\frac{\partial C}{\partial z}\right|_{i,j}\\
&-2\beta^2 k_\chi(z)(1-\chi^2)\chi\left.\frac{\partial C}{\partial\chi}\right|_{i,j}-K\left.\frac{\partial C}{\partial z}\right|_{i,j}=\delta(i)\delta(j-j_p),
\end{aligned}
$$

for $i = 2,\ldots,M$ and $j = 2,\ldots,N$ with the boundary conditions

$$C(1, j) = C(M+1, j) = 0, \qquad C(i,1) = C(i,N+1) = 0.$$

The fitted operators along χ and z directions are given as follows:

$$
\begin{aligned}
&\text{in } \chi \text{ direction:} \quad \sigma_1[q_1(\chi)] = q_1(\chi)\coth q_1(\chi)\\
&\text{where} \quad q_1(\chi) = \frac{u(z)\beta(1-\chi^2)h_1}{2\beta^2 k_\chi(z)(1-\chi^2)^2} = \frac{u(z)}{2\beta k_\chi(z)(1-\chi^2)M};\\
&\text{in } z \text{ direction:} \quad \sigma_2[q_2(z)] = q_2(z)\coth q_2(z)\\
&\text{where} \quad q_2(z) = \frac{-\omega_s h_2}{2k_z(z)} = \frac{-\omega_s}{2k_z(z)N}.
\end{aligned}
$$

Here, K is defined as $K = \frac{\partial}{\partial z}(k_z(z))$.

Numerical Results

The convection diffusion problem Equation 3 using fitted operator approach has been mentioned in , and a comparison is performed with the present numerical outcomes & the laboratory results of Raupach and Legg (1983) and numerical solutions of Sullivan and Yip (1987) when the settling velocity $\omega_s = 0$. In their experimental setup, Raupach and Legg (1983) executed their study of inert tracers by the way of affixing an uneven floor of 7 mm pebble glued into a wood basement. A point of heat supply was situated at 60 mm above the bed and thickness of the bearer stream was 0.54 m. The measured records produced by them was a log-law velocity profile of the form: $u^* = \frac{u_*}{\kappa}\log(z^*/z_0^*)$, with the height of roughness $z_0^* = 0.12$ mm and $\kappa = 0.38$.

For the numerical experiments presented here, it has been assumed that, $k_x(z) = k_z(z) = k_e$ which is a reasonable assumption as the present problem is asserted for a homogeneous and fully developed turbulent flow. Furthermore, the molecular diffusivity has been taken zero, i.e., $k_m = 0$, and the wake-strength parameter is considered to be $\Pi = .09$. For comparison purposes, vertical and longitudinal stations were non-dimensionalized using the height of source of heat h. Following Raupach and Legg (1983), concentration C was normalized with a scale of heat and its form is: $\theta^* = F/(z_p u(z_p))$, here F denotes the debris constant flux along the perpendicular to the flow.

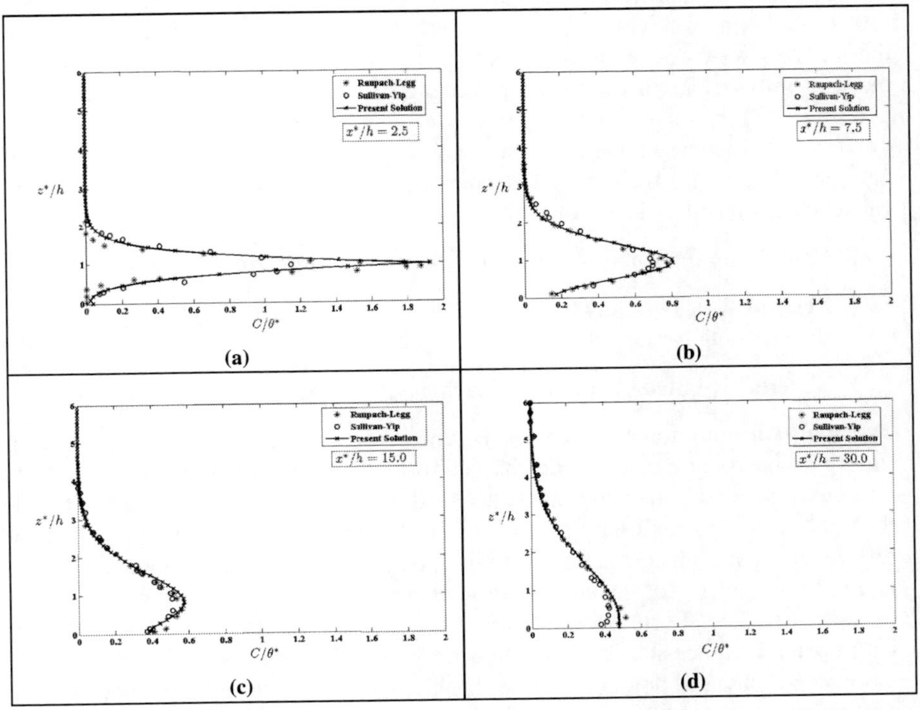

Figure 2. Contour lines for equi-concentration for steady transport of the suspended particles are compared at various downstream stations. These solutions are as follows: profiles generated using experimental result by Raupach and Legg $(***)$, by means of numerical study by Sullivan and Yip $(\circ\circ\circ)$, and the present result of Equation 1 using fitted operator approach $(-)$ For generating all the figures using fitted operator approach, we have taken uniform stretching factor $\beta = .1$.

In Figure 2, the dimensionless concentration distributions at different downstream positions $(x^*/h = 2.5, 7.5, 15.0, 30.0)$ are displayed when sediment velocity becomews negligible. They are matched with the profiles obtained using experimental result in Raupach and Legg (1983) and numerical data of Sullivan and Yip (1987). The concentration distributions at four distinct downstream locations found by applying the fitted operator approach are agreed well with those obtained by using data in (Raupach and Legg (1983), Sullivan and Yip (1987)). In particular, the layer of interior points for the nearest downstream position is sharper than rest of down-stream stations, the profile obtained by using fitted approach is in remarkable agreement with the profile obtained by means of the experimental data in Sullivan and Yip (1987). Additionally, it has been observed that the present technique gives relatively higher accuracy in particular at the closest downstream locations than the distributions revealed in the literature, see e.g., Mazumder and Bandyopadhyay (2001), Sullivan and Yip (1987). The schemes considered on uniform mesh in these papers were not adequate to capture the sharp layer phenomenon depicted at the very initial stage of the turbulent mixing of the suspended particles, and they overestimate the breadth of the layer.

Next, we compare three different numerical schemes and generate contours of iso-concentration for the time independent dispersion of the particles. The numerical schemes considered here involve:

1. **Scheme 1:** Central difference operators for all the terms.
2. **Scheme 2:** Upwinding for $x-$, and $z-$ direction convection terms and central differencing for rest of the terms.
3. **Scheme 3:** Fitted operator approach explained in .

The equi-concentration contours for the time-independent dispersion are shown in Figure 3 when the particles are discharged from the height $z_p = 0.5$ with the Dirichlet boundary conditions and with varies settling velocity, $\omega_s = 0, 0.2, 0.4, 0.6$. All the concentration profiles are plotted for the computational domain (χ, z). Central differencing for both convection and diffusion terms is applied for both convection and diffusion terms for generating these concentration profiles shown in Figure 3 (a, b, c, d). The spurious oscillations in the computed solution are spread over entire solution space starting from the source, and they are visible in both computational and physical domains. However, with an increase in settling velocity these oscillations tend to be reducing.

The plots Figure 3 (e, f, g, h) show contour lines of equi-concentration for steady dispersion, where we have used **Scheme 2**, the upwinding is used for both x, and z-direction convection terms and central differencing is used for rest of the terms, keeping all other parameters same as used for generating Figure 3 (a, b, c, d). Note that these contour plots corresponding to **Scheme 2** are free from spurious oscillations. However, few contour lines can be observed as numerical artifacts near the bed which appear for the combined impact of settling velocity, gravity, turbulence, and the smearing effect because of upwinding. The plots in Figure 3(i, j, k, l) show contour lines of equi-concentration corresponding to **Scheme 3**, where we have used our fitted operator approach. It can be seen that the solution is stable, free from spurious oscillations and for distinct values of ω_s it could capture the layer behavior. Thus, out of three different numerical schemes, the technique on the basis of fitted operator approach is very satisfactory to solve this problem.

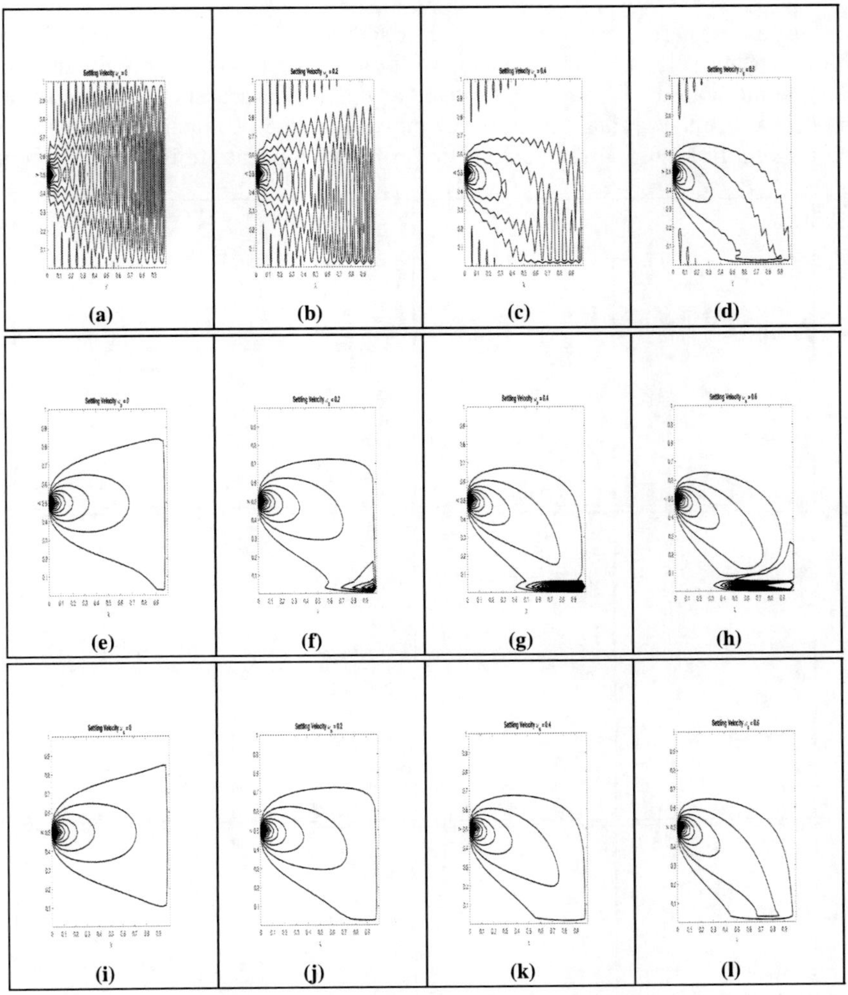

Figure 3. Contour lines of equi-concentration in the computational and physical domains for steady dispersion of suspended particles when the particles are discharged from $z_p = 0.5$ with various settling velocity. Upwinding in both x and z-directions used in conjunction with Dirichlet boundary conditions.

It has been observed in all the cases as shown in Figure 3(i, j, k, l) that the profiles of concentration turn into further expanded along the downstream direction because the problem is convection dominated which implies that the convection in longitudinal direction is significantly more in comparison to the diffusion in the transverse direction. It may also be interesting to note from the contour plots that the suspended particles get more concentrated near the bed with an enhancement in the settling velocity, and expansion of these distributions is more distinguished close to the bottom. It can be interpreted as the heavier tracers tend to travel near the bed where the gradient of flow velocity is higher in comparison to the rest of the region. In Figure 4, the contour lines of equi-concentration in both computa-

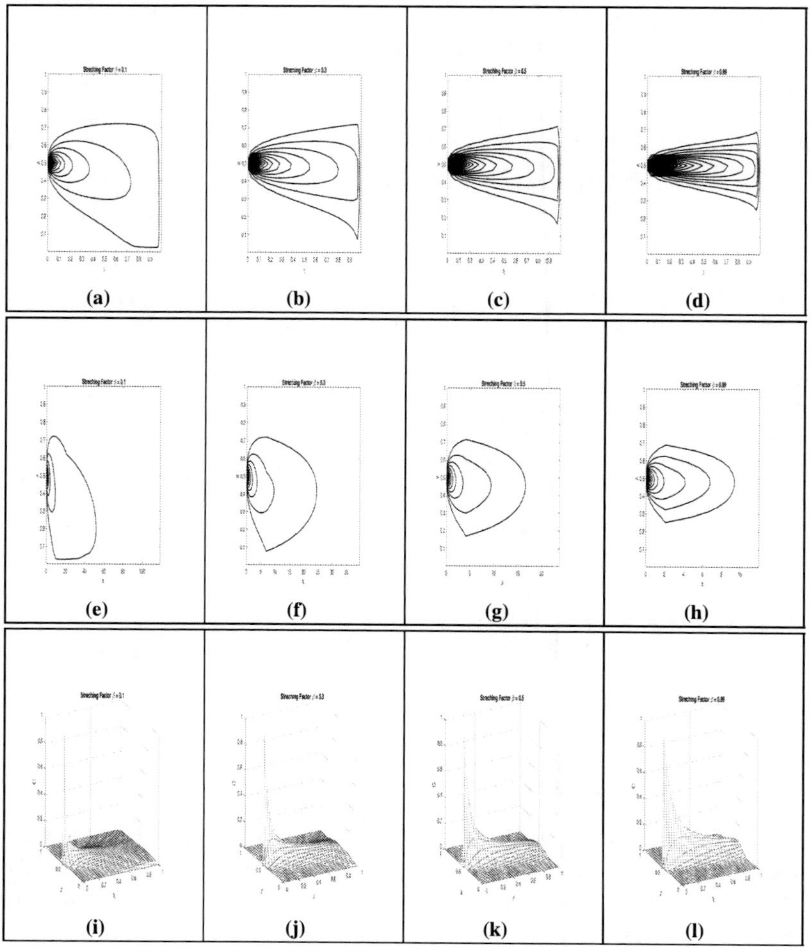

Figure 4. Contour lines of equi-concentration in the computational and physical domains for steady dispersion of suspended particles when the particles are discharged from $z_p = 0.5$ with settling velocity 0.2; different stretching factors are used. Fitted Operator used in conjunction with Dirichlet boundary conditions.

tional and physical domain are shown for various values of stretching factor used in *arctanh* transformation given in Equation 2, for these plots settling velocity is kept fixed as $w_s = .2$. Fitted operator approach is used to solve the problem, and the mesh plots for the computed solution corresponding various values of stretching values are also shown in Figure 4. From the plots it can be seen that the solute concentration distribution get expanded along downstream direction with an increase of stretching factor. Consequently, the tracers agglomeration close to the bed is reduced. An optimal value of this stretching factor for a problem is based on practical considerations, and numerical experiments. How to obtain an optimal value of this stretching factor theoretically for a given problem is an open problem which requires further investigations.

Conclusion

A fitted operator approach has been implemented to observe the flow-wise transport of inert suspended particles. The governing equation is a convection-diffusion equation with the Dirichlet boundary conditions; to accommodate the fact that the particles have been discharged from a continual elevated point-source into an pulsatile turbulent flow, boundary conditions have been adjusted, accordingly. At the free surface, the eddy diffusivity tends to zero which makes the problem convection dominated.

It is widely recognized in the literature that conventional numerical techniques fail to deal with convection dominated convection-diffusion problems as they generally depict sharp layer phenomenon. The results obtained here, using fitted operator approach, are in precise agreement with the numerical and experimental studies published in (Raupach and Legg (1983), Sullivan and Yip (1987)) for all four downstream locations. In particular, the results obtained here are more stable and accurate at the closest downstream location, a sharp layer phenomenon can be observed at this location, in comparison with the results reported in the literature, e.g., see Mazumder and Dalal (2000), Mazumder and Bandyopadhyay (2001), Mondal and Mazumder (2008), Sullivan and Yip (1987).

The study provided here can be prolonged to the version of various complicated physical problems, see e.g., Vitez and Travnicek (2011) and references therein. For instance, it has been shown here that how the blended effect of debris settling velocity, average shearing velocity, turbulence, and gravity can extensively effect the concentration distributions that may result in agglomeration of tracers near a point source of dispersion of particles. This observation may be useful for waste water treatment. For example, substances and impurities such as grit, metal ions, inert chemical waste can be separated from the waste water using the combined effect of the factors mentioned above. Another practical example is separation of minerals from ores by controlling the settling velocity and other related factors in a flowing wind environment. The same phenomenon holds true for controlling air pollution where vehicles and factories release toxic chemicals into our environment.

Acknowledgments

One of us (Nanda Poddar) is thankful to University Grants Commission, India for economical support to pursuing this work under Junior Research Fellowship grant 1164/(CSIR-UGC NET DEC. 2017). We also acknowledge the help given by Professor B. S. Mazumder, Indian Statistical Institute, Kolkata, India for his valuable comments for qualitative improvement of our work.

References

Aris R. On the Dispersion of a Solute in Pulsating Flow Through a Tube. *Proceedings of the Royal Society A: Mathematical, Physical and Engineering Sciences.* (1960) 259(1298):370-376. https://doi.org/10.1098/rspa.1960.0231

Coles D. The law of the wake in the turbulent boundary layer. *Journal of Fluid Mechanics.* (1956) 1(02):191-226 https://doi.org/10.1017/s0022112056000135

De DN, Allen G, Southwell RV. Relaxation methods applied to determine the Motion, in two dimensions, of a viscous fluid past a fixed cylinder. *The Quarterly Journal of Mechanics and Applied Mathematics.* (1955) 8(2):129-145 https://doi.org/10.1093/qjmam/8.2.129

Dhar S, Poddar N, Kairi RR, Mazumder BS, Mondal KK. Numerical study on dispersion of fine settling particles in a depth dominated wetland flow. *Commun Nonlinear Sci Numer Simul.* (2021) 96, 105707. https://doi.org/10.1016/j.cnsns.2021.105707

Doolan EP, Miller JJH, Schilders WHA. *Uniform Numerical Methods for Problems with Initial and Boundary Layers.* Boole Press, Dublin. (1980).

Il'in A. A difference scheme for a differential equation with a small parameter affecting the highest derivative. *Mat. Zametki.* (1969) 6:237-248 https://doi.org/10.1007/bf01093706

Islam S, Singh V, Kumar S. Estimation of Dispersion in an Open Channel from an Elevated Source Using an Upwind Local Meshless Method. *International Journal of Computational Methods.* (2017) 14(02):1750009 https://doi.org/10.1142/s0219876217500098

Madden N, Mondal KK. Improved Mathematical and Numerical Modelling of Dispersion of a Solute from a Continuous Source. *BAIL 2010 - Boundary and Interior Layers, Computational and Asymptotic Methods.* (2011) 177-185 https://doi.org/10.1007/978-3-642-19665-2_19

Mazumder BS, and Dalal D. C. Contaminant dispersion from an elevated time-dependent source. *Journal of Computational and Applied Mathematics.* (2000) 126(1-2):185-205 https://doi.org/10.1016/s0377-0427(99)00353-2

Mazumder BS, and Bandyopadhyay S. On solute dispersion from an elevated line source in an open-channel flow. *Journal of Engineering Mathematics.* (2001) 40:197-209. https://doi.org/10.1023/A:1017598215497

Miller J, O'Riordan E, Shishkin GI. Fitted numerical methods for singular perturbation problems. *World Scientific.* (1996).

Mondal KK, Mazumder BS. On dispersion of settling particles from an elevated source in an open-channel flow. *Journal of Computational and Applied Mathematics.* (2006) 193:22-37. https://doi.org/10.1016/j.cam.2005.04.068

Mondal KK, Mazumder BS. Dispersion of fine settling particles from an elevated source in an oscillatory turbulent flow. *European Journal of Mechanics - B/Fluids.* (2008) 27(6):707-725 https://doi.org/10.1016/j.euromechflu.2007.11.005

Mondal, K. K., Dhar, S., Mazumder, B. S. (2020). On dispersion of solute in steady flow through a channel with absorption boundary: an application to sewage dispersion. *Theor. Comput. Fluid Dyn.* 34, 643-658. https://doi.org/10.1007/s00162-020-00539-7

Munyakazi JB, Patidar KC, Sayi MT. A robust fitted operator finite difference method for singularly perturbed problems whose solution has an interior layer. *Mathematics and Computers in Simulation.* (2018). https://doi.org/10.1016/j.matcom.2018.12.010

Nezu I, and Nakagawa H. *Turbulence in open-channel flows.* IAHR Monograph, A.A. Balkema Publishers, Rotterdam. (1993) 281. https://doi.org/10.1201/9780203734902

Nezu, I, Rodi W. Open channel Flow Measurements with a Laser Doppler Anemometer. *Journal of Hydraulic Engineering.* (1986) 112(5):335-355 https://doi.org/10.1061/(asce)0733-9429(1986)112:5(335)

Poddar N, Mondal KK, Madden N. Layer-adapted meshes for solute dispersion in a steady flow through an annulus with wall absorption: Application to a catheterized artery. *Korea-Aust. Rheol. Journal.* (2021) 33, 11-24. https://doi.org/10.1007/s13367-021-0002-4

Poddar N, Dhar S, Mazumder, BS, Kairi RR, Mondal KK. Effects of bulk degradation and boundary absorption on dispersion of contaminant in wetland flow. *Int. J. Heat Mass Transf.* (2021) 179, 121669. https://doi.org/10.1016/j.ijheatmasstransfer.2021.121669

Raupach MR, Legg BJ. Turbulent dispersion from an elevated line source: measurements of wind-concentration moments and budgets. *Journal of Fluid Mechanics.* (1983). 136(-1):111-137 https://doi.org/10.1017/s0022112083002086

Roos HG, Stynes M, Tobiska L. *Numerical Methods for Singularly Perturbed Differential Equations. Convection Diffusion and Flow Problems*, Springer Verlag, Berlin. (1996).

Roos HG, Stynes M, Tobiska L. *Robust Numerical Methods for Singularly Perturbed Differential Equations*. Springer-Verlag Berlin, 2nd ed. (2008).

Sullivan, P. J., Yip, H. Near-field contaminant dispersion from an elevated line-source. *Journal of Applied Mathematics and Physics (ZAMP).* (1987) 38(3):409-423 https://doi.org/10.1007/bf00944959

Taylor GI. The Dispersion of Matter in Turbulent Flow through a Pipe. *Proceedings of the Royal Society A: Mathematical, Physical and Engineering Sciences.* (1954) 223(1155):446-468. https://doi.org/10.1098/rspa.1954.0130

Vitez T, Travnicek P. Study of settling velocity of sand particles located in wastewater treatment plant. *Acta Universitatis Agriculturae et Silviculturae Mendelianae Brunensis.* (2011) 59(1):249-254 https://doi.org/10.11118/actaun201159010249

Yasuda H. Longitudinal dispersion of matter due to the shear effect of steady and oscillatory currents. *Journal of Fluid Mechanics.* (1984) 148:383-403. https://doi.org/10.1017/S0022112084002391

Chapter 12

Propagation of SH-Wave in Anisotropic Porous Layer Lying over Viscoelastic Sandy Half-space

Naveen Kumar*
Dinesh Kumar Madan
Mathematics Department, Chaudhary Bansi Lal University, Bhiwani, India

Abstract

The present model discusses the SH-wave propagating in a prestressed anisotropic porous layer overlying viscoelastic sandy half-space. Layer and half-space's interface are supposed to have spring-like contact. The variable separation method is applied to derive the expressions for displacement for the half-space and layer. Appropriate boundary conditions are used to obtain frequency equation involving sandiness, dissipation, and imperfectness parameters. The real part of the frequency equation, known as the dispersion frequency equation, is analyzed graphically to obtain the effects of various parameters. MATLAB software is used for graphical plots. The findings of the current study could be useful in earthquake engineering, geophysics, and seismology.

Keywords: anisotropic porous, viscoelastic sandy, dissipation factor, dispersion equation

* Corresponding Author's Email: nkjangra521@gmail.com.

In: Emerging Trends in Mathematical Sciences and Computing
Editors: B. Basu Mallik, S. Ghosh, B. Kumar Pandey et al.
ISBN: 979-8-89113-751-6

Introduction

Theoretical studies on seismic wave propagation in layered media are critical because they provide a wealth of information about the earth's interior and aid in determining the nature of the earth's crust.

Earth is considered as a layered medium consisting of various rocks, and materials with different properties such as anisotropy, sandiness, and porosity. Studies regarding seismic wave propagation involving porous media help in understanding the Earth's crust nature and predicting seismic behavior in mountain roots, and continental regions. SH-waves cause horizontal shifting during earthquakes. Biot (1956) introduced elastic wave propagation theory for fluid-filled, porous media. Various researchers (Wang and Zhang, 1998; Yew and Jogi, 1976; Ghorai, Samal, and Mahanati, 2010) had carried out studies regarding seismic wave propagation considering porous media. Kundu et al. (2016) explored torsional wave propagation considering a porous layer overlying a sandy semi-infinite medium. Torsional surface wave propagation for a geometry comprised of two porous layers and a Gibson semi-infinite medium was investigated by Shekhar and Parvez (2016), deriving the dispersion frequency relation for torsional waves' phase velocity.

The layer made up of sand particles is referred to as a sandy layer. Weiskopf (1964) introduced the sandy soil mechanics, providing the proper relationship for the sandy soil i.e., $\frac{E}{\mu} = 2\eta(1+\sigma)$, where $\eta(>1)$ denotes the sandiness parameter and $\eta = 1$, refers to an elastic solid.

Viscoelasticity basically involves two properties, viscosity and elasticity. Materials such as sediments, tar, and coal can be modeled as viscoelastic materials. Kar, Pal, and Kalyani (1986) examined the propagation of Love waves considering sandy media in irregularity's presence. Pal and Ghorai (2015) explored the propagation of Love waves considering sand particle layer overlaying isotropic porous semi-infinite medium under gravity effects. Singh, Mistri, and Das (2016) investigated SH-wave propagation for a geometry comprised of a corrugated visco-sandy layer bounded by heterogeneous elastic and gravity affected viscoelastic semi-infinite medium, observing various parameters impacts such as heterogeneity, attenuation, and gravity parameters. The frequency relation for torsional waves propagating considering a sandy layer under the effects of pre-stress overlying an anisotropic porous semi-infinite medium with gravity effects was derived by Prasad and Kundu (2016).

Various layers of the earth are not in welded or perfect contact as seismic waves come across various types of irregularities or imperfect interfacial conditions due to mountain roots, basins, and ores. Various researchers discussed the effects of these boundary/interfacial conditions. Imperfectness parameter effects on Love wave propagation in a geometry consisting of layered graded composite structures were studied by Hua, Jia-Ling and Kai-Xin (2006). Sharma and Kumar (2017) derived the SH-wave dispersion frequency equation for a model comprised of a viscoelastic layer and a coupled stressed substrate with an imperfect interface and observed the impacts of heterogeneity, friction, and imperfectness. Deep and Verma (2020) investigated the effects of imperfection and sandiness factor on Love wave propagation involving sandy layer isotropic elastic media. Kumar and Madan (2021) studied the impacts of imperfectness and sandiness parameters for the propagation of Love waves in sandy media.

Seismic wave propagation in porous and viscoelastic sandy media remains still unexplored. An attempt to investigate the propagation of SH-wave in a prestressed anisotropic porous layer overlying viscoelastic sandy half-space has been made. The interface is considered spring-like contact. Analytical expressions for displacement fields are derived. The frequency equation is derived and analyzed graphically to obtain the effects of factors involved in the frequency relation. Validation of the problem is also verified. Various parameters such as imperfection, sandiness, and porosity are found to have significant effects on the SH-waves phase velocity. The present work could be beneficial in understanding the seismic wave propagation pattern in the presented geometry.

Problem Formulation and Solution

The present geometry is comprised of a prestressed anisotropic porous layer and viscoelastic sandy half-space. Cartesian co-ordinate system (-XYZ system) is used to solve the problem, with z-axis directed downwards and wave is in the x-direction. Interface is assumed in spring like contact (imperfect interface). For that, a parameter, 'G' is introduced to measure the degree of imperfectness. $G \to \infty$ corresponds to welded contact, i.e., perfect interface. The problem's geometry is given in Figure 1.

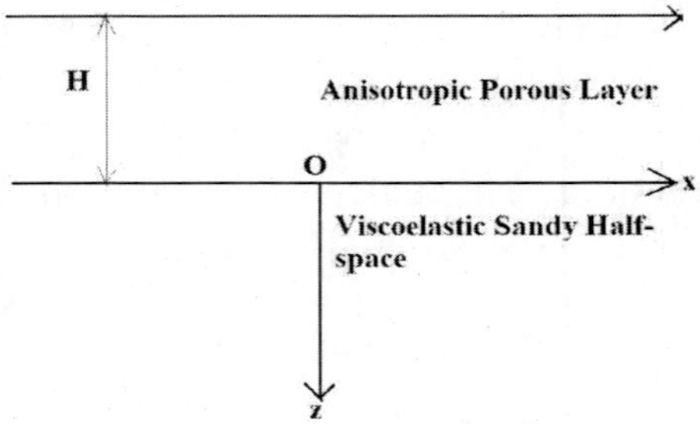

Figure 1. Model's geometry.

Conditions regarding SH-wave: Displacement components for SH-wave propagating in x-direction for -xz plane are independent of the y-coordinate and

$$u = w = u' = w' = U_x = W_x = 0 \text{ and } \frac{\partial}{\partial y} \approx 0$$
$$\text{and } V_y = V_y(x,z,t),\ v' = v'(x,z,t),\ v = v(x,z,t) \quad (1)$$

Dynamics of Anisotropic Porous Layer

For the prestressed anisotropic porous layer, (u,v,w) and (U_x, V_y, W_z) denotes components of displacement for solid and liquid parts respectively. For porous layer, dynamical equations of motion (obtained from Biot (1965)) are:

$$\left.\begin{aligned} \frac{\partial p_{xx}}{\partial x} + \frac{\partial p_{xy}}{\partial y} + \frac{\partial p_{xz}}{\partial z} - P\left(\frac{\partial \omega_z}{\partial y} - \frac{\partial \omega_y}{\partial z}\right) &= \frac{\partial^2}{\partial t^2}[\rho_{11}u + \rho_{12}U_x] \\ \frac{\partial p_{yx}}{\partial x} + \frac{\partial p_{yy}}{\partial y} + \frac{\partial p_{yz}}{\partial z} - P\left(\frac{\partial \omega_z}{\partial x}\right) &= \frac{\partial^2}{\partial t^2}[\rho_{11}v + \rho_{12}V_y] \\ \frac{\partial p_{zx}}{\partial x} + \frac{\partial p_{zy}}{\partial y} + \frac{\partial p_{zz}}{\partial z} - P\left(\frac{\partial \omega_x}{\partial y} - \frac{\partial \omega_y}{\partial x}\right) &= \frac{\partial^2}{\partial t^2}[\rho_{11}w + \rho_{12}W_z] \end{aligned}\right\} \quad (2)$$

$$\text{and} \left.\begin{aligned} \frac{\partial p}{\partial x} &= \frac{\partial^2}{\partial t^2}[\rho_{12}u + \rho_{22}U_x] \\ \frac{\partial p}{\partial y} &= \frac{\partial^2}{\partial t^2}[\rho_{12}v + \rho_{22}V_y] \\ \frac{\partial p}{\partial x} &= \frac{\partial^2}{\partial t^2}[\rho_{12}w + \rho_{22}V_y] \end{aligned}\right\} \quad (3)$$

where p = -fτ, where p, f and τ denote liquid part's stress vector, porosity and pressure of the fluid respectively and p_{ij} denotes stresses.

Also, the angular components can be defined as:

$$\left.\begin{aligned} \omega_x &= \frac{1}{2}\left(\frac{\partial w}{\partial y}-\frac{\partial v}{\partial z}\right)\\ \omega_y &= \frac{1}{2}\left(\frac{\partial u}{\partial z}-\frac{\partial w}{\partial x}\right)\\ \omega_y &= \frac{1}{2}\left(\frac{\partial v}{\partial x}-\frac{\partial u}{\partial y}\right) \end{aligned}\right\} \tag{4}$$

ρ_{11}, ρ_{12} and ρ_{22} denote mass coefficients and are related to the ρ, ρ_w *and* ρ_s denoting density of the layer, liquid, and solid part respectively

$$\rho_{12} + \rho_{22} = f\rho_w \text{ and } \rho_{11} + \rho_{12} = (1-f)\rho_s \tag{5}$$

The density of bulk material is:

$$\rho = \rho_{11} + 2\rho_{12} + \rho_{22} = \rho_s + f(\rho_w + \rho_s) \tag{6}$$

Also, mass coefficients hold the following relationships:

$$\rho_{11} > 0, \rho_{22} > 0, \rho_{12} < 0 \; and \; \rho_{11}\rho_{22} - \rho_{12}^2 > 0.$$

Using stress-strain, strain-displacement relations and Eq. (1) for prestressed anisotropic porous layer, we have

$$\left.\begin{aligned} p_{xx} = p_{yy} = p_{zz} = p_{xz} = 0\\ p_{xy} = N\frac{\partial v}{\partial x} \; and \; p_{yz} = L\frac{\partial v}{\partial z} \end{aligned}\right\} \tag{7}$$

where L and N denote elastic constants for the anisotropic layer. Using Eq. (2), Eq. (3), Eq. (4), and Eq. (7), the non-identically satisfied equations are

$$\left(N - \frac{P}{2}\right)\frac{\partial^2 v}{\partial x^2} + L\frac{\partial^2 v}{\partial z^2} = \frac{\partial^2}{\partial t^2}\left(\rho_{11}v + \rho_{12}V_y\right)$$

$$\text{and } \frac{\partial^2}{\partial t^2}\left(\rho_{12}v + \rho_{22}V_y\right) = 0 \tag{8}$$

From Eq. (8): $\left(N - \frac{P}{2}\right)\frac{\partial^2 v}{\partial x^2} + L\frac{\partial^2 v}{\partial z^2} = d'\frac{\partial^2 v}{\partial t^2}$ (9)

where $d' = \rho_{12}v + \rho_{22}V_y$

From Eq. (9), shear wave's phase velocity, along x and z-direction are $\sqrt{\frac{\left(N-\frac{P}{2}\right)}{d'}}$ *and* $\sqrt{\frac{L}{d'}}$ respectively.

Also SH-wave velocity along x-direction can be rewritten as:

$$\beta = \sqrt{\frac{\left(N-\frac{P}{2}\right)}{d'}} = \beta_1\sqrt{\frac{(1-\xi')}{d}} \tag{10}$$

where d $= \alpha_{11} - \frac{\alpha_{12}^2}{\alpha_{22}}, \beta_1 = \sqrt{\frac{N}{\rho}}$ and $\alpha_{11} = \frac{\rho_{11}}{\rho}, \alpha_{12} = \frac{\rho_{12}}{\rho}, \alpha_{22} = \frac{\rho_{22}}{\rho}$ and $\xi' = \frac{P}{2N}$.

α_{11}, α_{12}, α_{22} and ξ' are the non-dimensional parameter introduced as obtained by Biot (1965). Therefore,

d $\rightarrow$ 0, 1 corresponds that medium is non-porous solid or fluid respectively. Also 0<d<1 corresponds that layer is poroelastic.

Assume Eq. (9) solution as: v(x,z,t) = V(z) $e^{ik(x-ct)}$ (11)

Using Eq. (9) and Eq. (11): $\frac{d^2V}{\partial z^2} + k^2 l_1^2 \frac{\partial^2 V}{\partial z^2} = 0$ (12)

where $l_1^2 = \frac{d'c^2 - N + \frac{P}{2}}{L}$. Solving Eq. (12) we get:

$$V(z) = A\cos(kl_1 z) + B\sin(kl_1 z)$$

here A and B denote arbitrary constants. Using Eq. (11):

v(z) = $(A\cos(kl_1 z) + B\sin(kl_1 z))e^{ik(x-ct)}$ (13)

Eq. (13) represents displacement field for anisotropic porous layer.

Dynamics of Viscoelastic Sandy Half-Space

For viscoelastic sandy layer, non-vanishing equation of motion with zero external forces, is given by Biot (1965) as:

$$\frac{\partial p'_{yx}}{\partial x} + \frac{\partial p'_{yz}}{\partial z} = \rho' \frac{\partial^2 v'}{\partial t^2} \tag{14}$$

with stress components derived by using stress-strain and strain-displacement relations are as:

$$p'_{yx} = \bar{\mu}\frac{\partial v'}{\partial x}\,;\ \tau_{yz} = \bar{\mu}\frac{\partial v'}{\partial z} \tag{15}$$

$$\text{with } \bar{\mu} = \frac{\mu}{\eta} + \mu' \frac{\partial}{\partial t} \tag{16}$$

where ρ', η , μ, and μ' denote density, sandiness, rigidity and internal friction parameters respectively for the viscoelastic sandy layer.

Using Eq. (14), Eq. (15) in Eq. (16), we have

$$\left(\frac{\mu_1}{\eta} + \mu' \frac{\partial}{\partial t}\right)\left(\frac{\partial^2 v'}{\partial x^2} + \frac{\partial^2 v'}{\partial z^2}\right) = \rho \frac{\partial^2 v'}{\partial t^2} \tag{17}$$

Assuming Eq. (17) solution as:

$$v'(x,z,t) = V'(z)e^{ik(x-ct)} \tag{18}$$

Using Eq. (17) and Eq. (18): $\frac{d^2v'(z)}{dz^2} + k^2 l_2^2 v'(z) = 0$ (19)

$$\text{where } l_2^2 = \frac{c^2}{\beta_2^2(1-i\eta Q^{-1})} - 1 \text{ with } \beta_2^2 = \frac{\mu_1}{\eta\rho'} \text{ and } Q^{-1} = \frac{\mu' kc}{\mu_1} \tag{20}$$

Solution of (19) is obtained as: $V'(z) = C\,e^{-kl_2 z} + D\,e^{kl_2 z}$ (21)

where C and D are arbitrary constants. Then from Eq. (18):

$$v'(x,z,t) = (C\,e^{-kl_2 z} + D\,e^{kl_2 z})e^{ik(x-ct)} \tag{22}$$

Our problem requires that the component of displacement for half-space vanished with increasing depth, i.e., for $z \to \infty$, $v' \to 0$. So,

$$v'(x,z,t) = C\,e^{-kl_2 z}e^{ik(x-ct)} \tag{23}$$

Boundary Conditions and Frequency Relations

Appropriate conditions for SH-wave propagation in present model with spring contact are as:

1. The upper boundary is considered free from stresses, i.e., $p_{yz} = 0$ at z = -H.
2. Continuity of stresses for the interface between half space and layer i.e., $p_{yz} = p'_{yz}$ at z = 0.
3. As the considered interface is imperfect, so an imperfectness parameter 'G' is introduced. The stress vector is proportional to the difference in displacement fields, i.e., $p_{yz} = G(v' - v)$ at z = 0.

Using the displacements and stresses expression and the boundary conditions, following equations are obtained:

$$A \sin(kl_1 H) + B \cos(kl_1 H) = 0$$

$$AG + B - CG = 0 \tag{24}$$

$$BLl_1 + C\left(\frac{1}{\eta} - iQ^{-1}\right)\mu l_2 = 0$$

For the non-trivial solution of the homogeneous system represented by Eq. (24), the determinant formed must be zero. Determinant equating to zero gives

$$\tan(kl_1 H) = \frac{\left(\frac{1}{\eta} - iQ^{-1}\right)\mu l_2 G}{\left(\frac{1}{\eta} - iQ^{-1}\right)\mu l_2 + GLl_1} \tag{25}$$

The frequency relation for the propagation of SH-wave in the considered geometry with an imperfect interface is given in equation (25). The imaginary and real part of Eq. (25) gives absorption frequency relation and dispersion frequency relation for propagation of SH-wave in the considered model respectively.

Special Cases

1. If $G \to \infty$, then Eq. (25) becomes: $\tan(kHl_1) = \frac{\left(\frac{1}{\eta} - iQ^{-1}\right)\mu l_2}{Ll_1}$ (26)

Then, Eq. (26) represents the frequency equation for welded contact.

2. If $G \to \infty$, L= M, $\eta = 1$, $Q^{-1} \to 0$, then Eq. (25) becomes:

$\tan\left(kH\sqrt{\frac{c^2}{\beta_1^2} - 1}\right) = \frac{\mu\sqrt{\left(1 - \frac{c^2}{\beta_2^2}\right)}}{L\sqrt{\left(\frac{c^2}{\beta_1^2} - 1\right)}}$, already derived SH-wave Equation (Love, 1920) and validates the problem.

Numerical Computation and Discussion

Effects of various parameters on SH-waves phase velocity for propagating in a porous layer overlying viscoelastic sandy half-space are examined by analyzing the real part of Eq. (25), known as the dispersion equation. The following relevant parameters are considered to carry out the numerical results:

(a) For anisotropic porous layer (Chattraj and Samal, 2013):

$N = 2.774 \times 10^9$ N/m², f = 0.26

$L = 1.387 \times 10^9$ N/m²,
$\rho_{11} = 1926.137\ kg/m^3, \rho_{12} = -2.137\ kg/m^3, \rho_{22} = 215.337\ kg/m^3$

(b) For viscoelastic sandy half-space, assumed approx. 300 km depth of Earth's crust (Gubbbins, 1990):

$\mu = 6.54 \times 10^{10}\ N/m^2, \rho = 3409\ kg/m^3$

The modes obtained, are used to show the impacts of various factors. Impacts of various factors such as imperfectness, porosity, sandiness, and dissipation factor are depicted in Figures 2–5, respectively. Values used for various parameters are given in Table 1. Variation is shown using three values of these parameters for imperfect (spring) and perfect (welded) contact, respectively. From Figures 2 and 4, it can be depicted that the imperfectness and sandiness parameters have almost negligible effects on SH-wave's phase velocity. Figure 3 depicts porosity parameter impacts for imperfect and perfect interface. It can be depicted from the modes that the porosity parameter acts adversely to the phase velocity for imperfect as well as perfect interface. Effects of the dissipation parameter for imperfect and perfect interface is depicted in Figure 5. It is observed from the computed modes that phase velocity initially reduces but subsequently increases beyond a certain value of wave number.

Table 1. Values used in Figures 2-5

	Figure.2	Figure. 3(a), (b)		Figure. 4(a), (b)		Figure. 5(a),(b)	
Imperfectness(G)	-	30.5×10^9	∞	30.5×10^9	∞	30.5×10^9	∞
Porosity (d)	0.7	-	-	0.9	0.9	0.9	0.9
Sandiness(η)	1.5	1.8	1.8	-	-	1.5	1.5
Dissipation(Q^{-1})	0.003	0.003	0.003	0.003	0.003	-	-
Initial Stress(P)	0.5	0.5	0.5	0.5	0.5	0.5	0.5

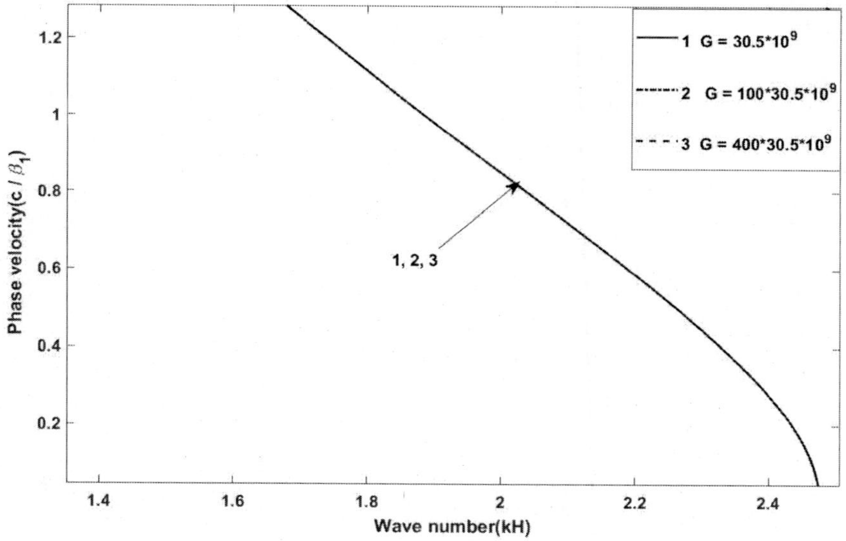

Figure 2. Imperfectness parameter effect.

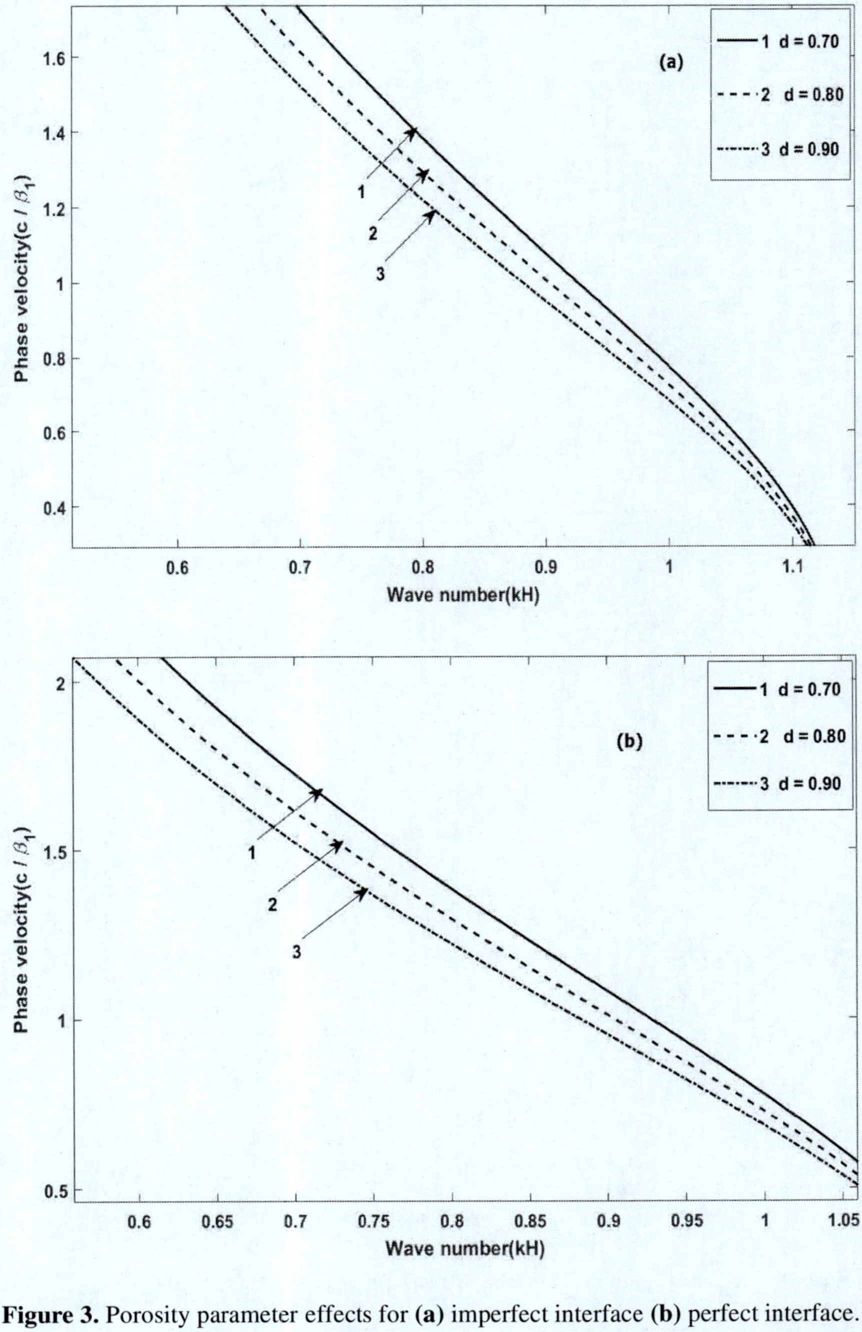

Figure 3. Porosity parameter effects for **(a)** imperfect interface **(b)** perfect interface.

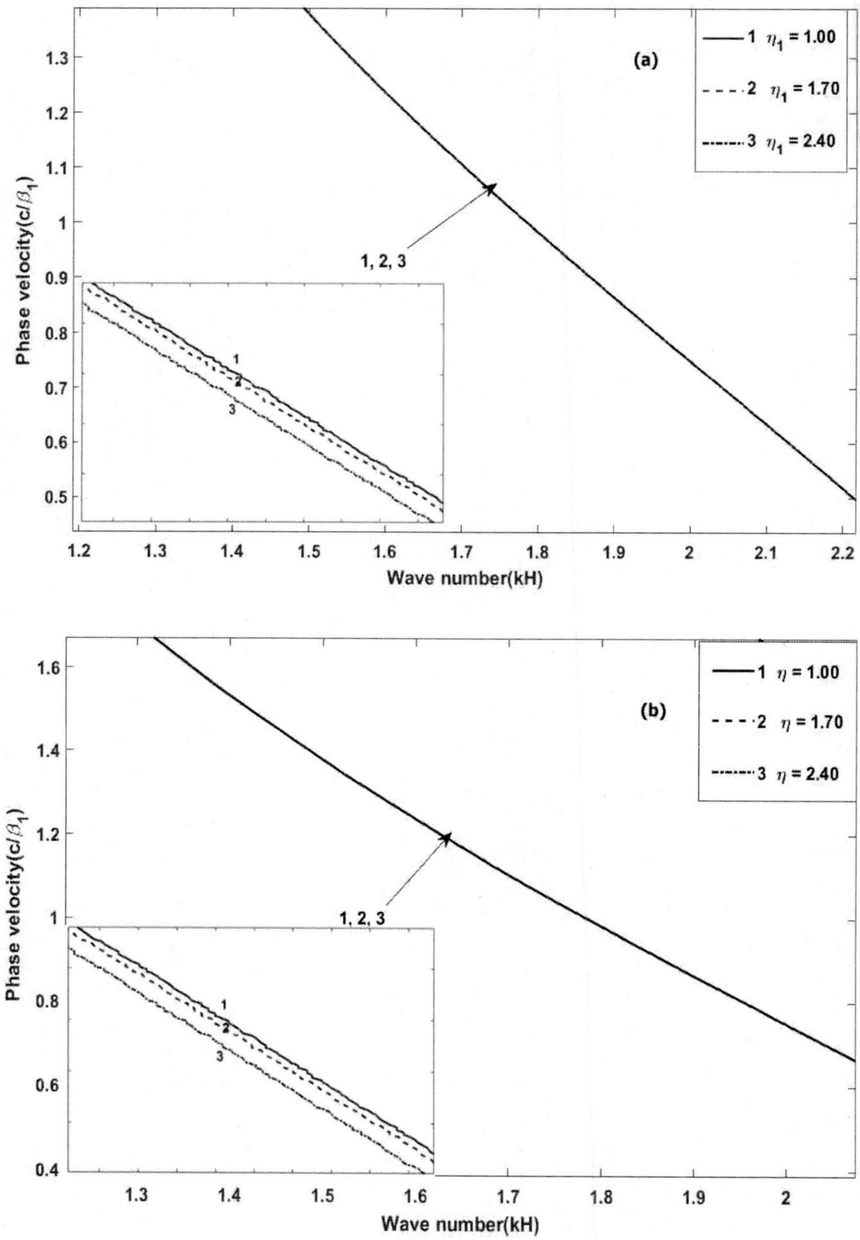

Figure 4. Sandiness parameter effects for **(a)** imperfect interface **(b)** perfect interface.

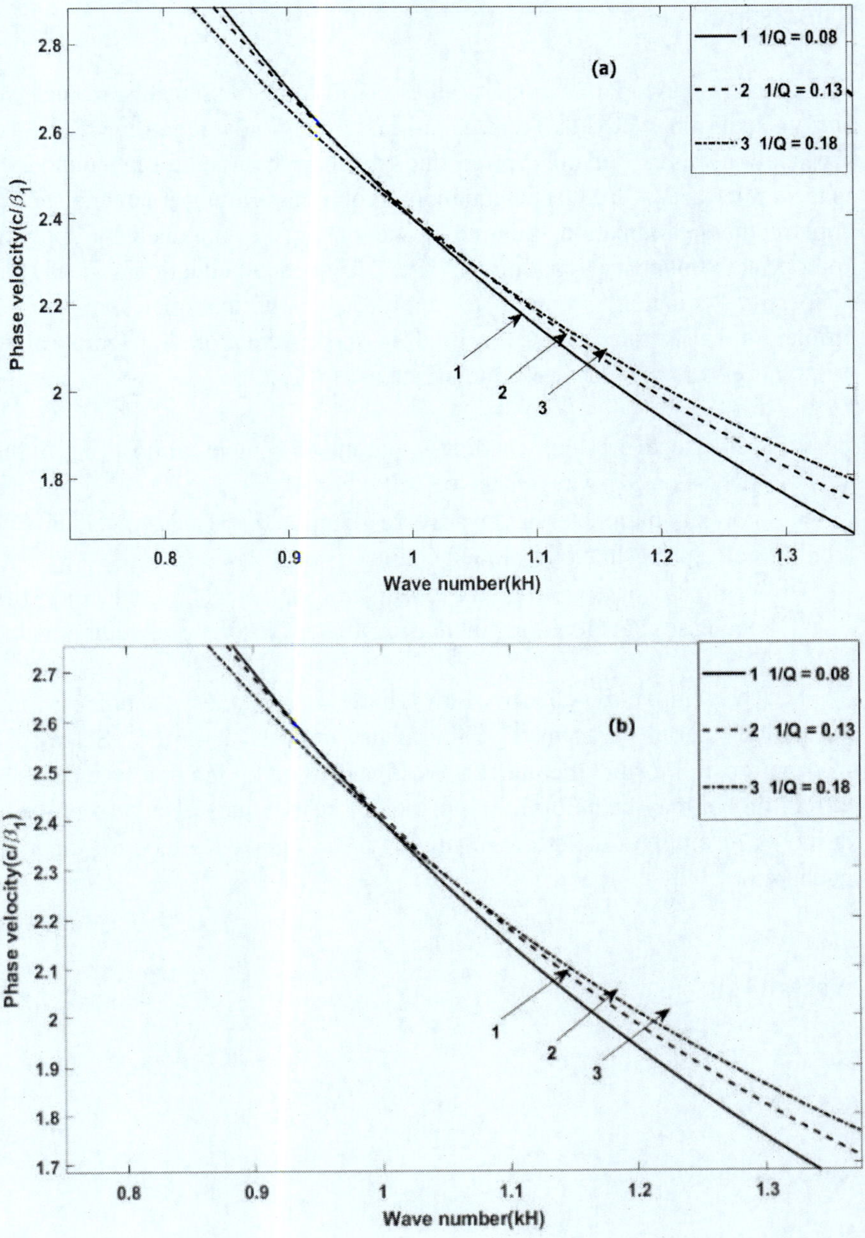

Figure 5. Dissipation parameter effects for **(a)** imperfect interface **(b)** perfect interface.

Conclusion

Within the framework of a model comprised of a pre-stressed anisotropic layer and viscoelastic sandy half-space, an analytical study regarding SH-wave propagation was carried out. Spring-like contact is assumed for layer and half-space's interface. A frequency equation involving various parameters such as imperfectness, dissipation, sandiness, and porosity is obtained by applying appropriate boundary conditions. The frequency equation's real part (dispersion equation) is used to analyze various parameter effects. A problem's validation is also verified in a particular case. Some salient observations of the study are summarized as:

- Imperfectness and sandiness parameters have almost negligible effects on SH-wave phase velocity.
- Porosity parameter has an adverse effect on the SH-wave velocity, for both spring-like and welded contact.
- With an increment in the dissipation factor, phase velocity first decreases but then starts increasing after a certain wave number value.

The present study clearly shows that imperfectness, sandiness, and dissipation parameters have significant impacts on the SH-wave's propagation. For further theoretical investigations involving porous media, the current model may be helpful. The presented results may also be useful in a variety of disciplines, including seismology, earthquake engineering, and soil mechanics.

Disclaimer

None.

References

Biot, M. A. (1956). Theory of propagation of elastic waves in a fluid saturated porous solid. *Journal of Acoustical Society of America,* 28(2),168-178.

Biot, M. A. (1965). Mechanics of Incremental Deformations. *John Wiley and Sons, New York.*

Chattaraj R., & Samal S. K. (2013). Love waves in the fiber-reinforced layer over a gravitating porous half- space. *Acta Geophys,* 61(5), 1170-1183.

Deep, S., & Verma, V. (2020) Love type waves in a dry sandy layer lying over an isotropic elastic half-space with imperf ect interface. *J. of Physics: Conference Series*, 1531.

Ghorai, A. P., Samal, S. K., & Mahanti, N. C. (2010). Love waves in a fluid saturated porous layer under rigid boundary and lying over an elastic half space under gravity, *Appl. Math. Model.,* 34, 1873–83.

Gubbins, D. (1990). *Seismology and plate tectonics*. Cambridge University Press, London.

Hua, L., Jia-Ling, Y., & Kai-Xin, L. (2006). Love waves in layered graded composite structures with imperfectly bonded interface, *Chin. J. Aeronaut.,* 20(3), 210-214.

Kar, B. K., Pal, A. K., & Kalyani, V. K. (1986). Propagation of Love waves in an irregular dry sandy layer. *Acta Geophys. Polonica*, 34, 157-170.

Kumar, N., & Madan, D. K. (2021). Propagation of Love waves in dry sandy medium laying over orthotropic semi-infinite medium with imperfect interface. *Int. Jour. Grid and Distributed Computing*, 14(1), 2057-2064.

Kundu, S., Prasad, R. M., Gupta, S., & Manna, S. (2016). Propagation of torsional surface waves in an anisotro-pic medium over a dry sandy half-space. *Int. J. Geomech.,* 16(2).

Love, A. E. H. (1920). Mathematical theory of elasticity. *Cambridge University Press,* London.

Pal, J., & Ghorai. A. P. (2015). Propagation of Love wave in sandy layer under initial stress above anisotropic porous half-space under gravity. *Transp Porous Med,* 109(2), 297-316.

Prasad, R. M., & Kundu, S. (2016). Torsional surface wave dispersion in prestressed dry sandy layer over a gravitating anisotropic porous half-space. *Z. Angew. Math. Mech.*

Sharma, V., & Kumar, S. (2017). Dispersion of SH waves in a viscoelastic layer imperfectly bonded with a couple stress substrate. *Journal of Theoretical and Applied Mechanics,* 83(1), 43-51.

Shekhar, S., & Parvez, I. A. (2016). Propagation of torsional surface waves in a double porous layer lying over a Gibson half-space. *Soil Dynamics and Earthquake Engineering,* 80, 56-64.

Singh, A. K., Mistri, K. C., & Das, A. (2016). Propagation of SH-wave in a corrugated viscous sandy layer sandwiched between two elastic half-spaces. *Waves in Random and Complex Media,* 27(2), 1-28.

Wang, Y. S., & Zhang, Z. M. (1998). Propagation of Love waves in a transversely isotropic fluid-saturated porous layered half-space, *J. Acous. Soc. Am.*, 103(2):695– 701.

Weiskopf, W. H. (1945). Stresses in soils under foundation. *J. Franklin Inst.,* 239, 445-465.

Yew, C. H., & Jogi, P. N. (1976). Study of wave motions in fluid-saturated porous rocks. *J. Acous. Soc. Am.,* 60, 2–8.

Chapter 13

A Pythagorean Fuzzy Distance Measure with Hesitancy Degree and Application in Decision Making

Naveen Kumar[*]
Juthika Mahanta
Department of Mathematics, NIT Silchar,
Assam, India

Abstract

The Pythagorean fuzzy sets have remarkably accommodated uncertainty in real-world problems. In a Pythagorean fuzzy environment, distance measures with a degree of hesitancy are commonly employed to manage uncertainty and distinguish between two objects. According to the literature, several distance functions currently in use must satisfy metric conditions. Additionally, specific measures are prone to calculation errors and may yield unreasonable outcomes. To address these concerns, we propose a new metric incorporating a degree of hesitancy for Pythagorean fuzzy sets in this study. The novel measure is compared to the prevailing distance metrics to demonstrate its improved efficacy. Numerical examples provided here successfully assess the efficiency and feasibility of the introduced measure in decision-making problems.

Keywords: fuzzy set, intuitionistic fuzzy set, Pythagorean fuzzy sets, distance measure, decision-making

---

[*] Corresponding Author's Email: naveen_rs@maths.nits.ac.in

In: Emerging Trends in Mathematical Sciences and Computing
Editors: B. Basu Mallik, S. Ghosh, B. Kumar Pandey et al.
ISBN: 979-8-89113-751-6

Introduction

In our daily lives, hesitancy is a common aspect of human decision-making. There are numerous instances where we must make complex choices, leading to moments of hesitation. Examples include selecting the top candidates for a job application, choosing the best university from a list of prestigious institutions, picking the 11 players for a cricket match, and selecting the best car. A decision can be evaluated both quantitatively and qualitatively. It depends on the needs of a person. Sometimes decision-making quantitatively can ease the work and help choose the best decision. MCDM (Multicriteria decision-making) is a highly relevant field for addressing this type of problem. MCDM helps us to choose the decision with both qualitative and quantitative factors. Decision-making has always been a tedious task due to the uncertainty involved. Many concepts encountered in the real world lack a clear boundary regarding belongingness. The ongoing theories needed to be more capable of accommodating such vagueness. Zadeh [1] introduced a fuzzy set (FS) as a mathematical tool to address the problem. The FS has a belongingness function that spans from 0 to 1, and it is an expansion of the crisp set which preserves the characteristic values of 0 or 1. An FS's MD (degree of belongingness) lies in the interval [0,1]. The NMD (non-belongingness degree) is one minus the MD, which also lies in the unit interval [0,1]. However, this may only sometimes be true because hesitancy occurs in many situations.
To handle uncertainty in decision-making, Atanassov [2] introduced intuitionistic fuzzy sets (IFSs) with parameters MD, NMD, and HD (hesitancy degree). The semantic representation of these sets has been the subject of significant interest, but they may be restricted if the sum of MD and NMD exceeds one. To overcome this, Yager [3, 4] proposed Pythagorean fuzzy sets (PFSs) as a generalization of IFSs, with a squared limit of MD and NMD less than or equal to 1. PFSs have been developed as useful tools for decision-making. For example, to demonstrate this situation: if $\alpha = \beta = \frac{1}{\sqrt{n}}$; $\forall\ 2 \leq n < 4$, then their sum is greater than 1, which cannot be explained using IFSs. However, it is best suited to utilize the PFSs since $\alpha^2 + \beta^2 \leq 1$. PFSs are more extended fields compared to IFSs to tackle the uncertainty in the real world using distance measures.
Distance measures (DMs) are remarkable tools for defining two objects' differences. Many researchers have done lot of work using this tool and applied them in decision making (personnel appointments, innovation management, etc.) [4, 5, 6, 7, 8, 9, 10, 11] with the help of Technique for order of preference by Similarity to Ideal Solution (TOPSIS) algorithm. TOPSIS is one of the most frequently used MCDM methods, developed by Hwang and Yoon [12] with further developments by Hwang [13]. Since then, researchers have widely used this technique as a productive tool. Zhang and Xu [14] introduced a DM between two PFS using three-parameter MD, NMD, and HD. Peng et al. [15] gave the axiomatic definition

consisting of five axioms of DM and normalized the existing Zhang DM. After this, Peng [16] realized that the existing Pythagorean fuzzy distance measures (PFDMs) do not obey the third or fourth axiom, are unable to distinguish between favorable and unfavorable distinctions, and cannot deal with the division by zero problems. To overcome such drawbacks, the author constructed a new DM between two PFS, which dealt with these issues and gave reliable results. Hussian and Yang [17] utilized the Hausdorff metric to describe the DM of PFS and applied it to decision-making problems using the TOPSIS approach. Li and Lu [18] extended the Hamming and Hausdorff distances, while Xiao and Ding [19] determined a unique divergence measure using the Jensen-Shannon divergence. Ejegwa and Awolola [20] proposed novel DMs for PFSs that incorporate conventional parameters and are useful in pattern recognition and decision-making for real-life problems. Chen [21] developed a novel Chebyshev DM for MCDM under Pythagorean fuzziness. Ejegwa [22] proposed a new DM that satisfies all metric conditions, as Zhang and Xu [14] existing DM did not meet the metric properties.

Additionally, He and Xiao [23] have observed that some of the current methods fail to effectively demonstrate the difference between PFSs and do not adhere to the metric property. To tackle this issue, they suggest a new distance metric for PFSs, which is constructed using a matrix that satisfies all of the metric conditions and subsequently applies to medical diagnosis. Mahanta and Panda [24] have also noted that the majority of the existing distance measures are a generalization of IFSs and only a few distances are normalized, while most of the measures are incapable of distinguishing high uncertainty for PFSs. To overcome these limitations, a new mathematical formula has been proposed to measure the distance of PFSs. This approach has been implemented to choose face masks using pattern recognition techniques. Recently many researchers have done lots of work in decision-making using the TOPSIS approach, VIKOR method, etc. However, the definition of the existing VIKOR function does not satisfy the axiom of DM, and some of the understanding solutions to the MCDM problem by the current VIKOR method used for PFSs do not yield a solution that is the most similar to the ideal positive outcome. To improve the ideas of remoteness and ranking indexes, M. J. Khan et al. [25] gave a new DM and refined the VIKOR method for PFSs. Also, no investigation focused on creating PFDMs and knowledge measures using t-norms. So A. H. Ganie [26] defines DM based on t-norm and applies it to solve decision-making problems. Yin et al. [27] constructed a DM based on the earth mover's distance since earth mover distance is an accurate distance metric. Furthermore, utilizing the distribution law approach to determine the distance between PFSs represents a fresh viewpoint that can be employed in multiple areas, such as MCDM, pattern recognition, and medical diagnosis. H. D. Arora et al. [28] defined an exponential DM and applied it in decision-making for selecting mobile phones for company employees using the TOPSIS approach. P. A. Ejegwa et al. [29] define a new PFDM and weighted DM based on the operator. M. Bhatia et al. [30] define a DM based on the sine function. For the stability of the proposed DM, they applied it in a real-life application through MCDM using the TOPSIS approach. The sudden increase in COVID-19 pandemic cases has accelerated the growth of online food delivery services (OFDAs) worldwide. In India, OFDAs are growing, opening up many opportunities for various platforms and encouraging competition. Although the present distance measures have some significance, they are only partially accurate and compatible with interval-valued PFSs. H. D. Arora et al. [31] re-examine existing distances for PFSs to choose better apps for online food delivery using the TOPSIS approach. During the literature survey, we realized that many existing DM's with hesitancy degree's primary purpose is to distinguish between two PFSs. However, there was always some error or flaw in existing measures. The limitations of the current approaches are

- Some of the existing distances do not satisfy the axioms of DM.
- Most of the existing DMs give absurd results and have zero divisor problems.
- Most of the existing DMs are a generalization of IFS distances.
- The existing DMs are unable to distinguish between PFSs with high uncertainty.

To overcome this shortcoming, we will determine a new DM with a hesitancy degree for PFSs, which can successfully deal with extremely unreliable results for PFSs. Consequently, the primary efforts of this work are

- Introducing a novel distance measure for PFSs.
- Analysing mathematical properties of the proposed definition.
- Conduction of comparative study with the existing ones.
- Applying the new distance measure to select smartphones for workers using the TOPSIS method in MADM (multiple attribute decision-making).

The remainder of the paper is structured as follows: Section explains PFSs mathematically, Section describes distance measures for PFSs that currently exist, Section produces a new distance measure for PFSs, Section provides a comparative analysis, Section discusses and investigates potential applications of the new distance measure proposed for PFSs, and Section concludes the paper and suggests future avenues for research.

Preliminaries

In this section, we present some mathematical definitions. Throughout this paper, X is a universal set, $PFS(X)$ be a collection of all PFSs on X, and $P, Q \in PFS(X)$ be two PFSs.

Definition 1. [1] F is a fuzzy set defined in the universal set X. It can be written as $F = \langle x, \alpha_F(x)\rangle : x \in X$, where $\alpha_F : X \longrightarrow [0, 1]$ is the belongingness degree of $x \in X$ with respect to F.

Definition 2. [2] Let I be an intuitionistic fuzzy set (IFS) defined in the universal set X, where I is expressed as $I = \{\langle x, \alpha_I(x), \beta_I(x)\rangle : x \in X\}$, and $\alpha_I, \beta_I : X \longrightarrow [0, 1]$ are the belongingness and non-belongingness degree of $x \in X$, respectively. It is required that $0 \leq \alpha_I(x) + \beta_I(x) \leq 1$ for all $x \in X$. The IF index or hesitation margin of I is defined as $\gamma_I(x) = 1 - \alpha_I(x) - \beta_I(x)$, which lies in the range $[0, 1]$.

Definition 3. [3] Let P be a Pythagorean fuzzy set (PFS) defined in the universal set X, where P are expressed as $P = \{\langle x, \alpha_P(x), \beta_P(x)\rangle : x \in X\}$, and $\alpha_P, \beta_P : X \longrightarrow [0, 1]$ are the belongingness and non-belongingness degree of $x \in X$, respectively. It is required that $0 \leq \alpha_P^2(x) + \beta_P^2(x) \leq 1$ for all $x \in X$. The PF index or hesitation margin of P is defined as $\gamma_P(x) = \sqrt{1 - \alpha_P^2(x) - \beta_P^2(x)}$, which lies in the range $[0, 1]$.

Some Existing Distance Measures for PFSs

In this section, we consider distance measures that incorporate a level of uncertainty.

1. Zhang and Xu distance measure [14]

$$D_{ZX}(P,Q)=\frac{1}{2}\sum_{i=1}^{n}\Big(\mid \alpha_P^2(x_i)-\alpha_Q^2(x_i)\mid + \mid \beta_P^2(x_i)-\beta_Q^2(x_i)\mid + \mid \gamma_P^2(x_i)-\gamma_Q^2(x_i)\mid\Big) \tag{1}$$

2. The Euclidean distance measure [32]

$$D_{EN}(P,Q)=\sqrt{\frac{1}{2n}\sum_{i=1}^{n}\mid \alpha_P^2(x_i)-\alpha_Q^2(x_i)\mid^2 + \mid \beta_P^2(x_i)-\beta_Q^2(x_i)\mid^2 + \mid \gamma_P^2(x_i)-\gamma_Q^2(x_i)\mid^2} \tag{2}$$

3. Arrora modified exponential distance measure [31]

$$D_{PFS}(P,Q)=1-\frac{3}{n}\sum_{i=1}^{n}\frac{2^{1-\frac{1}{3}\left[\left(|\alpha_P^2(x_i)-\alpha_Q^2(x_i)|+|\beta_P^2(x_i)-\beta_Q^2(x_i)|+|\gamma_P^2(x_i)-\gamma_Q^2(x_i)|\right)\right]}-1}{2^{1-\frac{1}{3}\left[\left(|\alpha_P^2(x_i)-\alpha_Q^2(x_i)|+|\beta_P^2(x_i)-\beta_Q^2(x_i)|+|\gamma_P^2(x_i)-\gamma_Q^2(x_i)|\right)\right]}+1} \tag{3}$$

4. Jensen-Shannon divergence [19]

$$D_X(P,Q)=\sqrt{\frac{1}{n}\sum_{i=1}^{n}\left[\sum_{K\in\alpha,\beta,\gamma}(K_P(x_i))^2\log\Big(\frac{2(K_P(x_i))^2}{(K_P(x_i))^2+(K_Q(x_i))^2}+\sum_{K\in\alpha,\beta,\gamma}(K_Q(x_i))^2\log\Big(\frac{2(K_Q(x_i))^2}{(K_Q(x_i))^2+(K_P(x_i))^2}\right]} \tag{4}$$

5. Hybrid Pythagorean fuzzy Hamming distance measure [33]

$$\begin{aligned}PFHD(P,Q)=\sum_{i=1}^{n}\Bigg[&\frac{\mid \alpha_P^2(x_i)-\alpha_Q^2(x_i)\mid + \mid \beta_P^2(x_i)-\beta_Q^2(x_i)\mid + \mid \gamma_P^2(x_i)-\gamma_Q^2(x_i)\mid}{4}\\ &+\frac{\max\left(\mid \alpha_P^2(x_i)-\alpha_Q^2(x_i)\mid, \mid \beta_P^2(x_i)-\beta_Q^2(x_i)\mid, \mid \gamma_P^2(x_i)-\gamma_Q^2(x_i)\mid\right)}{2}\Bigg)\Bigg]\end{aligned} \tag{5}$$

6. Zeng distance measure [33]

(I) Normalized Hamming-Hausdorff distance measure

$$D_{NH}(P,Q)=\frac{1}{n}\sum_{i=1}^{n}\max\left[\mid \alpha_P^2(x_i)-\alpha_Q^2(x_i)\mid, \mid \beta_P^2(x_i)-\beta_Q^2(x_i)\mid, \mid \gamma_P^2(x_i)-\gamma_Q^2(x_i)\mid\right] \tag{6a}$$

(II) Normalized Euclidean-Hausdorff distance measure

$$D_{NE}(P,Q)=\sqrt{\frac{1}{n}\sum_{i=1}^{n}\max(\alpha_P^2(x_i)-\alpha_Q^2(x_i))^2,(\beta_P^2(x_i)-\beta_Q^2(x_i))^2,(\gamma_P^2(x_i)-\gamma_Q^2(x_i))^2} \tag{6b}$$

7. Spherical distance measure [34]

$$D_{Gc}(P,Q) = \frac{2}{n\pi}\sum_{i=1}^{n} \arccos\Big[\alpha_P(x_i)\alpha_Q(x_i) + \beta_P(x_i)\beta_Q(x_i) + \gamma_P(x_i)\gamma_Q(x_i)\Big] \quad (7)$$

8. Modified Zhang and Xu distance [35]

$$D_{NHm}(P,Q) = \frac{1}{2n}\sum_{i=1}^{n}\Big(\mid \alpha_P^2(x_i) - \alpha_Q^2(x_i)\mid + \mid \beta_P^2(x_i) - \beta_Q^2(x_i)\mid + \mid \gamma_P^2(x_i) - \gamma_Q^2(x_i)\mid\Big) \quad (8)$$

9. Ejegwa robust weighted distance measure [36]

$$D_\alpha(P,Q) = \sqrt{\frac{1}{3n}\sum_{i=1}^{n}\alpha_i\Big(\big(\alpha_P(x_i) - \alpha_Q(x_i)\big)^2 + \big(\beta_P(x_i) - \beta_Q(x_i)\big)^2 + \big(\gamma_P(x_i) - \gamma_Q(x_i)\big)^2\Big)} \quad (9)$$

10. Ejegwa distance measure [20]

$$D_{PA}(P,Q) = \frac{1}{4n}\sum_{i=1}^{n}\Big[\mid \alpha_P(x_i) - \alpha_Q(x_i)\mid + \|\alpha_P(x_i) - \beta_P(x_i)\mid - \mid \alpha_Q(x_i) - \beta_Q(x_i)\| + \|\alpha_P(x_i) - \gamma_P(x_i)\mid - \mid \alpha_Q(x_i) - \gamma_Q(x_i)\|\Big] \quad (10)$$

11. Bhatia distance measure [30]

$$D_B(P,Q) = 1 - \frac{1}{n}\sum_{i=1}^{n}\sin\Big[\frac{\pi}{2} - \frac{\pi}{6}\Big(\mid \alpha_P^2(x_i) - \alpha_Q^2(x_i)\mid + \beta_P^2(x_i) - \beta_Q^2(x_i)\mid + \mid \gamma_P^2(x_i) - \gamma_Q^2(x_i)\mid\Big)\Big] \quad (11)$$

12. Ejegwa operator distance measure [29]

$$\Delta(P,Q) = \frac{1}{3n}\sum_{i=1}^{n}(\mid \alpha_P(x_i) - \alpha_Q(x_i)\mid + \mid \beta_P(x_i) - \beta_Q(x_i)\mid + \mid \gamma_P(x_i) - \gamma_Q(x_i)\mid) \quad (12)$$

The list mentioned above does not cover all the existing definitions, rather only a few are mentioned here among numerous sustaining ones.

The Proposed Definition for PFSs

This segment proposes a new distance function with a hesitancy degree.

Definition 4. If there is a finite universe X consisting of n elements $X = x_i | i = 1, 2, ..., n$, then the distance between any two PFSs (P and Q) is specified as follows:

$$D_{dis}(P, Q) = \frac{1}{n} \sum_{i=1}^{n} \frac{|\alpha_P^2(x_i) - \alpha_Q^2(x_i)| + |\beta_P^2(x_i) - \beta_Q^2(x_i)| + |\gamma_P^2(x_i) - \gamma_Q^2(x_i)|}{\alpha_P^2(x_i) + \alpha_Q^2(x_i) + \beta_P^2(x_i) + \beta_Q^2(x_i) + \gamma_P^2(x_i) + \gamma_Q^2(x_i)} \quad (13)$$

Subsequently, the following theorem can be stated.

Theorem 1. [15] "Let X be a non-empty set and $P, Q, R \in PFS(X)$. The introduced distance measure between P and Q is a function $D_{dis} : [0, 1] \times [0, 1] \to [0, 1]$ satisfies the following properties:

(a) Boundedness: $0 \leq D_{dis}(P, Q) \leq 1$

(b) Separability: $D_{dis}(P, Q) = 0 \Leftrightarrow P = Q$

(c) Symmetric: $D_{dis}(P, Q) = D_{dis}(Q, P)$

(d) Inequality: If R is a PFS in X and $P \subseteq Q \subseteq R$, then $D_{dis}(P, Q) \leq D_{dis}(P, R)$ and $D_{dis}(Q, R) \leq D_{dis}(P, R)$"

Proof. The new distance measures satisfy all four required conditions, which are listed below:

(a) Boundedness: $0 \leq D_{dis}(P, Q) \leq 1$

Proof. Given $\alpha_{PFSs}(x_i), \beta_{PFSs}(x_i), \gamma_{PFSs}(x_i) \in [0, 1]$, therefore, $0 \leq |\alpha_P(x_i) \pm \alpha_Q(x_i)| \leq 1$, $0 \leq |\beta_P(x_i) \pm \beta_Q(x_i)| \leq 1$ and $0 \leq |\gamma_P(x_i) \pm \gamma_Q(x_i)| \leq 1$. As the maximum value of each expression is 1, the distance measure $D_{dis}(P, Q)$ will be 1, and we can express it as: $D_{dis}(P, Q) = \frac{1}{1} \cdot \left(\frac{1+1+1}{3}\right) = 1$. Moreover, each expression is non-negative for all $x_i \in X$, so we can conclude that $D_{dis}(P, Q)$ is also non-negative: $D_{dis}(P, Q) \geq 0$. Since the maximum possible value of $D_{dis}(P, Q)$ is 1, we can further conclude that: $0 \leq D_{dis}(P, Q) \leq 1$. □

(b) Separability: $D_{dis}(P, Q) = 0 \Leftrightarrow P = Q$.

Proof. Given two PFSs P and Q in $X = \{x_i | i = 1, 2, ..., n\}$, if $P = Q$, then:
$\alpha_P^2(x_i) = \alpha_Q^2(x_i)$, $\beta_P^2(x_i) = \beta_Q^2(x_i)$, and $\gamma_P^2(x_i) = \gamma_Q^2(x_i)$ for all $i = 1, 2, ..., n$. Thus, we have: $|\alpha_P^2(x_i) - \alpha_Q^2(x_i)| = 0$, $\beta_P^2(x_i) - \beta_Q^2(x_i) = 0$, and $\gamma_P^2(x_i) - \gamma_Q^2(x_i) = 0$. Consequently, the distance between P and Q using the D_{dis} measure is equal to 0.
If $D_{dis}(P, Q) = 0$, this implies

$$\frac{|\alpha_P^2(x_i) - \alpha_Q^2(x_i)| + |\beta_P^2(x_i) - \beta_Q^2(x_i)| + |\gamma_P^2(x_i) - \gamma_Q^2(x_i)|}{\alpha_P^2(x_i) + \alpha_Q^2(x_i) + \beta_P^2(x_i) + \beta_Q^2(x_i) + \gamma_P^2(x_i) + \gamma_Q^2(x_i)} = 0$$

$\Rightarrow |\alpha_P^2(x_i) - \alpha_Q^2(x_i)| + |\beta_P^2(x_i) - \beta_Q^2(x_i)| + |\gamma_P^2(x_i) - \gamma_Q^2(x_i)| = 0$
$\Rightarrow |\alpha_P^2(x_i) - \alpha_Q^2(x_i)| = 0$, $|\beta_P^2(x_i) - \beta_Q^2(x_i)| = 0$ and $|\gamma_P^2(x_i) - \gamma_Q^2(x_i)| = 0$
Therefore $\alpha_P^2(x_i) = \alpha_Q^2(x_i)$, $\beta_P^2(x_i) = \beta_Q^2(x_i)$, and $\gamma_P^2(x_i) = \gamma_Q^2(x_i)$.
Hence $P = Q$. □

(c) Symmetric: $D_{dis}(P, Q) = D_{dis}(Q, P)$
Follows the definition of distance function and proof are straightforward.

(d) Inequality: Let R be a PFS in X, and let $P \subseteq Q \subseteq R$. Then we have:
$D_{dis}(P, Q) \leq D_{dis}(P, R)$, and $D_{dis}(Q, R) \leq D_{dis}(P, R)$.

Proof. Let $P \subseteq Q \subseteq R$, and let $x_i \in X$. Then we have:
$0 \leq \alpha_P(x_i) \leq \alpha_Q(x_i) \leq \alpha_R(x_i) \leq 1$, and $1 \geq \beta_P(x_i) \geq \beta_Q(x_i) \geq \beta_R(x_i) \geq 0$.
This implies that $0 \leq \alpha_P^2(x_i) \leq \alpha_Q^2(x_i) \leq \alpha_R^2(x_i) \leq 1$ and $1 \geq \beta_P^2(x_i) \geq \beta_Q^2(x_i) \geq \beta_R^2(x_i) \geq 0$. Thus, we have,

Case 1: $|\alpha_P^2(x_i) - \alpha_Q^2(x_i)| \leq |\alpha_P^2(x_i) - \alpha_R^2(x_i)|$; $|\alpha_Q^2(x_i) - \alpha_R^2(x_i)| \leq |\alpha_P^2(x_i) - \alpha_R^2(x_i)| \Rightarrow |\beta_P^2(x_i) - \beta_Q^2(x_i)| \leq |\beta_P^2(x_i) - \beta_R^2(x_i)|$; $|\beta_Q^2(x_i) - \beta_R^2(x_i)| \leq |\beta_P^2(x_i) - \beta_R^2(x_i)|$
And, $|\gamma_P^2(x_i) - \gamma_Q^2(x_i)| \leq |\gamma_P^2(x_i) - \gamma_R^2(x_i)|$; $|\gamma_Q^2(x_i) - \gamma_R^2(x_i)| \leq |\gamma_P^2(x_i) - \gamma_R^2(x_i)|$
Adding above equations

$$\begin{aligned} &|\alpha_P^2(x_i) - \alpha_Q^2(x_i)| + |\beta_P^2(x_i) - \beta_Q^2(x_i)| + |\gamma_P^2(x_i) - \gamma_Q^2(x_i)| \\ &\leq |\alpha_P^2(x_i) - \alpha_R^2(x_i)| + |\beta_P^2(x_i) - \beta_R^2(x_i)| + |\gamma_P^2(x_i) - \gamma_R^2(x_i)| \end{aligned} \tag{14}$$

$$\begin{aligned} &|\alpha_Q^2(x_i) - \alpha_R^2(x_i)| + |\beta_Q^2(x_i) - \beta_R^2(x_i)| + |\gamma_Q^2(x_i) - \gamma_R^2(x_i)| \\ &\leq |\alpha_P^2(x_i) - \alpha_R^2(x_i)| + |\beta_P^2(x_i) - \beta_R^2(x_i)| + |\gamma_P^2(x_i) - \gamma_R^2(x_i)| \end{aligned} \tag{15}$$

Case 2: $\alpha_P^2(x_i) + \alpha_Q^2(x_i) \leq \alpha_P^2(x_i) + \alpha_R^2(x_i)$; $\alpha_Q^2(x_i) + \alpha_R^2(x_i) \leq \alpha_P^2(x_i) + \alpha_R^2(x_i)$
$\Rightarrow \beta_P^2(x_i) + \beta_Q^2(x_i) \leq \beta_P^2(x_i) + \beta_R^2(x_i)$; $\beta_Q^2(x_i) + \beta_R^2(x_i) \leq \beta_P^2(x_i) + \beta_R^2(x_i)$
And, $\gamma_P^2(x_i) + \gamma_Q^2(x_i) \leq \gamma_P^2(x_i) + \gamma_R^2(x_i)$; $\gamma_Q^2(x_i) + \gamma_R^2(x_i) \leq \gamma_P^2(x_i) + \gamma_R^2(x_i)$
Adding above equations

$$\alpha_P^2(x_i) + \alpha_Q^2(x_i) + \beta_P^2(x_i) + \beta_Q^2(x_i) + \gamma_P^2(x_i) + \gamma_Q^2(x_i) \leq \alpha_P^2(x_i) + \alpha_R^2(x_i) + \beta_P^2(x_i) + \beta_R^2(x_i) + \gamma_P^2(x_i) + \gamma_R^2(x_i) \tag{16}$$

$$\alpha_Q^2(x_i) + \alpha_R^2(x_i) + \beta_Q^2(x_i) + \beta_R^2(x_i) + \gamma_Q^2(x_i) + \gamma_R^2(x_i) \leq \alpha_P^2(x_i) + \alpha_R^2(x_i) + \beta_P^2(x_i) + \beta_R^2(x_i) + \gamma_P^2(x_i) + \gamma_R^2(x_i) \tag{17}$$

Divide by equation (14) by $\alpha_P^2(x_i) + \alpha_Q^2(x_i) + \beta_P^2(x_i) + \beta_Q^2(x_i) + \gamma_P^2(x_i) + \gamma_Q^2(x_i)$, we get

$$\frac{|\alpha_P^2(x_i) - \alpha_Q^2(x_i)| + |\beta_P^2(x_i) - \beta_Q^2(x_i)| + |\gamma_P^2(x_i) - \gamma_Q^2(x_i)|}{\alpha_P^2(x_i) + \alpha_Q^2(x_i) + \beta_P^2(x_i) + \beta_Q^2(x_i) + \gamma_P^2(x_i) + \gamma_Q^2(x_i)}$$
$$\leq \frac{|\alpha_P^2(x_i) - \alpha_R^2(x_i)| + |\beta_P^2(x_i) - \beta_R^2(x_i)|}{\alpha_P^2(x_i) + \alpha_Q^2(x_i) + \beta_P^2(x_i) + \beta_Q^2(x_i)} \frac{+|\gamma_P^2(x_i) - \gamma_R^2(x_i)|}{+\gamma_P^2(x_i) + \gamma_Q^2(x_i)}$$
$$\leq \frac{|\alpha_P^2(x_i) - \alpha_R^2(x_i)| + |\beta_P^2(x_i) - \beta_R^2(x_i)| + |\gamma_P^2(x_i) - \gamma_R^2(x_i)|}{\alpha_P^2(x_i) + \alpha_R^2(x_i) + \beta_P^2(x_i) + \beta_R^2(x_i) + \gamma_P^2(x_i) + \gamma_R^2(x_i)}$$

$$\Rightarrow \frac{1}{n}\sum_{i=1}^{n} \frac{|\alpha_P^2(x_i) - \alpha_Q^2(x_i)| + |\beta_P^2(x_i) - \beta_Q^2(x_i)| + |\gamma_P^2(x_i) - \gamma_Q^2(x_i)|}{\alpha_P^2(x_i) + \alpha_Q^2(x_i) + \beta_P^2(x_i) + \beta_Q^2(x_i) + \gamma_P^2(x_i) + \gamma_Q^2(x_i)}$$
$$\leq \frac{1}{n}\sum_{i=1}^{n} \frac{|\alpha_P^2(x_i) - \alpha_R^2(x_i)| + |\beta_P^2(x_i) - \beta_R^2(x_i)|}{\alpha_P^2(x_i) + \alpha_R^2(x_i) + \beta_P^2(x_i) + \beta_R^2(x_i)} + \frac{|\gamma_P^2(x_i) - \gamma_R^2(x_i)|}{+\gamma_P^2(x_i) + \gamma_R^2(x_i)}$$

$\Rightarrow D_{dis}(P, Q) \leq D_{dis}(P, R)$
Similarly, we get
$\Rightarrow D_{dis}(Q, R) \leq D_{dis}(P, R)$ □

□

Comparative Study

This section compares the newly proposed distance measure and several existing distance measures, using numerical examples to illustrate the differences.

Example 2. Let $P, Q, R \in PFS(X)$ be three PFSs for $X = \{x_1, x_2, x_3, x_4, x_5\}$. Suppose

$$P = \left\{ \left\langle \frac{0.6, 0.4}{x_1} \right\rangle, \left\langle \frac{0.5, 0.7}{x_2} \right\rangle, \left\langle \frac{0.8, 0.4}{x_3} \right\rangle, \left\langle \frac{0.7, 0.2}{x_5} \right\rangle \right\}$$

$$Q = \left\{ \left\langle \frac{0.7, 0.3}{x_1} \right\rangle, \left\langle \frac{0.4, 0.7}{x_3} \right\rangle, \left\langle \frac{0.9, 0.2}{x_4} \right\rangle \right\}$$

$$R = \left\{ \left\langle \frac{0.6, 0.4}{x_2} \right\rangle, \left\langle \frac{0.7, 0.3}{x_3} \right\rangle, \left\langle \frac{0.5, 0.4}{x_4} \right\rangle \right\}$$

Then, the results obtained from existing and proposed measures are mentioned in Table 1. In Table 1, bold indicates unreasonable results.

Table 1. Distances generated by different methods

PFSs	$D(P, Q)$	$D(P, R)$	$D(Q, R)$
D_{ZX} [14]	**2.4900**	**3.1901**	**2.8101**
D_{EN} [32]	0.5259	0.6172	0.5795
D_{PFS}[31]	0.3202	0.4131	0.3646
D_X [19]	**NAN**	**NAN**	**NAN**
$PFHD$[33]	**2.1419**	**2.9555**	**2.4276**
D_{Gc} [34]	0.4450	0.5477	**NAN**
D_{PA} [20]	**0.3120**	**0.2480**	**0.2214**
D_{dis}	0.4785	0.6380	0.5254

Discussion

- Some existing methods can precisely detect the differences under the given example.
- However, the results produced by D_X , D_{Gc} which is absurd and irrational.
- The distances D_{ZX}, D_{PFHD} do not satisfy the first property of theorem 1 for DM in PFS, which is visible from the results in Table 1.
- In Table 1, we see that the existing distance D_{PA} fail the inequality property of theorem 1.

- **Remark:** The proposed distance D_{dis} is performing very well under any cases given in Table 1 to examine the distance between PFS, while other methods do not satisfy metric properties and give unreasonable results in some cases. A critical analysis of the mathematical properties of the distance functions portrays that few are metric while other fails to satisfy the metric properties.

Application of PFSs in the Selection Problem via TOPSIS

Overview of the TOPSIS algorithm

The proposed PFS TOPSIS has the following steps that are listed in order:

Step 1: Creating the PFS decision matrix
Let $A^{\diamond}$ be a set of n alternatives, where $\chi^{\diamond} = \{A_1^{\diamond}, A_2^{\diamond}, ..., A_n^{\diamond}\}$. Let C be a set of m alternatives related to criteria, where $C = \{c_1, c_2, ..., c_m\}$. We create a decision matrix $D = [d_{ij}^k]_{n\times m}$ to analyze the structure of the decision-making process for k experts or decision-makers. The value $d_{ij} = (\alpha_{ij}, \beta_{ij})$ represents their preference, where α_{ij} and β_{ij} are the belongingness and non belongingness values of alternative A_i with respect to criteria C_j. The hesitancy PFSs index is calculated by $\gamma_{ij} = \sqrt{1 - \alpha_{ij}^2 - \beta_{ij}^2}$, which indicates the extent of indecisiveness of the experts in assigning values to alternatives $A_i^{\diamond}$ based on criteria C_j.

Step 2: The process of converting the Pythagorean decision matrix into a normalized matrix
Normalizing the Pythagorean fuzzy decision matrix based on benefit and cost criteria involves swapping belongingness values with non-belongingness values for cost criteria, while benefit criteria are left unchanged.

Step 3: Find the "Pythagorean fuzzy positive ideal solution" (PFPIS) and the "Pythagorean fuzzy negative ideal solution" (PFNIS)
The TOPSIS method divides the assessment feature into two categories, "benefit and cost criteria", denoted by collections I and J, respectively. Using PFSs and the principle of the TOPSIS method, we can determine the PFPIS and PFNIS.

$$A^{\diamond k+} = \{r_1^{k+}, r_2^{k+}, ..., r_n^{k+}\} = \left\{\left(\max_i(r_{ij}^k), j \in I\right), \left(\min_i(r_{ij}^k), j \in J\right)\right\} \tag{18}$$

$$A^{\diamond k-} = \{r_1^{k-}, r_2^{k-}, ..., r_n^{k-}\} = \left\{\left(\min_i(r_{ij}^k), j \in I\right), \left(\max_i(r_{ij}^k), j \in J\right)\right\} \tag{19}$$

Step 4: Calculating the distance measures of each alternative from the PFPIS and PFPIS)

$$D_{dis}(A_i^{\diamond}, A^{\diamond +}) = \frac{1}{n}\sum_{i=1}^{n} w_i \left[\frac{|\alpha_P^2(x_i)-\alpha_Q^{2+}(x_i)|+|\beta_P^2(x_i)-\beta_Q^{2+}(x_i)|+|\gamma_P^2(x_i)-\gamma_Q^{2+}(x_i)|}{\alpha_P^2(x_i)+\alpha_Q^{2+}(x_i)+\beta_P^2(x_i)+\beta_Q^{2+}(x_i)+\gamma_P^2(x_i)+\gamma_Q^{2+}(x_i)}\right] \tag{20}$$

$$D_{dis}(A_i^{\diamond}, A^{\diamond -}) = \frac{1}{n}\sum_{i=1}^{n} w_i \left[\frac{|\alpha_P^2(x_i)-\alpha_Q^{2-}(x_i)|+|\beta_P^2(x_i)-\beta_Q^{2-}(x_i)|+|\gamma_P^2(x_i)-\gamma_Q^{2-}(x_i)|}{\alpha_P^2(x_i)+\alpha_Q^{2-}(x_i)+\beta_P^2(x_i)+\beta_Q^{2-}(x_i)+\gamma_P^2(x_i)+\gamma_Q^{2-}(x_i)}\right] \tag{21}$$

Step 5: Evaluating the closeness degree of each potential choice
For every decision expert, the evaluation of the proximity coefficient between the alternatives and the ideal solution of PFSs is found with this formula

$$R_i = \frac{D_{dis}(A_i^{\diamond}, A^{\diamond -})}{D_{dis}(A_i^{\diamond}, A^{\diamond -}) + D_{dis}(A_i^{\diamond}, A^{\diamond +})} \tag{22}$$

where $0 \leq R_i, \leq 1, i = 1, 2, ...n$

Step 6: Ranking of the alternatives
Arranging the various choices in a particular sequence based on their performance. The alternatives can be ranked according to high to low values of R_i.

A Case Study [28]

A multinational corporation needs to buy smartphones for its white-collar workers, which is crucial since many phones will be purchased. They have appointed a Procurement Manager (D) to choose the best smartphone from five options: $M_{(Models)} = \{A_1^{\diamond}, A_2^{\diamond}, A_3^{\diamond}, A_4^{\diamond}, A_5^{\diamond}\}$. An expert will assist the manager in making this decision using five selection criteria: storage capacity (GB) (C_1), weight (Gms) (C_2), camera specifications (Px) (C_3), the screen size (In) (C_4), and battery life (Hrs) (C_5). These $M_{(Models)}$ have been selected because they are similarly priced in the Indian market. w= $\{0.25, 0.35, 0.20, 0.12, 0.08\}$ are the weights the organization gives to each of these criteria.

Step 1: Creating the PFS decision matrix:- The PFS evaluations of the alternatives based on the pairwise comparison of options for each criterion by decision maker D are presented in Table 2.

Step 2: Normalizing the Pythagorean decision matrix:- To make the normalization process less complicated, the decision-maker assigns C_1, C_2, and C_4 as criteria that provide benefits and C_3 and C_5 as criteria that result in costs. When

Table 2. Data set in the form of Pythagorean fuzzy decision matrix (X) of the decision maker (D)

Decision maker	Alternatives vs Criteria	C_1	C_2	C_3	C_4	C_5
	$A_1^\diamond$	$\langle 0.8, 0.5\rangle$	$\langle 0.6, 0.7\rangle$	$\langle 0.2, 0.9\rangle$	$\langle 0.6, 0.5\rangle$	$\langle 0.4, 0.9\rangle$
	$A_2^\diamond$	$\langle 0.3, 0.8\rangle$	$\langle 0.5, 0.6\rangle$	$\langle 0.7, 0.6\rangle$	$\langle 0.9, 0.2\rangle$	$\langle 0.1, 0.8\rangle$
D	$A_3^\diamond$	$\langle 0.4, 0.8\rangle$	$\langle 0.8, 0.2\rangle$	$\langle 0.6, 0.4\rangle$	$\langle 0.4, 0.8\rangle$	$\langle 0.6, 0.6\rangle$
	$A_4^\diamond$	$\langle 0.1, 0.9\rangle$	$\langle 0.3, 0.9\rangle$	$\langle 0.7, 0.7\rangle$	$\langle 0.7, 0.5\rangle$	$\langle 0.5, 0.7\rangle$
	$A_5^\diamond$	$\langle 0.4, 0.9\rangle$	$\langle 0.9, 0.2\rangle$	$\langle 0.6, 0.4\rangle$	$\langle 0.3, 0.9\rangle$	$\langle 0.8, 0.5\rangle$

dealing with a Pythagorean fuzzy environment, the normalization matrix can be derived by replacing the values of belongingness and non-belongingness in the cost criteria while keeping the benefit criteria the same. The normalized matrix is shown in Table 3.

Table 3. Normalized the Pythagorean fuzzy decision matrix (X) of the decision maker (D)

Decision maker	Alternatives vs Criteria	C_1	C_2	C_3	C_4	C_5
	$A_1^\diamond$	$\langle 0.8, 0.5\rangle$	$\langle 0.6, 0.7\rangle$	$\langle 0.9, 0.2\rangle$	$\langle 0.6, 0.5\rangle$	$\langle 0.9, 0.4\rangle$
	$A_2^\diamond$	$\langle 0.3, 0.8\rangle$	$\langle 0.5, 0.6\rangle$	$\langle 0.6, 0.7\rangle$	$\langle 0.9, 0.2\rangle$	$\langle 0.8, 0.1\rangle$
D	$A_3^\diamond$	$\langle 0.4, 0.8\rangle$	$\langle 0.8, 0.2\rangle$	$\langle 0.4, 0.6\rangle$	$\langle 0.4, 0.8\rangle$	$\langle 0.6, 0.6\rangle$
	$A_4^\diamond$	$\langle 0.1, 0.9\rangle$	$\langle 0.3, 0.9\rangle$	$\langle 0.7, 0.7\rangle$	$\langle 0.7, 0.5\rangle$	$\langle 0.7, 0.5\rangle$
	$A_5^\diamond$	$\langle 0.4, 0.9\rangle$	$\langle 0.9, 0.2\rangle$	$\langle 0.4, 0.6\rangle$	$\langle 0.3, 0.9\rangle$	$\langle 0.5, 0.8\rangle$

Step 3: Determine the Pythagorean fuzzy positive and negative ideal (PFPIS and PFNIS We compute PFPIS and PFNIS using equations 18 and 19. The obtained result is shown in Table 4.

Step 4: Calculating the distance measures of each alternative from the PFPIS and PFNIS
Table 5 presents the distance measures of each evaluated alternative from the Pythagorean fuzzy positive ideal solution (PFPIS) and negative ideal solution (PFNIS) using Equations 20 and 21.

Step 5: Calculating the closeness coefficient of each alternative
The Pythagorean fuzzy TOPSIS approach calculates each alternative's relative

Table 4. Pythagorean fuzzy positive and negative ideal for decision maker

FPIS and FNIS	C_1	C_2	C_3	C_4	C_5
P^+	$\langle 0.8, 0.5\rangle$	$\langle 0.9, 0.2\rangle$	$\langle 0.9, 0.2\rangle$	$\langle 0.9, 0.2\rangle$	$\langle 0.9, 0.1\rangle$
P^-	$\langle 0.1, 0.9\rangle$	$\langle 0.3, 0.9\rangle$	$\langle 0.4, 0.7\rangle$	$\langle 0.3, 0.9\rangle$	$\langle 0.5, 0.8\rangle$

Table 5. Decision maker's impact on ideal solution separation measures

Alternatives	$D_{dis}(A_i^\diamond, A^{\diamond+})$	$D_{dis}(A_i^\diamond, A^{\diamond-})$	R_i	Ranking
$A_1^\diamond$	0.0447	0.1023	0.7184	1
$A_2^\diamond$	0.0874	0.0766	0.4581	4
$A_3^\diamond$	0.0874	0.0762	0.4900	2
$A_4^\diamond$	0.1162	0.0329	0.2275	5
$A_5^\diamond$	0.0826	0.0666	0.4647	3

closeness, R_i, with higher values indicating a higher ranking and better performance. The ranking results obtained using Equation 22 are presented in Table 5.

Discussion: According to the decision maker (D), Table 5 presents the ranking of the five smartphones considered, with M_{Models} $(A_1^\diamond)$ identified as the best-performing smartphone.

Comparative Study

The proposed weighted distance measure is validated by presenting specific numerical examples and contrasting them with the existing measures to demonstrate its superiority. A comprehensive analysis of PFS distance measures is presented in Table 6. The results show that existing distance measures yield the same conclusion as the proposed measure, with M_{Models} $(A_1^\diamond)$ being identified as the best smartphone. This suggests that the proposed measure is aligned with the majority and outperforms existing measures.

Conclusion

This paper introduces a new DM with a hesitancy degree for PFSs, proven to be a metric for PFSs and superior to existing measures. The proposed DM is applied

Table 6. Comparison of existing distance measures with proposed approach

Measure	Ranking
X Zhang et al. [14]	$A_1^\diamond > A_3^\diamond > A_5^\diamond > A_2^\diamond > A_4^\diamond$
P.A.Ejegwa et al. [29]	$A_1^\diamond > A_3^\diamond > A_5^\diamond > A_2^\diamond > A_4^\diamond$
M. Bhatia et al. [30]	$A_1^\diamond > A_3^\diamond > A_5^\diamond > A_2^\diamond > A_4^\diamond$
H.D.Arora et al. [31]	$A_1^\diamond > A_3^\diamond > A_5^\diamond > A_2^\diamond > A_4^\diamond$
P.A.Ejegwa [35]	$A_1^\diamond > A_3^\diamond > A_5^\diamond > A_2^\diamond > A_4^\diamond$
P.A.Ejegwa et al. [36]	$A_1^\diamond > A_3^\diamond > A_5^\diamond > A_2^\diamond > A_4^\diamond$
Proposed DM	$A_1^\diamond > A_3^\diamond > A_5^\diamond > A_2^\diamond > A_4^\diamond$

to find the best smartphones for white-collar workers using the TOPSIS method, demonstrating its suitability for various real-life applications. In the future, the proposed DM can address complex MADM issues, clustering problems, and image processing. Moreover, it can encompass Fermatean fuzzy sets and q-ROF sets. The paper's results demonstrate the applicability of the proposed DM to a wide variety of genuine problems that occur in daily life. And provide a reliable tool for handling uncertainty. The proposed approach is expected to contribute to the development of more accurate and making decisions in the future. This study highlights the potential of PFSs and DMs as powerful tools for handling uncertainty and opens up opportunities for further research in this area.

References

[1] Lotfi A Zadeh. Fuzzy sets. *Information and control*, 8(3):338–353, 1965.

[2] K Atanassov. *Intuitionistic fuzzy sets. fuzzy sets and systems* 20 (1), 87-96, 1986.

[3] Ronald R Yager. Pythagorean fuzzy subsets. In *2013 joint IFSA world congress and NAFIPS annual meeting (IFSA/NAFIPS)*, pages 57–61. IEEE, 2013.

[4] Ronald R Yager. Properties and applications of pythagorean fuzzy sets. In *Imprecision and Uncertainty in Information Representation and Processing*, pages 119–136. Springer, 2016.

[5] Harish Garg. A novel correlation coefficients between pythagorean fuzzy sets and its applications to decision-making processes. *International Journal of Intelligent Systems*, 31(12):1234–1252, 2016.

[6] Yi Liu, Jun Liu, and Ya Qin. Pythagorean fuzzy linguistic muirhead mean operators and their applications to multiattribute decision-making. *International Journal of Intelligent Systems*, 35(2):300–332, 2020.

[7] Rajkumar Verma and José M Merigó. On generalized similarity measures for pythagorean fuzzy sets and their applications to multiple attribute decision-making. *International Journal of Intelligent Systems*, 34(10):2556–2583, 2019.

[8] Harish Garg. A new generalized pythagorean fuzzy information aggregation using einstein operations and its application to decision making. *International Journal of Intelligent Systems*, 31(9):886–920, 2016.

[9] Peijia Ren, Zeshui Xu, and Xunjie Gou. Pythagorean fuzzy todim approach to multi-criteria decision making. *Applied Soft Computing*, 42:246–259, 2016.

[10] Xiaolu Zhang. Multicriteria pythagorean fuzzy decision analysis: A hierarchical qualiflex approach with the closeness index-based ranking methods. *Information Sciences*, 330:104–124, 2016.

[11] PA Ejegwa. Generalized tri parametric correlation coefficient for pythagorean fuzzy sets with application to mcdm problems. *Granular Computing*, 6(3):557–566, 2021.

[12] Ching Lai Hwang and Kwangsun Yoon. Methods for multiple attribute decision making. In *Multiple attribute decision making*, pages 58–191. Springer, 1981.

[13] Ching Lai Hwang, Young Jou Lai, and TingYun Liu. A new approach for multiple objective decision making. *Computers & operations research*, 20(8):889–899, 1993.

[14] Xiaolu Zhang and Zeshui Xu. Extension of topsis to multiple criteria decision making with pythagorean fuzzy sets. *International Journal of Intelligent Systems*, 29(12):1061–1078, 2014.

[15] Xindong Peng, Huiyong Yuan, and Yong Yang. Pythagorean fuzzy information measures and their applications. *International Journal of Intelligent Systems*, 32(10):991–1029, 2017.

[16] Xindong Peng. New similarity measure and distance measure for pythagorean fuzzy set. *Complex & Intelligent Systems*, 5(2):101–111, 2019.

[17] Zahid Hussian and Miin Shen Yang. Distance and similarity measures of pythagorean fuzzy sets based on the hausdorff metric with application to fuzzy topsis. *International Journal of Intelligent Systems*, 34(10):2633–2654, 2019.

[18] Zengxian Li and Mao Lu. Some novel similarity and distance measures of pythagorean fuzzy sets and their applications. *Journal of Intelligent & Fuzzy Systems*, 37(2):1781–1799, 2019.

[19] Fuyuan Xiao and Weiping Ding. Divergence measure of pythagorean fuzzy sets and its application in medical diagnosis. *Applied Soft Computing*, 79:254–267, 2019.

[20] PA Ejegwa and JA Awolola. Novel distance measures for pythagorean fuzzy sets with applications to pattern recognition problems. *Granular Computing*, 6(1):181–189, 2021.

[21] Ting Yu Chen. New chebyshev distance measures for pythagorean fuzzy sets with applications to multiple criteria decision analysis using an extended electre approach. *Expert Systems with Applications*, 147:113164, 2020.

[22] Paul Augustine Ejegwa. Distance and similarity measures for pythagorean fuzzy sets. *Granular Computing*, 5(2):225–238, 2020.

[23] Yuanpeng He. A new distance measure of pythagorean fuzzy sets based on matrix and its application in medical diagnosis. *arXiv preprint arXiv:2102.01538*, 2021.

[24] Juthika Mahanta and Subhasis Panda. Distance measure for pythagorean fuzzy sets with varied applications. *Neural Computing and Applications*, 33(24):17161–17171, 2021.

[25] Muhammad Jabir Khan, Muhammad Irfan Ali, Poom Kumam, Wiyada Kumam, Muhammad Aslam, and Jose Carlos R Alcantud. Improved generalized dissimilarity measure-based vikor method for pythagorean fuzzy sets. *International Journal of Intelligent Systems*, 37(3):1807–1845, 2022.

[26] Abdul Haseeb Ganie. Some t-conorm-based distance measures and knowledge measures for pythagorean fuzzy sets with their application in decision-making. *Complex & Intelligent Systems*, pages 1–21, 2022.

[27] Longjun Yin, Qinghua Zhang, Fan Zhao, Qiong Mou, and Sidong Xian. A new distance measure for pythagorean fuzzy sets based on earth moverâĂŹs distance and its applications. *Journal of Intelligent & Fuzzy Systems*, (Preprint):1–14, 2022.

[28] HD Arora and Anjali Naithani. Significance of topsis approach to madm in computing exponential divergence measures for pythagorean fuzzy sets. *Decision Making: Applications in Management and Engineering*, 5(1):246–263, 2022.

[29] Paul Augustine Ejegwa, Yuming Feng, Shuyu Tang, Johnson Mobolaji Agbetayo, and Xiangguang Dai. New pythagorean fuzzy-based distance operators and their applications in pattern classification and disease diagnostic analysis. *Neural Computing and Applications*, pages 1–13, 2022.

[30] Mansi Bhatia, HD Arora, Anjali Naithani, and Surbhi Gupta. Distance measures of pythagorean fuzzy sets based on sine function in property selection under topsis approach. In *2022 12th International Conference on Cloud Computing, Data Science & Engineering (Confluence)*, pages 1–7. IEEE, 2022.

[31] HD Arora, Anjali Naithani, and Surbhi Gupta. Distance measures of pythagorean fuzzy topsis approach for online food delivery apps. *International Journal of Engineering*, 35(10):1877–1886, 2022.

[32] Ting Yu Chen. Remoteness index-based pythagorean fuzzy vikor methods with a generalized distance measure for multiple criteria decision analysis. *Information Fusion*, 41:129–150, 2018.

[33] Wenyi Zeng, Deqing Li, and Qian Yin. Distance and similarity measures of pythagorean fuzzy sets and their applications to multiple criteria group decision making. *International Journal of Intelligent Systems*, 33(11):2236–2254, 2018.

[34] Fatma Kutlu Gündoğdu and Cengiz Kahraman. Spherical fuzzy sets and spherical fuzzy topsis method. *Journal of intelligent & fuzzy systems*, 36(1):337–352, 2019.

[35] Paul Augustine Ejegwa. Modified zhang and xuâĂŹs distance measure for pythagorean fuzzy sets and its application to pattern recognition problems. *Neural Computing and Applications*, 32(14):10199–10208, 2020.

[36] Paul Augustine Ejegwa and Idoko Charles Onyeke. A robust weighted distance measure and its applications in decision-making via pythagorean fuzzy information. *Journal of the Institute of Electronics and Computer*, 3(1):87–97, 2021.

Chapter 14

Stability of General Radical Quadratic Functional Equation in Modular Spaces

Shalini Tomar*, PhD
Department of Mathematics, Kanya Mahavidyalaya Kharkhoda,
Sonipat, Haryana, India

Abstract

The goal of this chapter is to study the Generalized Hyers - Ulam - Rassias (H.U.R.) stability of general radical quadratic functional equation (RQFE)

$$\sum_{l=2}^{k} f\left(\sqrt{\tilde{s}o_1^2 + (\tilde{s}+1)o_l^2}\right) = (k-1)\tilde{s}f(o_1) + (\tilde{s}+1)\sum_{l=2}^{k} f(o_l)$$

in modular spaces using fixed point (FP) and direct method, where k is an integer greater than one and s˜ is a positive integer.

Keywords: fixed point, generalized Hyers - Ulam - Rassias stability, radical quadratic functional equation, modular spaces

AMS Subject Classification: 39B52, 39B72 and 46A80

Introduction

Foremost, let's recall the chronicle in the stability theory for functional equations (FEs). The stability problem for the FEs referring to the stability of group homo-morphisms was addressed by Ulam (1964). The Ulam's question was to an extent solved by Hyers (1941). Aoki (1950), Th.M. Rassias (1978), Gavruta (1994) and other mathematicians gradually expanded the Hyers' original result.

* Corresponding Author's Email: shalini.tomar3636@gmail.com.

In: Emerging Trends in Mathematical Sciences and Computing
Editors: B. Basu Mallik, S. Ghosh, B. Kumar Pandey et al.
ISBN: 979-8-89113-751-6

Radical FEs is one of the most frequently investigated areas within the theory of stability. Brzdek (2015) gave a general solution of the following radical F.E.

$$\mathfrak{R}(\sqrt{x^2+y^2}) = \mathfrak{R}(x) + \mathfrak{R}(y). \tag{1}$$

Every solution to (1) is labeled as a *Radical Quadratic Function*. Specifically, a real-valued mapping $\Upsilon : \mathbb{R} \to \mathbb{R}$ satisfies (1) $\Leftrightarrow \Upsilon(r) = \mathfrak{A}(r^2)$, $r \in \mathbb{R}$, where $\mathfrak{A} : \mathbb{R} \to \mathbb{R}$ is additive. Kim et al. (2012) and Gordji and Parviz (2009) investigated the H.U.R. stability of (1). Nowadays, many articles on radical FE stability and hyperstability are covered in various fields (see in Alizadeh and Ghazanfari, 2016; El-Fassi, 2018; EL-Fassi, 2018; Gordji et al., 2012; Gordji and Parviz, 2009; Khodaei et al., 2012, and references therein).

Next, let's talk about some fundamental modular space properties and ideas. The theory of modulars on linear spaces was instituted by Nakano (1950). Koshi and Shimogaki (1961), Yamamuro (1959) and others thoroughly elaborated the corresponding theory of modular linear spaces.

Definitions (Nakano, 1950)

" Let V_m be a vector space over a field say $K \in \{\mathbb{C}, \mathbb{R}\}$. A generalized functional $\rho_m : V_m \to [0, \infty]$ is labeled as a *modular* if for arbitrary $m_1, m_2 \in V_m$, ρ_m satisfies:

MS1 $\rho_m(m_1) = 0 \Leftrightarrow m_1 = 0$,

MS2 $\rho_m(\kappa_1 m_1) = \rho_m(m_1)$, for every scalar κ_1 with $|\kappa_1| = 1$,

MS3 $\rho_m(\kappa_1 m_1 + \kappa_2 m_2) \le \rho_m(m_1) + \rho_m(m_2)$, whenever $\kappa_1, \kappa_2 \ge 0$ & $\kappa_1 + \kappa_2 = 1$.

If we replace (MS3) by

MS3* $\rho_m(\kappa_1 m_1 + \kappa_2 m_2) \le \kappa_1 \rho_m(m_1) + \kappa_2 \rho_m(m_2)$, for $\kappa_1, \kappa_2 \ge 0$ and $\kappa_1 + \kappa_2 = 1$,

then, the modular ρ_m is called *convex*. Moreover, in case we replace (MS3) by

MS3$^\blacklozenge$ $\rho_m(\kappa_1 m_1 + \kappa_2 m_2) \le \kappa_1^t \rho_m(m_1) + \kappa_2^t \rho_m(m_2)$, whenever $\kappa_1, \kappa_2 \ge 0$; $t \in (0, 1]$ and $\kappa_1^t + \kappa_2^t = 1$,

then, the modular ρ_m is labeled as *t-convex*. Thus, we can assert that *convex modulars* are *1-convex modulars*. The corresponding *modular space*, denoted by V_{ρ_m} is defined as

$$V_{\rho_m} = \{x \in V_m : \rho_m(\lambda x) \to 0 \ as\ \lambda \to 0\}."$$

Remarks (Nakano, 1950)

{R1} "For a convex modular ρ_m, we have $\rho_m(x) \leq \delta\rho_m\left(\frac{x}{\delta}\right)$ for all $x \in V_{\rho_m}$, where $0 < \delta \leq 1$.

{R2} The modular function ρ_m has *Fatou property* if $\rho_m(x) \leq \lim_{n\to\infty} inf \rho_m(x_n)$ whenever sequence $\{x_n\}$ is $\rho_m - convergent$ to x i.e. $\rho_m(x_n - x) \to 0$ as $n \to \infty$.

{R3} $\{x_n\}$ is labeled as $\rho_m - Cauchy$ if for any $\varepsilon > 0$, we have $\rho_m(x_n - x_m) < \varepsilon$ for sufficiently large $m, n \in \mathbb{N}$. And if every $\rho_m - Cauchy$ sequence is $\rho_m - convergent$ then, the modular space V_{ρ_m} is labeled as $\rho_m - complete$.

{R4} A modular function ρ_m is labeled to obey $\Delta_\alpha - condition$ $(\alpha \in \mathbb{N}, \alpha \geq 2)$ if there exists $\kappa > 0$ such that $\rho_m(\alpha x) \leq \kappa\rho_m(x)$, for all $x \in V_{\rho_m}$.

{R5} Given a modular space V_{ρ_m}, a non-empty set $C \subset V_{\rho_m}$ along with a mapping $\top : C \to C$, the orbit of $\top$ around point x $\in C$ is:

$$O_\top = \{x, \top x, \top^2 x, \ldots\}.$$

Further, the orbital diameter is the quantity $\delta_{\rho_m}(x) = sup\{\rho_m(r - s) : r, s \in O_\top\}$. Finally, if $\delta_{\rho_m}(x) < \infty$ then we say $\top$ has a bounded orbit at x."

Example

Park et al. (2019) gave the following example:

"Let $\psi : [0, \infty) \to \mathbb{R}$ be expounded as:

$$\psi(0) = 0 \ \& \ \psi(t) > 0, \forall\, t > 0 \text{ and } \lim_{t\to\infty} \psi(t) = \infty.$$

If ψ is continuous, non-decreasing and convex, then it is labeled as an *Orlicz function*. For example, we can take $\psi(t) = e^{t^2} - 1$. For some measure space (X, Σ, μ), assume that $L^0(\mu)$ is the set of all measurable functions on X. For each $f \in L^0(\mu)$, expound

$$\rho_\psi(f) = \int_X \psi(|f|)d\mu.$$

Then, ρ_ψ is a modular and the corresponding modular space is labeled as an *Orlicz space* and denoted by

$$L_\psi = \{f \in L^0(\mu) | \rho_\psi(\lambda f) \to 0 \ as \ \lambda \to 0\}.$$

Here, we can assert that L_ψ is ρ_ψ *-complete*."

In this chapter, we will prove the Generalised H.U.R. Stability of following RQFE

$$\sum_{l=2}^{k} f(\sqrt{\tilde{s}o_1^2+(\tilde{s}+1)o_l^2}) = (k-1)\tilde{s}f(o_1)+(\tilde{s}+1)\sum_{l=2}^{k} f(o_l) \tag{2}$$

in modular spaces. It is fairly obvious that $f(\sqrt{o}) = co^2$ is solution of (2), therefore it is natural to label general RQFE (2) as a cubic reciprocal F.E.

Stability of (2) in Modular Spaces Using Direct Method (Without Δ_2 - Condition)

Throughout this chapter, we assume V and V_m to be a linear space, ρ_m be a convex modular which satisfies Fatou property and V_{ρ_m} as ρ_m-complete convex modular space. Also, let us define the difference operator $D_k f(o_1,o_2,....,o_k) : V \to V_m$ as

$$D_k f(o_1,o_2,...,o_k) =$$

$$\sum_{l=2}^{k} f(\sqrt{\tilde{s}o_1^2+(\tilde{s}+1)o_l^2}) - (k-1)\tilde{s}f(o_1) - (\tilde{s}+1)\sum_{l=2}^{k} f(o_l), \tag{3}$$

for all $o_i \in V$; i = 1,..., k.

1. Theorem

Let $\Psi : V^k \to [0,\infty)$ be a mapping which satisfy the inequality

$$\psi(o_1,...,o_n) = \sum_{l=1}^{\infty} \frac{1}{\tilde{s}^l} \Psi(\sqrt{\tilde{s}}^{l-1} o_1,...,\sqrt{\tilde{s}}^{l-1} o_k) < \infty, \tag{4}$$

$\forall\, o_i \in V;\ i = 1\ to\ k$. Assume that $f : V \to V_{\rho_m}$ be a mapping which maps zero to zero and obeys following inequality

$$\rho_m(D_k f(o_1,o_2,...,o_k)) \le \Psi(o_1,o_2,...,o_k), \tag{5}$$

for all $v_i \in V;\ i = 1\ to\ k$. Then, there exists a unique radical quadratic mapping say $Q_{rad} : V \to V_{\rho_m}$ which obeys RQFE (2) and

$$\rho_m(f(o) - Q_{rad}(o)) \le \frac{\psi(o,o,....,o)}{\bar{k}}, \tag{6}$$

where $\bar{k}$ = k-1 and Q_{rad} is defined as

$$Q_{rad}(o) = \rho_m - \lim_{r\to\infty} \frac{1}{\tilde{s}q^r} f(\sqrt{\tilde{s}}^r o),$$

for every $o \in V$.

Proof- Existence: Setting o_i as o ; i = 1,2,3,...,k in (5), we get

$$\rho_m(\bar{k}f(\sqrt{\tilde{s}}o) - \bar{k}\tilde{s}f(o)) \leq \Psi(o,o,...,o).$$

Since ρ_m is convex, we obtain,

$$\begin{aligned}\rho_m\Big(\frac{1}{\tilde{s}}f(\sqrt{\tilde{s}}o) - f(o)\Big) = \rho_m\Big(\frac{\bar{k}}{\tilde{s}\bar{k}}f(\sqrt{\tilde{s}}o) - \frac{\bar{k}}{\bar{k}}f(o)\Big) \\ = \rho_m\Big(\frac{1}{\tilde{s}\bar{k}}(\bar{k}f(\sqrt{\tilde{s}}o) - \bar{k}\tilde{s}f(o) \\ + \Big(\frac{\tilde{s}\bar{k}-1}{\tilde{s}\bar{k}}\Big)0\Big) \\ \leq \frac{1}{\bar{k}\tilde{s}}\Psi(o,o,...,o), \end{aligned} \tag{7}$$

$\forall\, o \in V$. Replacing o with $\sqrt{\tilde{s}}o$ in (7) we arrive at,

$$\rho_m\Big(\frac{1}{\tilde{s}}f(\tilde{s}o) - f(\sqrt{\tilde{s}}o)\Big) \leq \frac{1}{\bar{k}\tilde{s}}\Psi(\sqrt{\tilde{s}}o, \sqrt{\tilde{s}}o, ..., \sqrt{\tilde{s}}o),$$

for each $o \in V$. Moreover,

$$\begin{aligned}\rho_m\Big(\frac{1}{\tilde{s}^2}f(\tilde{s}o) - \frac{1}{\tilde{s}}f(\sqrt{\tilde{s}}o)\Big) = \rho_m\Big(\frac{1}{\tilde{s}}\Big(\frac{1}{\tilde{s}}f(\tilde{s}o) - f(\sqrt{\tilde{s}}o)\Big)\Big) \\ \leq \frac{1}{\bar{k}\tilde{s}^2}\Psi(\sqrt{\tilde{s}}o, \sqrt{\tilde{s}}o, ..., \sqrt{\tilde{s}}o),\end{aligned} \tag{8}$$

for each $o \in V$.
Next, by using (7) and (8), we can say that

$$\begin{aligned}\rho_m\Big(\frac{1}{\tilde{s}^2}f(\tilde{s}o) - f(o)\Big) = \rho_m\Big(\frac{1}{\tilde{s}}\Big(\frac{1}{\tilde{s}}f(\tilde{s}o) - f(\sqrt{\tilde{s}}o)\Big) + \frac{1}{\tilde{s}}\Big(f(\sqrt{\tilde{s}}o) - \tilde{s}f(o)\Big)\Big) \\ \leq \frac{1}{\bar{k}\tilde{s}}\Big[\Psi(o,...,o,..,o) + \frac{1}{\tilde{s}}\Psi(\sqrt{\tilde{s}}o,....,\sqrt{\tilde{s}}o)\Big],\end{aligned} \tag{9}$$

for every $o \in V$.
Therefore by induction, we can assert that

$$\rho_m\Big(\frac{1}{\tilde{s}^m} f(\sqrt{\tilde{s}}^m o) - f(o)\Big) \leq \sum_{l=1}^{m} \frac{1}{\bar{k}\tilde{s}^l} \Psi(\sqrt{\tilde{s}}^{l-1} o, \ldots, \sqrt{\tilde{s}}^{l-1} o), \tag{10}$$

for all $o \in V$. Let r and s be non-negative integers with $r > s$, then by (10), we obtain

$$\begin{aligned} \rho_m\Big(\frac{1}{\tilde{s}^r} f(\sqrt{\tilde{s}}^r o) - \frac{1}{\tilde{s}^s} f(\sqrt{\tilde{s}}^s o)\Big) &= \rho_m\Big(\frac{1}{\tilde{s}^s}\Big(\frac{1}{\tilde{s}^{r-s}} f(\sqrt{\tilde{s}}^{r-s}\sqrt{\tilde{s}}^s o) - f(\sqrt{\tilde{s}}^s o)\Big)\Big) \\ &\leq \sum_{l=s+1}^{r} \frac{1}{\bar{k}\tilde{s}^l} \Psi(\sqrt{\tilde{s}}^{l-1} o, .., \sqrt{\tilde{s}}^{l-1} o), \end{aligned} \tag{11}$$

for all $o \in V$. Thus (4) and (11) yield that sequence

$$\{\frac{1}{\tilde{s}^r} f(\sqrt{\tilde{s}}^r o)\}$$

is a $\rho_m - \textit{Cauchy}$ in V_{ρ_m} which directly makes the sequence $\rho_m - \textit{convergent}$ in V_{ρ_m}. Thus, we can define a mapping $Q_{rad}(o) : V \to V_{\rho_m}$ as

$$Q_{rad}(o) = \rho_m - \lim_{r\to\infty} \frac{1}{\tilde{s}^r} f(\sqrt{\tilde{s}}^r o), \tag{12}$$

$\forall o \in V$. Next, we claim that

$$Q_{rad}(\sqrt{\tilde{s}} o) = \tilde{s} Q_{rad}(o) \tag{13}$$

Consider,

$$\begin{aligned} \rho_m\Big(\frac{Q_{rad}(\sqrt{\tilde{s}}o) - \tilde{s}Q_{rad}(o)}{\tilde{s}^3}\Big) &= \rho_m\Big(\frac{1}{\tilde{s}^3}\Big(Q_{rad}(\sqrt{\tilde{s}}o) - \frac{1}{\tilde{s}^r} f(\sqrt{\tilde{s}}^{r+1} o)\Big) \\ &\quad + \frac{1}{\tilde{s}^2}\Big(\frac{1}{\tilde{s}^{r+1}} f(\sqrt{\tilde{s}}^{r+1} o) - Q_{rad}(o)\Big)\Big) \\ &\leq \frac{1}{\tilde{s}^3}\rho_m\Big(\Big(Q_{rad}(\sqrt{\tilde{s}}o) - \frac{1}{\tilde{s}^r} f(\sqrt{\tilde{s}}^{r+1} o)\Big) \\ &\quad + \frac{1}{\tilde{s}^2}\rho_m\Big(\frac{1}{\tilde{s}^{r+1}} f(\sqrt{\tilde{s}}^{r+1} o) - Q_{rad}(o)\Big)\Big), \end{aligned} \tag{14}$$

for every $o \in V$. Following from (12), the right hand side of (14) tends to 0 as $r \to \infty$, which proves (13).

Next, since $\sum_{l=1}^{r}\frac{1}{\tilde{s}^l}+\frac{1}{\tilde{s}}<1$, thus we have

$$\begin{aligned}
\rho_m(Q_{rad}(o)-f(o)) &= \rho_m\Big(\sum_{l=1}^{r}\frac{f(\sqrt{\tilde{s}}^{l}o)-\tilde{s}f(\sqrt{\tilde{s}}^{l-1}o)}{\tilde{s}^l}+Q_{rad}(o)-\frac{f(\sqrt{\tilde{s}}^{r}o)}{\tilde{s}^r}\Big)\\
&= \rho_m\Big(\sum_{l=1}^{r}\frac{f(\sqrt{\tilde{s}}^{l}o)-\tilde{s}f(\sqrt{\tilde{s}}^{l-1}o)}{\tilde{s}^l}+\frac{1}{\tilde{s}}(Q_{rad}(\sqrt{\tilde{s}}o)-\frac{f(\sqrt{\tilde{s}}^{r}o)}{\tilde{s}^{r-1}})\Big)\\
&\le \sum_{l=1}^{r}\frac{1}{\tilde{s}^l}\rho_m(f(\sqrt{\tilde{s}}^{l}o)-\tilde{s}f(\sqrt{\tilde{s}}^{l-1}o))\\
&\quad +\frac{1}{\tilde{s}}\rho_m(Q_{rad}(\sqrt{\tilde{s}}o)-\frac{f(\sqrt{\tilde{s}}^{r-1}(\sqrt{\tilde{s}}o))}{\tilde{s}^{r-1}})\\
&\le \sum_{l=1}^{r}\frac{1}{\tilde{s}^l\bar{k}}\Psi(\sqrt{\tilde{s}}^{l-1}o,\ldots..,\sqrt{\tilde{s}}^{l-1}o))\\
&\quad +\frac{1}{\tilde{s}}\rho_m(Q_{rad}(\sqrt{\tilde{s}}o)-\frac{f(\sqrt{\tilde{s}}^{r-1}(\sqrt{\tilde{s}}o))}{\tilde{s}^{r-1}}).
\end{aligned} \tag{15}$$

Thus, by letting $r\to\infty$ in (14), we get (6).
Next, for all $i=1,2,\ldots,k$ replace o_i by $(\sqrt{\tilde{s}}^{(l-1)}o_i)$ in (5), to get

$$\begin{aligned}
\rho_m\Big(\frac{1}{\tilde{s}^l}D_kf(\sqrt{\tilde{s}}^{(l-1)}o_1,..,\sqrt{\tilde{s}}^{(l-1)}o_k)\Big) &\le \frac{1}{\tilde{s}^l}\rho_m(D_kf(\sqrt{\tilde{s}}^{(l-1)}o_1,\ldots,\sqrt{\tilde{s}}^{(l-1)}o_k)\\
&\le \frac{1}{\tilde{s}^l}\Psi(\sqrt{\tilde{s}}^{(l-1)}o_1,\ldots,\sqrt{\tilde{s}}^{(l-1)}o_k)\\
&\to 0 \quad as \quad l\to\infty,
\end{aligned} \tag{16}$$

for all $o_i\in V$; $i=1,2,\ldots,k$. Thus it follows that $Q_{rad}(o)$ is a quadratic radical mapping.

Uniqueness: Lastly, to ratify the oneness of Q_{rad}, let us assume that Q'_{rad} is one more quadratic radical mapping which also obeys (6).
Then, we can write

$$\begin{aligned}
\rho_m\Big(\frac{Q'_{rad}(o)-Q_{rad}(o)}{2}\Big) &= \rho_m\Big(\frac{1}{2}\Big(\frac{Q'_{rad}(\sqrt{\tilde{s}}^{j}o)}{\tilde{s}^i}-\frac{f(\sqrt{\tilde{s}}^{j}o)}{\tilde{s}^i}\Big)\\
&\quad +\frac{1}{2}\Big(\frac{f(\sqrt{\tilde{s}}^{j}o)}{\tilde{s}^i}-\frac{Q_{rad}(\sqrt{\tilde{s}}^{j}o)}{\tilde{s}^i}\Big)\Big)
\end{aligned}$$

$$\leq \frac{1}{2}\rho_m\Big(\frac{Q'_{rad}(\sqrt{\tilde{s}}^{j} o)}{\tilde{s}^{i}} - \frac{f(\sqrt{\tilde{s}}^{j} o)}{\tilde{s}^{i}}\Big) + \frac{1}{2}\rho_m\Big(\frac{f(\sqrt{\tilde{s}}^{j} o)}{\tilde{s}^{i}} - \frac{Q_{rad}(\sqrt{\tilde{s}}^{j} o)}{\tilde{s}^{i}}\Big)$$

$$\leq \frac{1}{2\tilde{s}^{i}}\rho_m(Q'_{rad}(\sqrt{\tilde{s}}^{j} o) - f(2\tilde{s}^{i} o)) + \frac{1}{2\tilde{s}^{i}}\rho_m(f(\sqrt{\tilde{s}}^{j} o) - Q_{rad}(\sqrt{\tilde{s}}^{j} o))$$

$$\leq \frac{1}{\tilde{s}^{i}\bar{k}}\psi(\sqrt{\tilde{s}}^{j} o, \sqrt{\tilde{s}}^{j} o, ..., \sqrt{\tilde{s}}^{j} o)$$
$$= \sum_{l=i+1}^{\infty} \frac{1}{\tilde{s}^{l}\bar{k}}\Psi(\sqrt{\tilde{s}}^{(l-1)} o, ..., \sqrt{\tilde{s}}^{(l-1)} o)$$
$$\to 0 \quad as \qquad l \to \infty. \tag{17}$$

This implies that $Q'_{rad} = Q_{rad}$, which completes the proof.
Next we obtain following corollaries from Theorem 2.1 concerning the H.U. stability and H.U.R. stability respectively

2. Corollary

Assume V as a linear space and ρ_m as a convex modular with V_{ρ_m} as a ρ_m-complete modular space. Let $f : V \to V_{\rho_m}$ be a mapping so that

$$\rho_m(D_k f(o_1, o_2, ..., o_{k-1}, o_k)) \leq \varepsilon, \tag{18}$$

with f(0) = 0, $\forall\, o_i \in V;\ i = 1 \ to \ k$. Then, there occurs a unique radical quadratic mapping $Q_{rad} : V \to V_{\rho_m}$ which obeys RQFE (2) and

$$\rho_m(f(o) - Q_{rad}(o)) \leq \frac{\varepsilon}{\bar{k}(q-1)}, \tag{19}$$

for each $o \in V$.

Proof: The claim can be easily reproduced by replacing $\Psi = \varepsilon$ in Theorem 2.1.

3. Corollary

Assume V as a normed linear space, ρ_m as a convex modular, V_{ρ_m} as ρ_m-complete modular space, $\delta > 0$ & $0 < p < 2$ be real numbers. Also, consider $f : V \to V_{\rho_m}$ as a mapping with f(0) = 0 and

$$\rho_m(D_k f(o_1, o_2, ..., o_k)) \leq \delta \sum_{i=1}^{k} (||o_i||_{\beta}^{p}), \tag{20}$$

for all $o_i \in V$. Then, there occurs one and only one radical quadratic mapping $Q_{rad} : V \to V_{\rho_m}$ satisfying RQFE (2) with

$$\rho_m(f(o) - Q_{rad}(o)) \leq \frac{k\delta}{\bar{k}(\tilde{s} - \tilde{s}^{p/2})} ||o||_{\beta}^{p}, \tag{21}$$

$\forall o \in V$.

Proof: Proof can be easily reproduced by replacing $\Psi = \delta \sum_{i=1}^{k} (||o_i||_{\beta}^{p})$ in Theorem 2.1.

Stability of (2) in Modular Spaces Using FP Method

In this segment, we consider the stability of the RQFE (2) using FP method. To continue with the proof, let us recall a lemma proved by Khamsi (2008).

Lemma (Khamsi, 2008)

"Let V_{ρ_m} be a modular space whose induced modular satisfy Fatou property and also $C \subset V_{\rho_m}$ be a $\rho_m - complete$ subset. If $T : C \to C$ is a $\rho_m - contraction$ i.e. there is a constant $k \in [0, 1)$ such that

$$\rho_m(Tx - Ty) \leq k\rho_m(x - y), \quad \forall x, y \in C,$$

and T has a bounded orbit at a point $x_0 \in C$, then the sequence $\{T^n x_0\}$ is $\rho_m - convergent$ to a point $c \in C$."

4. Theorem

Let $\Psi : V \to [0,\infty)$ be a mapping which satisfy

$$\lim_{l\to\infty} \frac{1}{\tilde{s}^l}\Psi(\sqrt{\tilde{s}}^l o_1, \sqrt{\tilde{s}}^l o_2, ..., \sqrt{\tilde{s}}^l o_k) = 0 \tag{22}$$

and

$$\Psi(\sqrt{\tilde{s}}o_1, \sqrt{\tilde{s}}o_2, ..., \sqrt{\tilde{s}}o_n) \leq \tilde{s}L\Psi(o_1, o_2, ..., o_n), \tag{23}$$

$\forall\, o_i \in V$ where i varies from 1 to k, with $0 < L < 1$. Assume that $f : V \to V_{\rho_m}$ satisfies (5) for every $o_i \in V$ where i varies from 1 to k and $f(0) = 0$. Then, there occurs one and only one mapping $Q_{rad} : V \to V_{\rho_m}$ which obeys

$$\rho_m(Q_{rad}(o) - f(o)) \leq \frac{1}{(1-L)\bar{k}\tilde{s}}\Psi(o,o,..,o), \tag{24}$$

$\forall\, o \in V$ with $\bar{k} = k - 1$.

Proof: Let

$$\Omega = \{h : V \to V_{\rho_m}, g(0) = 0\}$$

and characterize the function $\bar{\rho_m}$ on Ω along following lines,

$$\bar{\rho_m}(h) = inf\{\kappa > 0 : \rho_m(h(o)) \leq \kappa\Psi(o,o,...,o), \forall o \in V\}.$$

We can easily show that $\bar{\rho_m}$ is a convex modular on Ω. It is simple to justify that $\bar{\rho_m}$ obeys the properties (MS1) & (MS2) of a modular. Next, let $\varepsilon > 0$ be given and there exists real constants $\kappa_1 > 0$ and $\kappa_2 > 0$ so as

$$\bar{\rho_m}(g) \leq \kappa_1 \leq \bar{\rho_m}(g) + \varepsilon, \qquad \bar{\rho_m}(h) \leq \kappa_2 \leq \bar{\rho_m}(h) + \varepsilon.$$

Consequently, we have

$$\rho_m(g(o)) \leq \kappa_1\Psi(o,...,o,...,o), \qquad \rho_m(h(o)) \leq \kappa_2\Psi(o,...,o,...,o),$$

for all $o \in V$. Thus, if r + s = 1 with r, s ≥ 0, then we get

$\rho_m(\mathrm{r}g(o)+\mathrm{s}\,h(o)) \leq \mathrm{r}\rho_m(g(o))+\mathrm{s}\,\rho_m(h(o)) \leq (\kappa_1\mathrm{r}+\kappa_2\mathrm{s}\,)\Psi(o,o,...,o),$
so that

$$\bar{\rho_m}(\mathrm{r}g+\mathrm{s}\,h) \leq \mathrm{r}\bar{\rho_m}(g) + \mathrm{s}\,\bar{\rho_m}(h) + (\mathrm{r}+\mathrm{s}\,)\varepsilon,$$

that is,

$$\bar{\rho_m}(\mathrm{r}g+\mathrm{s}\,h) \leq \mathrm{r}\bar{\rho_m}(g)+\mathrm{s}\,\bar{\rho_m}(h),$$

$\forall\, g,h \in \Omega$.

Hence, $\bar{\rho_m}$ is convex modular on Ω.
Now, we show that the corresponding modular space $\Omega_{\bar{\rho_m}}$ is $\bar{\rho_m}$-complete. Let $\{h_n\}$ be $\bar{\rho_m}-$ Cauchy sequence in $\Omega_{\bar{\rho_m}}$ and $\varepsilon > 0$ be given, then $\exists\ n_0 \in \mathbb{Z}^+$ such that

$$\bar{\rho_m}(h_n - h_m) < \varepsilon,$$

$\forall m, n \geq n_0$. Considering the definition, we get

$$\rho_m(h_n(o) - h_m(o)) \leq \varepsilon\Psi(o, o, ..., o), \tag{25}$$

$\forall\ o \in V$ and $m, n \geq n_0$. Hence, sequence $\{h_n(o)\}$ is ρ_m-Cauchy in V_{ρ_m}. For this reason,

$$V_{\rho_m} \text{ is } \rho_m- \text{ complete} \Rightarrow \{h_n(o)\} \text{ is } \rho_m-\text{convergent in } V_{\rho_m},$$

$\forall o \in V$. Thus, we can set a mapping $h : V \to V_{\rho_m}$ as

$$h(o) = \lim_{n\to\infty} h_n(o), \tag{26}$$

for all $o \in V$. Next, since ρ_m satisfies the Fatou property, thus by (25)

$$\rho_m(h_n(o) - h(o)) \leq \lim_{m\to\infty} inf \rho_m(h_n(o) - h_m(o)) \leq \varepsilon\Psi(o, o, ..., o). \tag{27}$$

for $n \geq n_0$. So,

$$\bar{\rho_m}(h_n - h) \leq \varepsilon, \tag{28}$$

for all $n \geq n_0$. Thus, $\{h_n\}$ is $\bar{\rho_m}$-convergent, which implies that $\Omega_{\bar{\rho_m}}$ is $\bar{\rho_m}$-complete.
We next demonstrate that $\bar{\rho_m}$ fulfills the Fatou property. Consider a sequence say $\{h_n\}$ in $\Omega_{\bar{\rho_m}}$, which is $\bar{\rho_m}$- convergent to $h \in \Omega_{\bar{\rho_m}}$. For given $\varepsilon > 0$ and each $n \in \mathbb{N}$, let κ_n be a constant so as

$$\bar{\rho_m}(h_n) \leq \kappa_n \leq \bar{\rho_m}(h_n) + \varepsilon. \tag{29}$$

Thus we have,

$$\rho_m(g_n(o)) \leq \kappa_n\Psi(o, o, ..., o), \tag{30}$$

$\forall o \in V$. Now since, ρ_m obeys the Fatou property, therefore

$$\begin{aligned}\rho_m(h(o)) \leq \lim_{n\to\infty} inf \rho_m(h_n(o)) &\leq \lim_{n\to\infty} inf \kappa_n\Psi(o, o, ..., o) \\ &\leq [\lim_{n\to\infty} inf \bar{\rho_m}(h_n) + \varepsilon]\Psi(o, o, ..., o)\end{aligned} \tag{31}$$

Hence,

$$\bar{\rho_m}(h) \leq \lim_{n\to\infty} inf \bar{\rho_m}(h_n) + \varepsilon.$$

Therefore, $\bar{\rho_m}$ obeys the Fatou property.
Next, consider $\top : \Omega_{\bar{\rho_m}} \to \Omega_{\bar{\rho_m}}$ defined as:

$$\top h(o) = \frac{1}{\tilde{s}} h(\sqrt{\tilde{s}}o),$$

for all $o \in V$ and $h \in \Omega_{\bar{\rho_m}}$. Let $g, h \in \Omega_{\bar{\rho_m}}$ and $\kappa \in [0, \infty]$ be an undetermined constant with $\bar{\rho_m}(g-h) \leq \kappa$. Using the formulation of $\bar{\rho_m}$, we have

$$\rho_m(g(o) - h(o)) \leq \kappa\Psi(o, o, ..., o), \qquad \forall\, o \in V.$$

So that

$$\begin{aligned} \rho_m(\frac{1}{\tilde{s}} h(\sqrt{\tilde{s}}o) - \frac{1}{\tilde{s}} g(\sqrt{\tilde{s}}o)) &\leq \frac{1}{\tilde{s}} \rho_m(h(\sqrt{\tilde{s}}o) - g(\sqrt{\tilde{s}}o)) \\ &\leq \frac{1}{\tilde{s}} \kappa\Psi(\sqrt{\tilde{s}}o, \sqrt{\tilde{s}}o, ..., \sqrt{\tilde{s}}o) \\ &\leq \kappa L\Psi(o, o, ..., o), \end{aligned} \tag{32}$$

for all $o \in V$. Hence,

$$\bar{\rho_m}(\top h - \top g) \leq L\bar{\rho_m}(h-g),$$

for all $g, h \in \Omega_{\bar{\rho_m}}$, thus we get that, $\top$ is a $\bar{\rho_m}$-contraction.
Following that, we claim that orbit of $\top$ at f is bounded. For this, using (10) from Theorem 2.1, we can say

$$\begin{aligned} \rho_m\Big(\frac{1}{\tilde{s}^m} f(\sqrt{\tilde{s}}^m o) - f(o)\Big) &\leq \sum_{l=1}^{m} \frac{1}{\bar{k}\tilde{s}^l} \Psi(\sqrt{\tilde{s}}^{l-1} o, ..., \sqrt{\tilde{s}}^{l-1} o) \\ &\leq \frac{1}{L\bar{k}\tilde{s}} \Psi(o, o, ..., o) \sum_{l=1}^{m} L^l \\ &\leq \frac{1}{(1-L)\bar{k}\tilde{s}} \Psi(o, o, ..., o), \forall o \in V. \end{aligned} \tag{33}$$

It follows from inequality (33) that,

$$
\begin{aligned}
\rho_m\Big(\frac{1}{\tilde{s}^m}f(\sqrt{\tilde{s}}^m o)-\frac{1}{\tilde{s}^n}f(\sqrt{\tilde{s}}^n o)\Big)
&=\rho_m\Big(\frac{1}{\tilde{s}^n}\Big(\frac{1}{\tilde{s}^{m-n}}f(\sqrt{\tilde{s}}^{m-n}\sqrt{\tilde{s}}^n o)-f(\sqrt{\tilde{s}}^n o)\Big)\\
&\leq\frac{1}{\tilde{s}^n}\rho_m\Big(\Big(\frac{1}{\tilde{s}^{m-n}}f(\sqrt{\tilde{s}}^{m-n}\sqrt{\tilde{s}}^n o)-f(\sqrt{\tilde{s}}^n o)\Big)\\
&\leq\frac{1}{\tilde{s}^n}\sum_{l=n+1}^{m}\frac{1}{\bar{k}\tilde{s}^l}\Psi(\sqrt{\tilde{s}}^{l-1}o,..,\sqrt{\tilde{s}}^{l-1}o)\\
&\leq\frac{1}{(1-L)\bar{k}s^{\tilde{n+1}}}\Psi(o,o,...,o),
\end{aligned}
\tag{34}
$$

for all $o\in V$ and $m,n\in\mathbb{N}$ with $m>n$. Thus, by the definition of $\bar{\rho_m}$, we assert

$$
\bar{\rho_m}(\top^m f-\top^k f)\leq\frac{\kappa}{(1-L)\bar{k}\tilde{s}}<\infty.
$$

This suggests that an orbit of $\top$ at f is bounded. From Lemma 3.1 assert that, the sequence $\{\top^m f\}$ $\bar{\rho_m}$-converges to $Q_{rad}\in\Omega_{\bar{\rho_m}}$.
Now, using $\bar{\rho_m}$-contractivity of $\top$, we can say

$$
\bar{\rho_m}(\top Q_{rad}-\top^{m+1}f)\leq L\bar{\rho_m}(Q_{rad}-\top^m f).
$$

Taking the limit $m\to\infty$ and using the Fatou property of $\bar{\rho_m}$, we get that

$$
\begin{aligned}
\bar{\rho_m}(\top Q_{rad}-Q_{rad})&\leq\lim_{m\to\infty}inf\,\bar{\rho_m}(\top Q_{rad}-\top^{(m+1)}f)\\
&\leq L\lim_{m\to\infty}inf\,\bar{\rho_m}(Q_{rad}-\top^m f)=0.
\end{aligned}
$$

Hence, Q_{rad} is a fixed point of $\top$. Letting o_i as $(\sqrt{\tilde{s}}^{(l-1)}o_i)$ in (5), we get

$$
\begin{aligned}
\rho_m\Big(\frac{1}{\tilde{s}^l}D_k f(\sqrt{\tilde{s}}^{(l-1)}o_1,...,\sqrt{\tilde{s}}^{(l-1)}o_k)\Big)&\leq\frac{1}{\tilde{s}^l}\Psi(\sqrt{\tilde{s}}^{(l-1)}o_1,...,\sqrt{\tilde{s}}^{(l-1)}o_k)\\
&\to 0\qquad as\qquad l\to\infty,
\end{aligned}
\tag{35}
$$

for all $o_i\in V; i=1,2,3...,k$. Then it follows that $Q_{rad}(o)$ is a quadratic radical mapping.

To prove the uniqueness of Q_{rad} we can present the identical argument that was employed to prove Theorem 2.1.

Conclusion

In this chapter, we managed to prove the stability of general RQFE in modular spaces. Main tools used in the investigation are fixed-point and direct methods. This work may be further generalized in different spaces.

References

Alizadeh, Z. and Ghazanfari, A. (2016). On the stability of a radical cubic functional equation in quasi-β-spaces. *Journal of fixed point theory and applications*, 4(18):843–853.

Aoki, T. (1950). On the stability of the linear transformation in banach spaces. *Journal of the Mathematical Society of Japan*, 2(1-2):64–66.

Brzdek, J. (2015). Remark 3 in: Report of meeting of 16th international conference on functional equations and inequalities. *Ann. Univ. Paedagog. Crac. Stud. Math.*, 14:163–202.

EL-Fassi, I.-I. (2018). A new type of approximation for the radical quintic functional equation in non-archimedean (2, β)-banach spaces. *Journal of Mathematical Analysis and Applications*, 457(1):322–335.

EL-Fassi, I.-I. (2018). On the general solution and hyperstability of the general radical quintic functional equation in quasi-β-banach spaces. *Journal of Mathematical Analysis and Applications*, 466(1):733–748.

Gavruta, P. (1994). A generalization of the hyers-ulam-rassias stability of approximately additive mappings. *Journal of Mathematical Analysis and Applications*, 184(3):431–436.

Gordji, M. E., Khodaei, H., Ebadian, A., and Kim, G. (2012). Nearly radical quadratic functional equations in p-2-normed spaces. *Abstract and applied analysis*, 2012.

Gordji, M. E. and Parviz, M. (2009). On the hyers-ulam stability of the functional equation $f\sqrt[2]{(x^2+y^2)} = f(x)+f(y)$. *Nonlinear functional analysis and applications*, 14:413–420.

Hyers, D. H. (1941). On the stability of the linear functional equation. *Proceedings of the National Academy of Sciences*, 27(4):222–224.

Khamsi, M. (2008). Quasicontraction mappings in modular spaces without δ_2-condition. *Fixed Point Theory and Algorithms for Sciences and Engineering*.

Khodaei, H., Gordji, M. E., Kim, S., and Cho, Y. (2012). Approximation of radical functional equations related to quadratic and quartic mappings. *Journal of mathematical analysis and applications*, 395(1):284–297.

Kim, S., Cho, Y., and Gordji, M. (2012). On the generalized Hyers-Ulam-Rassias stability problem of radical functional equations. *Journal of Inequalities and Applications*, 2012.

Koshi, S. and Shimogaki, T. (1961). On f-norms of quasi-modular spaces. *Journal of the Faculty of Science Hokkaido University. Ser. 1 Mathematics*, 15(3-4):202–218.

Nakano, H. (1950). *Modulared semi-ordered linear spaces*. Maruzen Company.

Park, C., Rassias, J., Bodaghi, A., and Kim, S. O. (2019). Approximate homomorphisms from ternary semigroups to modular spaces. *Revista de la Real Academia de Ciencias Exactas, Físicas y Naturales. Serie A. Matemáticas*, 113(3):2175–2188.

Rassias, T. M. (1978). On the stability of the linear mapping in banach spaces. *Proceedings of the American mathematical society*, 72(2):297–300.

Ulam, S. M. (1964). *Problems in Modern Mathematics*. Science Editions, John Wiley and Sons, NY, USA.

Yamamuro, S. (1959). On conjugate spaces of nakano spaces. *Transactions of the American Mathematical Society*, 90(2):291–311.

Chapter 15

Health Care Waste Recycling Technology Selection Using Fermatean Fuzzy Multi-Criteria Group Decision Making

Saima Debbarma*
Sayanta Chakraborty
Apu Kumar Saha
Department of Mathematics, National Institute of Technology Agartala, Tripura, India

Abstract

The aim of the present study is to identify the best healthcare waste recycling technique (HCWRT) for sustainable environmental development using Fermatean Fuzzy Aggregation Operator (FFAO) based multi-criteria group decision making (MCGDM). To carry out this research, FF weighted power average operator (FFWPAO) based Stepwise Weight Assessment Ratio Analysis (SWARA) and Weighted Aggregated Sum Product Assessment (WASPAS) method have been developed. To validate the applicability of the proposed integrated model, the problem of HCWRT selection has been modeled and solved. Through comparative and sensitivity analyses, the consistency and robustness of this technique have been verified. The proposed integrated technique has identified Red2Green (R2G) as the optimal HCWR alternative.

Keywords: HCWRT, Fermatean fuzzy set, FFWPAO, MCGDM

---

* Corresponding Author's Email: debbarmasaima123@gmail.com.

In: Emerging Trends in Mathematical Sciences and Computing
Editors: B. Basu Mallik, S. Ghosh, B. Kumar Pandey et al.
ISBN: 979-8-89113-751-6

Introduction

Highly contaminated human waste from hospitals and other health centers poses serious potential risks to the environment and public health (Antoniadou et al., 2021). The globalization of the medical industry has contributed to an increase in healthcare waste (HCW) production. Making HCW reusable is referred to as Healthcare Waste Recycling (HCWR) (Chakraborty and Saha, 2022a). Healthcare waste management (HCM) involves making efficient use of resources created during healthcare operations for waste disposal (Krishankumar et al., 2022). Separating HCWs that could go through a process to make them usable is essential. Determining such techniques for recycling these wastes is so crucial. Recycling HCW enables waste volume reduction while also protecting the environment. Recycling waste is one of the best strategies to manage HCW. There are few studies (Chakraborty and Saha, 2023) that have focused on identifying HCWRT. So, the problem of HCWRT selection could be viewed as a Multi-Criteria Decision Making (MCDM) problem. It has already been proved that various real-world problems can be solved by converting them to an MCDM problem. Some of those can be seen in (Soni, 2022; Choudhury et al., 2020; Simic et al., 2022; Choudhury et al., 2021; Krishankumar et al., 2022; Choudhury et al., 2022; Saha et al., 2017). Our aim is to find the optimal HCWRT to get a pollution-free, safe environment as a part of HCW management. A few HCWRTs are taken into consideration as HCWR alternatives in the current study, namely, Anaerobic Digestion (AD), Combustion (CB), Plasma Gasification Melting (PGM), and Red2Green (R2G). Uncertainty is widespread during the recycling of disposable HCWs because of different restrictions, a lack of understanding, and the unexpected nature of situations. Fuzzy set theory (FST) and its generalizations must be used in decision-making to deal with such scenarios. Uncertainty in real-world situations cannot be explained by fuzzy set theory, despite the fact that it is quite good at resolving ambiguity or partial truth problems. Atanassov (1986) developed intuitionistic fuzzy sets (IFS), which link each element to both membership degrees (MDs) and non-MDs (NMDs). Yager (2013) introduced the Pythagorean fuzzy set (PFS) to resolve ambiguity if the sum of squares of MD and NMD is less than or equal to one. Senapati and Yager (2019a) proposed the concept of FFS, where the sum of cubes of MD and NMD is constrained to one. FFSs are therefore more effective and successful than IFSs and PFSs in resolving uncertain MCDM issues due to their broader scope. Aggregation Operators (AO) are used to aggregate decisions of multiple experts. There are many operational rule-based AOs provided by researchers. Furthermore, there is a rising trend to combine AOs with FFNs to solve MCGDM difficulties. Senapati and Yager (2019b) introduced various FFAO. These AOs help in group decision making for solving various real-life decision making (Chakraborty and Saha, 2022b; Simic et al., 2022; Chakraborty and Saha, 2022c) problems. The aim of the study is to find optimal HCWRT using FFWPAO based integrated MCGDM technique.

The main contributions of the present research are given below:

a. Based on FFWPAO, two popular MCDM techniques, SWARA and WASPAS have been integrated.
b. The proposed method has been illustrated by modeling and solving the HCWRT selection problem.
c. To verify the consistency and dependability of the suggested method for environmental sustainability through HCWR, a number of comparison and sensitivity assessments have been done.

The organization of the rest of the paper is as follows: In the section "Basic Concepts" Fermatean Fuzzy Number, Score, and Accuracy Function, Operational Laws, and FFWPAO are discussed. In the section "Proposed FFAO based MCGDM", FFWPAO based SWARA and FFWPAO based WASPAS has been introduced. Section "Application of proposed FFAO based SWARA-WASPAS in HCWR" contains the application of proposed integrated SWARA-WASPAS. In the "Results and Discussions" section, Comparative Analysis with respect to existing MCDMs and Sensitivity Analysis have been carried out. The last section includes the Conclusion and Perspectives.

Basic Concepts

Here we have discussed a few concepts of FFN and its operational laws.

Fermatean Fuzzy Number (FFN)

Let X be a universal set (Senapati and Yager, 2019a). A FFS F in X is an object such that $F = \{< x, \Phi(x), \Psi(x) >: x \in X\}$, where the function $\Phi(x): X \to [0,1]$ and $\Psi(x): X \to [0,1]$, having the condition for all $x \in X$, $0 \leq (\Phi(x))^3 + (\Psi(x))^3 \leq 1$.

The numbers $\Phi(x)$ and $\Psi(x)$ denote MD and NMD of the elements $x \in X$, respectively. For any FFS F and for all $x \in X$, the hesitancy degree is defined as $\pi(x) = \sqrt[3]{1 - (\Phi(x))^3 - (\Psi(x))^3}$. For convenience, we call $F = (\Phi(x), \Psi(x))$ a FFN.

Score and Accuracy Function

For any FFN $F = (\Phi, \Psi)$, SF and AF of F are defined as follows:

$$S(F) = \Phi^3 - \Psi^3, \text{ where } S(F) \in [-1,1]. \quad (1)$$
$$A(F) = \Phi^3 + \Psi^3, \text{ where } A(F) \in [0,1].$$

Operational Laws

Let $F_1 = (\Phi_1, \Psi_1)$, $F_2 = (\Phi_2, \Psi_2)$ and $F = (\Phi, \Psi)$ be the three FFNs, the operational laws are as follows:

$$F_1 \oplus F_2 = (\sqrt[3]{(\Phi_1)^3 + (\Phi_2)^3 - (\Phi_1)^3(\Phi_2)^3}, \Psi_1\Psi_2)$$
$$F_1 \otimes F_2 = (\Phi_1\Phi_2, \sqrt[3]{(\Psi_1)^3 + (\Psi_2)^3 - (\Psi_1)^3(\Psi_2)^3})$$
$$\lambda F = (\sqrt[3]{1 - (1 - \Phi^3)^\lambda}, \Psi^\lambda)\ \lambda > 0$$
$$F^\lambda = (\Phi^\lambda, \sqrt[3]{1 - (1 - \Psi^3)^\lambda}, \lambda > 0$$
$$F^C = (\Psi, \Phi).$$

FFWPAO

Let $F_i = (\Phi_{F_i}, \Psi_{F_i})(i = 1,2, \dots, n)$ be FFNs and $w = (w_1, w_2, \dots, w_n)^T$ be weight vector of F_i with $\sum_{i=1}^n w_i = 1$. FFWPAO is a function $FFWPAO: F^n \to F$, where

$$FFWPAO(F_1, F_2, \dots, F_n) = \left((\sum_{i=1}^n w_i \Phi_{ij}^3)^{\frac{1}{3}}, (\sum_{i=1}^n w_i \Psi_{ij}^3)^{\frac{1}{3}} \right) \quad (2)$$

Theorem: Let $F_i = (\Phi_{F_i}, \Psi_{F_i})$ are FFNs, then the aggregated value obtained by applying the FFWPA operator is also an FFN.

Example: Let $F_1 = (0.5,0.3)$, $F_2 = (0.8,0.4)$ be two FFNs, and suppose that $w = (0.5,0.5)^T$ be the weight vector.

$$FFWPAO(F_1, F_2, \ldots, F_n) = \left((\Sigma_{i=1}^{n} w_i \Phi_{ij}^3)^{\frac{1}{3}}, (\Sigma_{i=1}^{n} w_i \Psi_{ij}^3)^{\frac{1}{3}} \right)$$

$$= \left(((w_1 * \Phi_1^3) + (w_2 * \Phi_2^3))^{\frac{1}{3}}, ((w_1 * \Psi_1^3) + (w_2 * \Psi_2^3))^{\frac{1}{3}} \right)$$

$= (0.68292, 0.357002)$ which is also a FFN.

Proposed FFAO Based MCGDM

Here the FFAO based SWARA-WASPAS technique has been discussed.

Let there are m alternatives $A_i (i = 1, 2, \ldots, m)$, n criteria $C_j (j = 1, 2, \ldots, n)$ and let the weighting vector be w_j and r $(r = 1, 2, \ldots, l)$ experts, the given FF evaluation matrix is $M = [A_{ij}^r]_{m \times n} = (\Phi_{ij}^r, \Psi_{ij}^r)$; where $\Phi_{ij}^r \in [0, 1]$ denotes the MD and $\Psi_{ij}^r \in [0, 1]$ denotes the NMD.

Proposed FFWPAO Based SWARA

Kersuliene et al. (2010) presented the SWARA approach with which criteria that should be utilized in evaluating alternatives are ranked from most significant weight value to least significant one. Each criterion is then selected by DMs and less important ones are discarded. The algorithm of FFWPAO based SWARA method is as follows:

Step 1. The decision maker (DM) decides the priority of criteria and accordingly assigns criteria value. The more the importance of criteria more is the value assigned to it and so is the value assigned to less important criteria. We have l DM and n number of criteria.

Step 2. Aggregation of individual evaluation of all decision makers is carried out by using FFWPAO, where p_j' denotes the merged relative importance score for each criterion.

$$p_j' = \left((\Sigma_{i=1}^{n} w_i \Phi_{ij}^3)^{\frac{1}{3}}, (\Sigma_{i=1}^{n} w_i \Psi_{ij}^3)^{\frac{1}{3}} \right) \quad (3)$$

Step 3. SF of each criterion is calculated using (1).

Step 4. The criterion with the highest score is ranked first and accordingly criteria with their relative importance are ranked in descending order. Relative significance of criterion j with respect to previous criterion $(j-1)$ is calculated, denoted by s_j.

$$s_j = p'_{j-1} - p'_j,\ j = 2, \dots, n. \tag{4}$$

Step 5. Coefficients of each criteria are obtained by binary comparison and denoted as C_j. Coefficients show importance of criterion $(j-1)$ with respect to criterion j. Value C_j for each criterion is calculated as follows:

$$C_j = \begin{cases} 1, j = 1; \\ s_j + 1, j = 2, \dots, n \end{cases} \tag{5}$$

Step 6. Corrected weights (s'_j) for all criteria are calculated as follows:

$$s'_j = \begin{cases} 1, j = 1 \\ \frac{s'_{j-1}}{C_j}, j = 2, \dots, n \end{cases} \tag{6}$$

Step 7. The final criteria weight w_j is calculated as follows:

$$w_j = \frac{s'_j}{\sum_{j=1}^{n} s'_j} \tag{7}$$

Proposed FFWPAO based WASPAS

Zavadskas et al. (2012) introduced the WASPAS approach to rank alternatives. This approach combines the weighted sum model (WSM) and the weighted product model (WPM). The steps of WASPAS are given below:

Step 1. Create a fuzzy evaluation matrix for FFN as shown below:

$$M = [A^r_{ij}]_{m\times n} = \left(\Phi^r_{ij}, \Psi^r_{ij}\right)$$

$$M = [A^r_{ij}]_{m\times n} = \begin{matrix} & C_1 & C_2 & \cdots & C_n \\ A_1 & (\Phi^r_{11}, \Psi^r_{11}) & (\Phi^r_{12}, \Psi^r_{12}) & \cdots & (\Phi^r_{1n}, \Psi^r_{1n}) \\ A_2 & (\Phi^r_{21}, \Psi^r_{21}) & (\Phi^r_{22}, \Psi^r_{22}) & \cdots & (\Phi^r_{2n}, \Psi^r_{2n}) \\ \vdots & \vdots & \vdots & \vdots & \vdots \\ A_m & (\Phi^r_{m1}, \Psi^r_{m1}) & (\Phi^r_{m2}, \Psi^r_{m2}) & \cdots & (\Phi^r_{mn}, \Psi^r_{mn}) \end{matrix} \tag{8}$$

where $A^r_{ij} = \left(\Phi^r_{ij}, \Psi^r_{ij}\right)$ denotes FFN with alternatives A_i and criteria C_j by rth DM.

Step 2. Aggregated decision matrix by using FFWPAO is given below:

$$m' = [A_{ij}]_{m\times n} = \begin{array}{c} \\ A_1 \\ A_2 \\ \vdots \\ A_m \end{array} \begin{array}{c} \begin{array}{cccc} C_1 & C_2 & \cdots & C_n \end{array} \\ \begin{bmatrix} (\Phi_{11}, \Psi_{11}) & (\Phi_{12}, \Psi_{12}) & \cdots & (\Phi_{1n}, \Psi_{1n}) \\ (\Phi_{21}, \Psi_{21}) & (\Phi_{22}, \Psi_{22}) & \cdots & (\Phi_{2n}, \Psi_{2n}) \\ \vdots & \vdots & \vdots & \vdots \\ (\Phi_{m1}, \Psi_{n1}) & (\Phi_{m2}, \Psi_{m2}) & \cdots & (\Phi_{mn}, \Psi_{mn}) \end{bmatrix} \end{array} \tag{9}$$

where $A_{ij} = \left(\Phi_{ij}, \Psi_{ij}\right)$ denotes aggregated FFN, with alternatives A_i and criteria C_j by the DM.

Step 3. Normalization of aggregated matrix $m' = [A_{ij}]_{m\times n}$ respective of the type of each criterion by the given formula:

$$\tilde{N}_{ij} = \begin{cases} A_{ij} & \text{if } j \in BC \\ Com(A_{ij}) & \text{if } j \in CC \end{cases} \tag{10}$$

BC and CC is beneficiary and cost criterion respectively.

Step 4. Calculate WSM and WPM measures as follows:

$$\tilde{Q}_i^S = \oplus_{j=1}^n \left(w_j \otimes \tilde{N}_{ij}\right) \tag{11}$$

$$\tilde{Q}_i^P = \otimes_{j=1}^n \left(\tilde{N}_{ij}{}^{w_j}\right) \tag{12}$$

Step 5. Calculate $\tilde{Q}_i$ using

$$\tilde{Q}_i = \lambda\tilde{Q}_i^S \oplus (1-\lambda)\tilde{Q}_i^P \tag{13}$$

Step 6. Rank alternatives based on scores of $\tilde{Q}_i$.

Application of Proposed FFAO Based SWARA-WASPAS in HCWR

This work provides an integrated SWARA-WASPAS technique based on FFAO for choosing the best HCWRT for sustainable environmental development. The selection of the HCWRT problem has been modeled and solved in this section.

In this research, four potential treatment options are suggested in relation to nine HCW recycling criteria for material recycling, reuse, or recovery. Summary of criteria and alternatives are depicted in Table 1 and Table 2 respectively. A panel of two DMs, DM1 and DM2 has been put together for the case study to choose the most practical and efficient HCWRT. To rate options and criteria, DMs used a 9-level set of linguistic elements that are described in Table 3, and DM's linguistic assessment of criteria is depicted in Table 4 using FFNs.

Application of Proposed Integrated SWARA-WASPAS

The algorithm of the proposed integrated approach is as follows:

Step 1. Using (2), decision matrices are aggregated by assigning weights to DMs as (0.5, 0.5).

Step 2. Using (7), FF weights of criteria corresponding to each DM have been determined and scored using (1), which is presented in Table 5.

Step 3. Assessments of DMs for alternatives corresponding to each criterion are presented in Table 6.

Step 4. To apply FFAO based WASPAS, decision matrices are aggregated using (2), considering weight vector (0.5, 0.5), and are presented in Table 7.

Step 5. Aggregated decision matrix is normalized using Step 3 of the proposed FF-WASPAS.

Step 6. Finally using (13), the performance of each alternative has been determined and accordingly ranked. The result is furnished in Table 8 and shown in Figure 1.

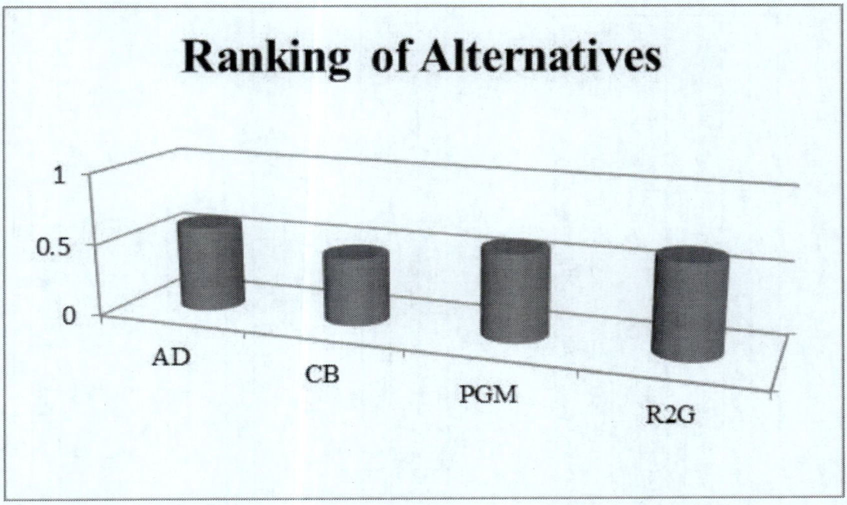

Figure 1. Ranking of alternatives.

The results indicate that alternative R2G is the top choice for the proposed integrated SWARA-WASPAS for HCWR. The consequences of this research result are briefly covered in section that follows.

Table 1. Criteria proposed for HCW

Criteria	Description	Criteria Type
Ct1	Investment Cost	Cost
Ct2	Energy recovery efficiency	Beneficiary
Ct3	Effect on Environment	Cost
Ct4	Operational conditions	Beneficiary
Ct5	Human resource requirement	Cost
Ct6	Effects on Public Health	Cost
Ct7	Reduction of Waste Volume	Beneficiary
Ct8	Infrastructure requirement	Beneficiary
Ct9	Occupational hazards	Cost

Table 2. Description of HCWRT

Sl. No.	HCWRT	Description
1	AD	In the absence of oxygen, a sequence of processes known as AD cause bacteria to decompose into biodegradable material.
2	CB	In combustion, a high-temperature exothermic redox chemical process, a reductant (fuel) reacts with an oxidant (often ambient oxygen) to create oxidized, frequently gaseous products in a mixture known as smoke.
3	PGM	A syngas (synthesis gas) is created by the high-temperature, plasma-based process of plasma gasification, which consists primarily of hydrogen and carbon monoxide.
4	R2G	CDC and state-approved methods are used to treat regulated medical wastes in the R2G recycling process after they are collected from research and manufacturing facilities. The treated bi-product is then sent to a firm that turns it into recycled plastic.

Table 3. 9-level scale using FFNs

Extreme Low	Very Low	Low	Moderate Low	Moderate	Moderate High	High	Very High	Extreme High
EL	VL	L	ML	M	MH	H	VH	EH
(0.2,0.18)	(0.3,0.15)	(0.4,0.13)	(0.45,0.1)	(0.5,0.08)	(0.6,0.07)	(0.7,0.05)	(0.8,0.03)	(0.9,0.01)

Table 4. DM's linguistic assessment of criteria using FFNs

	Ct1	Ct2	Ct3	Ct4	Ct5	Ct6	Ct7	Ct8	Ct9
DM1	(0.5,0.08)	(0.5,0.08)	(0.8,0.03)	(0.7,0.05)	(0.7,0.05)	(0.8,0.03)	(0.5,0.08)	(0.5,0.08)	(0.8,0.03)
DM2	(0.5,0.08)	(0.4,0.13)	(0.7,0.05)	(0.5,0.08)	(0.4,0.13)	(0.8,0.03)	(0.5,0.08)	(0.5,0.08)	(0.7,0.05)

Table 5. Criteria weights

	Ct1	Ct2	Ct3	Ct4	Ct5	Ct6	Ct7	Ct8	Ct9
weights	0.0975	0.09458	0.1294	0.1084	0.1051	0.1404	0.0975	0.0975	0.1294

Table 6. Linguistic assessments of alternatives provided by DMs

		Ct1	Ct2	Ct3	Ct4	Ct5	Ct6	Ct7	Ct8	Ct9
DM1	AD	(0.5,0.08)	(0.5,0.08)	(0.2,0.18)	(0.7,0.05)	(0.5,0.08)	(0.7,0.05)	(0.5,0.08)	(0.5,0.08)	(0.7,0.05)
	CB	(0.4,0.13)	(0.7,0.05)	(0.2,0.18)	(0.5,0.08)	(0.5,0.08)	(0.7,0.05)	(0.5,0.08)	(0.5,0.08)	(0.7,0.05)
	PGM	(0.7,0.05)	(0.8,0.03)	(0.2,0.18)	(0.5,0.08)	(0.5,0.08)	(0.7,0.05)	(0.3,0.15)	(0.7,0.05)	(0.7,0.05)
	R2G	(0.3,0.15)	(0.4,0.13)	(0.9,0.01)	(0.6,0.07)	(0.5,0.08)	(0.2,0.18)	(0.4,0.13)	(0.5,0.08)	(0.3,0.15)
DM2	AD	(0.4,0.13)	(0.7,0.05)	(0.4,0.13)	(0.5,0.08)	(0.5,0.08)	(0.4,0.13)	(0.4,0.13)	(0.5,0.08)	(0.5,0.08)
	CB	(0.5,0.08)	(0.4,0.13)	(0.7,0.05)	(0.7,0.05)	(0.5,0.08)	(0.5,0.08)	(0.4,0.13)	(0.5,0.08)	(0.7,0.05)
	PGM	(0.8,0.03)	(0.5,0.08)	(0.4,0.13)	(0.7,0.05)	(0.5,0.08)	(0.4,0.13)	(0.5,0.08)	(0.8,0.03)	(0.5,0.08)
	R2G	(0.5,0.08)	(0.5,0.08)	(0.4,0.13)	(0.5,0.08)	(0.5,0.08)	(0.4,0.13)	(0.5,0.08)	(0.5,0.08)	(0.4,0.13)

Table 7. Aggregated decision matrix

	Ct1	Ct2	Ct3	Ct4	Ct5	Ct6	Ct7	Ct8	Ct9
AD	(0.46,0.11)	(0.62,0.07)	(0.33,0.16)	(0.62,0.07)	(0.5,0.08)	(0.59,0.11)	(0.46,0.11)	(0.5,0.08)	(0.62,0.07)
CB	(0.46,0.11)	(0.59,0.11)	(0.56,0.14)	(0.62,0.07)	(0.5,0.08)	(0.62,0.07)	(0.46,0.11)	(0.5,0.08)	(0.7,0.05)
PGM	(0.75,0.04)	(0.68,0.06)	(0.33,0.16)	(0.62,0.07)	(0.5,0.08)	(0.59,0.11)	(0.42,0.12)	(0.75,0.04)	(0.62,0.07)
R2G	(0.42,0.12)	(0.46,0.11)	(0.73,0.103)	(0.55,0.08)	(0.5,0.08)	(0.33,0.16)	(0.46,0.11)	(0.5,0.08)	(0.36,0.14)

Table 8. Ranking of alternatives

Alternatives	Score	Ranking
AD	0.591706	3
CB	0.46117	4
PGM	0.592979	2
R2G	0.633131	1

Results and Discussion

According to the model formulation, suggested FFAO based integrated SWARA-WASPAS displays numerous important consequences and impacts of the selection of optimal HCWR approaches. According to integrated SWARA-WASPAS, R2G is the HCWRT in this application that performs the best. The consistency of results is further illustrated by comparing them to those obtained using alternative strategies. R2G is one of the best and most well-liked systems for HCWR due to its lower running costs, increased treatment capacity, and improved recycling potential for transforming waste into energy. In addition to getting rid of viruses and dangerous organic waste, it considerably reduces amount of waste. Order of waste recycling methods obtained through proposed FFWPAO based integrated technique is presented in Table 8 and shown in Figure 1.

Key benefits of R2G process are as follows:

1. For reuse of disposable HCW, R2G has been demonstrated to be the most cost-effective waste recycling technology.
2. It eliminates infections and organic hazardous waste while also reducing the volume of waste. In R2G processing plant, it collects predetermined medical wastes, sterilizes them and then recycles them.
3. It is environmentally friendly because it helps to create a pollutant-free atmosphere in addition to disposing of HCW in a methodical way.

Furthermore, comparative analyses have been conducted to examine reliability of ranking outcomes obtained using suggested AO based integrated approach.

Comparative Analysis with Respect to Existing MCDMs

To check robustness and effectiveness of rankings produced by suggested FFWPAO, we have also solved problem of HCWRT selection using FF Weighted Sum Model (FF-WSM), FF Weighted Product Model (FF-WPM) and FF Multi Attributive Border Approximation Area Comparison (FF-MABAC). The ranking results are furnished in Table 9 and shown in Figure 2. This comparison shows that all the methods — proposed FFAO based FF-WASPAS, FF-WPM, FF-WSM and FF-MABAChave indicated alternative R2G, as optimal HCWRT, and CB as the worst HCWRT. However, FF-WASPAS and FF-WSM have selected PGM as the second best HCWRT, whereas FF-WPM and FF-MABAC have identified AD as the second best HCWRT.

Table 9. Comparison of MCDM

MCDM	Ranking
FF-WASPAS	R2G $> PGM > AD > CB$
FF-WPM	R2G $> AD > PGM > CB$
FF-WSM	R2G $> PGM > AD > CB$
FF-MABAC	R2G $> AD > PGM > CB$

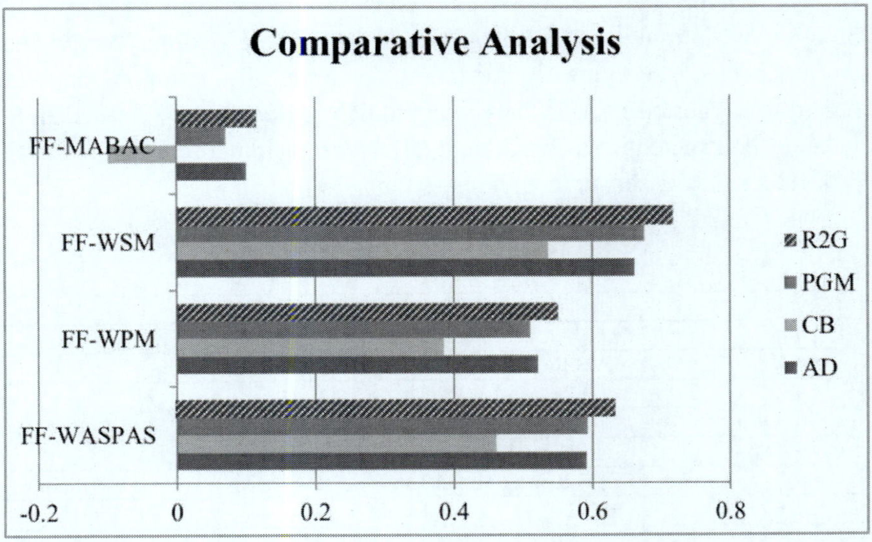

Figure 2. Comparative analysis on comparison of MCDMs.

This has occurred as various ranking techniques used by MCDM approaches to choose options. Spearman's rank correlation coefficient (SRCC) is employed in this case to look at how HCWRT preferences have changed. SRCCs between proposed integrated approach and FF-WPM, FF- WSM and FF-MABAC have been obtained as (0.8, 1.00, 0.8). As a result, it can be said that ranking results are consistent because SRCC is always greater than 0.7. Therefore, it can be argued that the recommended method is a novel addition because it takes into account all important MCDM issues for resolving practical decision-making issues under FFE.

Sensitivity Analysis

This subsection performs sensitivity analysis (SA) to evaluate reliability and consistency of rankings produced by suggested FFWPAO-based integrated approach. As the parameter λ has a significant impact on the findings, it is very much pertinent to check flexibility and sensitivity of results in respect of the variation of parameter λ. Table 10 shows the outcomes of ranking.

The results show that the ranking of alternatives is the same for $\lambda = 0$ to $\lambda = 0.4$ Case 1 to Case 5, for $\lambda = 0.5$ to $\lambda = 1$, again ranking orders are same. In all cases, R2G has been identified as the best alternative for HCWR, whereas CB is selected as the worst. A modest violation orders could be observed in ranking order of AD and PGM. These findings demonstrate that parameter λ significantly affects the outcomes of decision-making with regard to suggested FFAO. Thus, it could be concluded that variation in the value of λ, depicted in Figure 3 could affect the ranking order and hence the proposed model is sensitive with respect to λ.

Table 10. Variation in λ

Values of λ	Ranking
$\boldsymbol{\lambda = 0}$	R2G $> AD > PGM > CB$
$\boldsymbol{\lambda = 0.1}$	R2G $> AD > PGM > CB$
$\boldsymbol{\lambda = 0.2}$	R2G $> AD > PGM > CB$
$\boldsymbol{\lambda = 0.3}$	R2G $> AD > PGM > CB$
$\boldsymbol{\lambda = 0.4}$	R2G $> AD > PGM > CB$
$\boldsymbol{\lambda = 0.5}$	R2G $> PGM > AD > CB$
$\boldsymbol{\lambda = 0.6}$	R2G $> PGM > AD > CB$
$\boldsymbol{\lambda = 0.7}$	R2G $> PGM > AD > CB$
$\boldsymbol{\lambda = 0.8}$	R2G $> PGM > AD > CB$
$\boldsymbol{\lambda = 0.9}$	R2G $> PGM > AD > CB$
$\boldsymbol{\lambda = 1}$	R2G $> PGM > AD > CB$

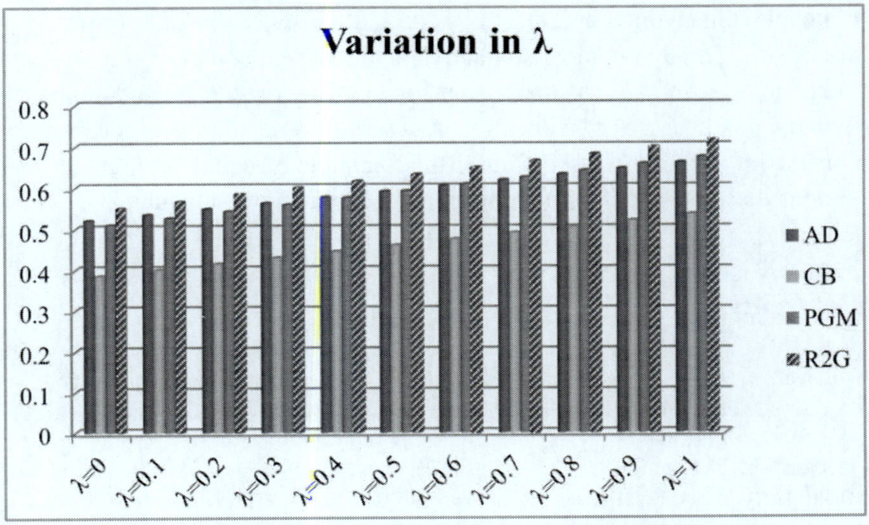

Figure 3. Sensitivity analysis on variation in λ.

Hence it can be inferred from these comparisons that proposed method is completely consistent and effective to handle real-world uncertainty.

Perspectives

The main focus of this paper is to identify the optimal HCWRT for recycling the waste produced by different healthcare sectors. The high amount of HCW production may cause harmful effects to both living beings and the environment as well. Therefore, to protect human health and the environment HCWRT selection problem has been modeled in terms of the MCGDM problem and solved using the proposed integrated technique. The proposed technique has identified R2G as the best recycling technology.

Conclusion

Due to the volume of HCWs and rising urbanization, HCWR has grown to be a serious issue in emerging nations. In this paper, we have proposed FFWPAO based integrated SWARA-WASPAS technique, to select the best HCWRT. The proposed model has chosen R2G as the best HCWRT and has developed a novel framework for selecting optimal HCWRT in the presence of ambiguity. Through comparison and SAs, the dependability of the suggested integrated technique has been confirmed. The outcomes show that the integrated technique is workable, trustworthy, and effective for handling unclear information. In the future, this technology could be used to solve various decision-making problems in an uncertain environment.

References

Antoniadou M., Varzakas T. and Tzoutzas I. Circular Economy in Conjunction with Treatment Methodologies in the Biomedical and Dental Waste Sectors, *Circ. Econ. Sust.* (2021).

Atanassov K. T. Intuitionistic Fuzzy Sets. *Fuzzy Sets and Systems* (1986) 20:87-96.

Chakraborty S. and Saha A. K. A framework of LR fuzzy AHP and fuzzy WASPAS for health care waste recycling technology, *Appl. Soft Comput* (2022a) 127 (109388).

Chakraborty S. and Saha A. K. Novel Fermatean Fuzzy Bonferroni Mean aggregation operators for selecting optimal health care waste treatment technology, *Engineering Applications of Artificial Intelligence* (2023) 119:105752.

Chakraborty S. and Saha A. K. Selection of Forklift Unit for Transport Handling using Integrated MCDM under Neutrosophic Environment. *FactaUniversitatis, Series:Mechanical Engineering* (2022b).

Chakraborty S. and Saha A. K. Selection of optimal lithium ion battery recycling process: A multi-criteria group decision making approach, *Journal of Energy Storage* (2022c) 55: Part B.

Choudhury S., Howladar P., Majumder M, and Saha A. K. Application of novel MCDM for location selection of surface water treatment plant. *IEEE Transactions on Engineering Management* (2022) 69 (5):1865-1877.

Choudhury S., Majumdar A., Saha A. K. and Majumdar P. Evaluating the preparedness of Indian States against COVID-19 pandemic risk: a fuzzy multi-criteria decision-making approach. *Risk Anal* (2021) 42 (1):85–96.

Choudhury S., Saha A. K. and Majumder M. Optimal location selection for installation of surface water treatment plant by gini coefficient-based analytical hierarchy process. *Environ. Dev. Sustain* (2020) 22 (5): 4073–4099.

Kersuliene V., Zavadskas E. K. and Turskis Z. Selection of rational dispute resolution method by applying new step-wise weight assessment ratio analysis (SWARA), *Journal of Business Economics and Management* (2010) 11(2):243-258.

Krishankumar R., Mishra A. R., Rani P., Zavadskas E. K., Ravichandran K. S. and Kar S. A new decision model with integrated approach for healthcare waste treatment technology selection with generalized orthopair fuzzy information, *Information Sciences* (2022) 610:1010-1028. ISSN 0020-0255.

Saha A. K., Choudhury S. and Majumder M. Performance efficiency analysis of water treatment plants by using MCDM and neural network model. *MATTER: international, J. Sci. Technol* (2017) 3 (1): 27–35.

Senapati T. and Yager R. R. Some new operations over Fermatean fuzzy numbers and application of Fermatean fuzzy WPM in multiple criteria decision making, *Informatica* (2019a) 30(2):391–412.

Senapati T. and Yager R. R. Fermatean fuzzy weighted averaging/geometric operators and its application in multi-criteria decision-making methods, *Engineering Applications of Artificial Intelligence* (2019b) 85:112-121.

Simic V., Torkayesh A. E. and Maghsoodi A. I. Locating a disinfection facility for hazardous healthcare waste in the COVID-19 era: a novel approach based on Fermatean fuzzy ITARA-MARCOS and random forest recursive feature elimination algorithm. *Ann Oper Res*. (2022).

Soni A., Chakraborty S., Das P. K. and Saha A. K. Materials selection of reinforced sustainable composites by recycling waste plastics and agro-waste: An integrated multi-criteria decision making approach, *Construction and Building Materials* (2022) 348:128608. ISSN 0950-0618.

Yager R. R. Pythagorean membership grades in multi criteria decision making, *Technical report MII*-3301. Machine Intelligence Institute. Iona College. New Rochelle (2013).

Zavadskas E. K., Turskis Z., Antucheviciene J. and Zakarevicius A. Optimization of weighted aggregated sum product assessment, *Elektron. Elektrotechnika* (2012) 122:3–6.

Index

T

U

V

W